THE TRIBAL WORLD AND ITS TRANSFORMATION

Xth ICAES SERIES

1. Ideas and Trends in World Anthropology/ Charles Frantz (Ed.)
2. Man and His Environment/ Indera P. Singh and S.C. Tiwari (Eds.)
3. The Communication of Ideas/ J.S. Yadava and Vinayshil Gautam (Eds.)
4. The Tribal World and Its Transformation/ Bhupinder Singh and J. S. Bhandari (Eds.)

About the Editors

BHUPINDER SINGH entered the Indian Administrative Service in 1956 and has been associated with tribal development work since 1957 when he was posted to Orissa. His interest in this field continued with his active involvement in Tribal welfare work in Orissa and Madhya Pradesh.

His doctoral thesis was based on research on the Saora tribe in Orissa. He has also contributed papers to several learned journals.

As Joint Secretary in the Home Ministry he looks after tribal development in the country.

J.S. BHANDARI was educated at Lucknow University where he also taught, and has done extensive field work among various tribes in the Western Himalayas and the Brahmaputra Valley. The results of these studies have appeared in several academic journals of repute.

In addition to contributing a paper to the Xth ICAES, he was co-chairperson of two of its sessions.

He now teaches social anthropology at delhi University and its currently engaged in a study sponsored by the UGC.

Xth ICAES SERIES NO. 1
General Editor : LALITA P. VIDYARTHI

THE TRIBAL WORLD AND ITS TRANSFORMATION

Edited by
BHUPINDER SINGH
J.S. BHANDARI

CONCEPT PUBLISHING COMPANY PVT. LTD.
NEW DELHI-110059

The royalty for the volume will be payable to the Indian Anthropological Association.

ISBN: 978-93-5594-632-4

Edition 2023

Published and Printed by

Concept Since 1974

Concept Publishing Company Pvt. Ltd.
A/15-16, Commercial Block, Mohan Garden,
New Delhi-110059 (India)
T: 91-11-41101460
E: publishing@conceptpub.com, *W*: www.conceptpub.com

GENERAL EDITOR'S INTRODUCTION

THE International Congress of Anthropological and Ethnological Sciences (ICAES) has been meeting quadrennially since the year 1934* excluding, of course, the World War II years. It has, however, taken forty-four long years before the venue could be shifted to a Third World country. The time gap is significant and indicates the general trend of the growth of the discipline.

Anthropology was once considered a tool for discovering the relative practices and customs of peoples who were destined to be governed, and thereby at best to be discovered in order to serve the purpose of the superior, the "civilised" industrialised nations. Very often the study of such peoples also provided insights to help in sound colonial administration. Physical anthropology, besides tracing the ascent of man, was used at times to find out if there was indeed a fundamental difference between the races. As a result of all this activity much data was recorded and the scientists of the industrial-urban cultures of Europe and America became aware of the less developed half of the world. Whether this meant real advancement of scientific knowledge in all such cases may be open to question; for that matter, it may even cause one to wonder about the meaning and quality of the cultural encounter of the colonial period. This is bound to be very different from exchanges between groups of people who respect each other. Such an encounter between equals would perhaps have provided a lasting base both for understanding and for an enduring relationship. But as the pattern of anthropological investigation emerged in such exploitative contexts, apparently plausible sets of reasons were given to discredit anthropological inquiry of this kind.

World War II, however, proved to be catalytic in the changes that it effected in the "science of man". Its repercussions were many and widespread. The post-war years heralded

---

* Until 1968 after which it has been held quinquennially.

the disintegration of the colonial empires and with it a transformation in the attitude towards those who had hitherto been under the colonial yoke. On another plane speedier modes of travel and communication and other significant advances in technology have brought the peoples of the world closer to each other.

More and more international gatherings have opened up new vistas of research and study. Each nation has applied the motto : *know thyself*, while attempting to project its image abroad. The vision is no longer constricted; the analyses no longer partial. This localization and internationalization have stimulated the formulation of theories and working models in the social sciences; the anthropological and ethnological sciences are the foremost among these sciences to have set the trend. The results have been spectacular : witness the success of the ten congresses held all over the world up to 1978.

It is but fitting that the first of the congresses to be held in the Third World countries should have been held in India. This country was perhaps the earliest to shake off the yoke of colonialism and blaze the trail of independence.

I have maintained elsewhere that up to a point the history of the congresses is the history of the growth of anthropology. Accordingly I have periodised the congresses in the following manner : *Institutionalisation* : *The Early Phase* : the London Congress (1934), the Copenhagen Congress(1938); *Anthropology in a World Reborn* : the Brussels Congress (1948); *The Age of Consolidation* : the Vienna Congress (1952), the Philadelphia Congress (1956), the Paris Congress (1960) ; *Towards a Richer Mix* : The Moscow Congress (1964), the Tokyo Congress(1968), the Chicago Congress (1973); *The Third World Orientation* : the Delhi Congress (1978).

The 1978 Congress in Delhi provided an opportunity to survey the terrain of anthropology from a different vantage point. Two things emerged very clearly from the papers presented at the various sessions. One, that the nature of data available as a result of anthropological studies was copious and abundant but very often unrelated. Little sustained effort has been made to read and study them in a fashion which would lead to the deciphering of meaningful patterns. The second was the reinforcement at a specific level of a view which many hold but is rarely so well brought out, viz., anthropology as a science of man being the most pervading and all embracing. Sessions during the Congress ranged from linguistics to management, from tribes to industrial cultures. Several levels of researches on the physical evolution of man in diverse environmental settings were reported.

While it is accepted that international conferences play a vital role in the dissemination of ideas and information and provide a forum for the exchange of such views, the printed word has a far wider impact and reaches a larger audience. Necessarily therefore, its utility is far greater and more lasting. Hence the publication of the papers presented at the Xth ICAES assumes great importance. The fact that their publication is being undertaken in this country is doubly significant. It is in many ways symbolic of the change that has come about in the sciences themselves.

Motivated by the urge to place this wealth of material before a wider audience we have taken upon ourselves the task of editing and publishing the various papers presented during the Congress. The point of the whole exercise is to collate much valuable research effort, and by this endeavour to achieve a normative upgrading of the status of research in the world of anthropology, thus contributing our mite to the summum bonum of human knowledge.

As one surveys the scene on the eve of the last two decades of this century it seems increasingly clear that whereas symbolic anthropology and psycho-social inter-face studies shall continue to be made, the anthropology of the future would be broader and deeper in context than it has been so far. Beyond the searches for epistemology, analysis of bio-social interface, genetic studies, analysis of strategic problems in culture history, shall emerge a richer anthropology which might serve as the integration of much information, analysis and insight. There is an urgent need to bring this about keeping in view the needs of a threatened human ecology, a rapidly deteriorating energy situation, an increasing consideration for the sub-cultures of various nationalities, growing substitutes involved in optimising natural, financial and human resources and thereby managing development.

It is our hope that the volumes in this series shall make some contribution towards the emergence of a more integrated growth of anthropology as the real science of man. The strength of this area of activity is really the combined strength of a whole range of other disciplines all of which relates to the study of some aspect of man. Accordingly the series shall be very comprehensive. This alone shall reflect that the Delhi Congress was able to achieve a high watermark in anthropological studies which many believed would serve as a trend setter for the future.

The delegates to the Xth ICAES were nearly 3,500 representing 63 countries. The participants contributed about 1000 papers covering a wide range of topics.

Our task here has been merely to collate the mass of material and present it in a series of handy readable volumes. Posterity shall be the judge of its merits as it shall be the chief user of its content. The groupings of the papers in each volume have been done in a vaguely discernible pattern so as to make each one independent of the other. The whole series, however, presents itself as a record of a period in the history of human society.

By providing wider perspectives and deeper insights, this voluminous project should secure the foundations for a meaningful study of man which will help in reducing disparities among peoples and imbalances in the development of societies.

We are not unaware of the challenging nature of the task before us in undertaking to publish this series of volumes. The success of this venture will depend ultimately on the efforts of all those interested in anthropological studies. That the International Council for Philosophy and Humanistic Studies has provided the initial grant for the first three volumes to commence the publication project is certainly a heartening indication of this interest.

Most of the papers included in the volume were presented in the Post-Plenary Congress held at Ranchi. I am grateful to the members of the staff and students of the Department of Anthropology, Ranchi University, the Vice-Chancellor of the University, Dr. N.L. Nodda and the Government of Bihar for e xtending all facilities for holding the Post-Congress.

We are extremely happy that Concept Publishing Company

have undertaken the arduous task of bringing out these volumes. We are confident that they will complete the entire project both efficiently and expeditiously.

We would like to express our thanks to the editors of the individual volumes for their cooperation in bringing this task to fruition.

One word more in conclusion: The views expressed in these volumes are not necessarily those of the editors or the ICAES. The responsibility for them rests solely with the contributors.

Ranchi University
Ranchi, Bihar,
India.
November, 1979

Lalita P. Vidyarthi
President
Xth ICAES &
IUAES (1973-78)

INTRODUCTION

THE CENTRAL theme of the Xth International Congress of Anthropological and Ethnological Sciences was "Anthropology and the Challenges of Development". It marked a departure from the conventional themes to which the social scientists have been accustomed. The further fact that the Congress was held in a Third World country like India, promised a fresh, exciting and challenging experience.

Indeed, the two facts are highly significant. They symbolise a shift in focus. They reflect the desideratum that the social sciences should be intensely concerned with social processes in developing societies as much as they have been involved in the industrialised societies. The idiom and content of the social sciences have hitherto been riddled with the mores and ethos of the western society which lived off the resources of their colonies. With prolonged exploitation, the schism between the western elite and the colonial subjects was riven deep. The social sciences were used as tools of the western societies, partly to reinforce their hegemonic designs and partly to satisfy their curiosity. The present day trends tend to call a halt to distortion in the use of these rational sciences. Man has roused himself to an assertion of his personality. No continent is now dark. There is a tremendous upsurge of the dignity of the individual. The social sciences can afford to ignore the revolutionary wave at great peril.

In this country, we stand at the cross-roads of history. After three decades of freedom from the colonial yoke, we face the daring challenge of passage into modernity through the eradication of poverty, illiteracy and under-nourishment. In common with other developing countries, we have a future to work for and a goal to attain. However, like such nations, our young nation-society is beset with a host of dilemmas and problems in the matrix of ethnic pluralism. For parts of it comprising over 250 scheduled tribe communities speaking not less than 105 different languages (in addition to a plethora of castes, communities, and languages not to talk of dialects) in the throes of development travails, the experience is likely to leave a lasting impression. The classical view about tribal societies is valid no more. The study of static societies and placid polities is yielding place to a study of the dynamics of development and forces of ferment. The change impels rethinking and reformulation of concepts and ideas. But before that, a full grasp of the scenario is imperative.

Some two decades ago, a Panchsheel policy of tribal transformation was implanted :

(i) Development should be along the lines of the genius of the tribal community and nothing should be imposed on them.

(ii) Tribal rights on land and forests should be respected.

(iii) Members of the tribes should be trained for undertaking their own administration and development.

(iv) Over-administration of tribal areas should be avoided and work should be done through their own cultural and social institutions.

(v) Results should be judged by the quality of human character that is evolved.

Today, it retains its freshness and validity. But it needs re-vivification. The transformation will be relevant and meaningful to the extent that the sensitivity and susceptibility of each tribal community modulates the character of the programmes and the processes.

Along with policy, attitudes are important, particularly in this case. The two parties are the development-agents, predominantly non-tribals, and the more or less passive tribal beneficiaries. The categories of non-tribal sections, the opponents, the do-gooders and the apathetic can all be a menace. As in other walks of life, one must strike a happy balance. Hence, positive participation in the development processes of the tribal communities themselves should be inter-faced with change-agents. With the largest concentration of tribals, this country can hope to make the democratic experiment successful only with their fullest involvement in planning and implementation.

The Xth International Congress of Anthropological and Ethnological Sciences held in Delhi in December 1978, provided a meeting ground for social scientists from all over the world. At both the plenary and the post-plenary sessions, a wide range of topics was discussed. New findings were presented and examined, new methods of research analysed. This book, the first in a series, is an attempt to collate the findings of only one of the many aspects discussed at the conference—that of transformation and change in the tribal ethos. The essays in this volume are a selection of the papers presented at the Congress. They cover a wide spectrum ranging from studies of the change brought about in the tribes of India by the impact of urbanisation and modernisation, to studies of the Canadian Indians, the Andamanese and of African and Melanesian societies. Some essays are purely descriptive, others analytical.

Of the eighteen essays presented in this volume, several deal with transformation and change among the tribals in the subcontinent Almut Mey presents an analysis of modernization in the Chittagong Hill Tracts based on a sample of 600 households in twenty-four villages of eight different tribes, as opposed to analyses based on an intensive study of one village. The essay shows how external factors such as construction of the Kaptai dam and other new schemes started by the government, as well as the fact of tribal land being opened up for sale, have displaced the tribals and, in some cases, led them to near-starvation. Ali Nawas, in his paper deals with the religion of the Garo hill tribes of Bangladesh, describing in detail their life-styles. K.K. Verma and Ramesh Sinha speak of socio-political movements among the Munda and the Oraon, two preponderant tribes of Bihar. They describe how the spread of Christianity and the movement of non-tribals into tribal areas has led to tribals becoming more organised. This has given rise to several movements where tribals have militated against non-tribals. The tribal areas of India, which are currently the scene of much ferment and discontent as well as the source of anxious interest on the part of the government, have been extensively dealt with in these essays. Sachchidananda speaks of the challenge modernism has presented to the Munda and the change this has wrought in their political institutions. Maheshwari Prasad's essay on the impact of urbanisation on a village, studies the village of Tusmu in Chotanagpur. The author examines not only the impact of urbanisation, but also the bearings of varying socio-cultural backgrounds on the process of adaptation and change and shows how Tusmu has been affected by its nearness to Ranchi. Another study of the Chotanagpur area by Bhabesh Chakraborty and Sumita Kundu, looks at the vanishing crafts in this area. It analyses the vital role of craftsmen in socio-economic and ritual life and shows how their will to live has been strengthened by the revival of native skill and craft. Three other studies look at the tribal areas of India—a subject of perennial interest for the social anthropologist. J.P. Singh makes a study of the changing patterns of tribal political organisation among the Santal; Satish Kumar looks at the Gond of Ranchi, while B.B. Goswami has a wider perspective and looks at the impact of Christianity on the hill tribesmen of North-East India. He perceives Christianity as a positive factor enabling the tribals to take advantage of the developmental programmes for material benefits. His study takes into account Mizoram and Nagaland. In all the essays, whether micro or macro studies, the impact of both Christianity and urbanisation, two important factors in the life of the tribes of India, are extensively discussed.

P.C. Ray discusses socio-political and technical factors in transformation by looking at the demand for a separate Jharkhand State and the factors that have led to this. Sarita Bhowmick in her article on the Andamanese, shows how the Greater Andamanese, from being one of the world's most primitive communities, are on the verge of extinction. She analyses the gradual decimation of population that has been caused due to disease, and the inability of the Andamanese to adjust to the new facilities that have been provided them. The social, economic and political organisation of the Saora of Orissa in the context of the current development programmes of government are scrutinised by Bhupinder Singh. His focus is on Saora leadership in the role of a catalyst for development. He concludes that this leadership is on the threshold and needs to be fostered for the take-off.

The studies of tribals in other countries also cover a wide spectrum and reveal an identity of interests. Stephen Inglis makes an interesting case study of the materials seized by the Canadian Museum after a "potlatch" and the subsequent controversial "theft" of cultural valuables by other museums. He looks at the Kwagitul, one of the largest language groups of the Northwest Coast people in Canada. B.J. Terwiel from the Australian National University speaks of the Tais—a people widely distributed over mainland Southeast Asia. Machiko Aoyagi from St Paul's University in Tokyo, makes a case study of the transformation of a traditional religion under Christian influence in Palau, Western Caroline Islands, Micronesia and G.T. Nurse discusses labour migration as an agent of change in African and Melanesian societies.

The papers collected here may not scan minutely the transformation that has so far taken place nor do they presage the direction it is likely to take. Yet, they offer a glimpse into various facets and illumine dark corners. They should serve to spur future scientists and researchers to new voyages of discovery to add to the summun bonum of knowledge that is basic to both theory and practice. Above all, they should lead to new dimensions in the social sciences.

Bhupinder Singh
Ministry of Home Affairs,
Government of India
New Delhi.

J.S. Bhandari
Department of Anthropology
University of Delhi
Delhi.

CONTENTS

LIST OF CONTRIBUTORS

Machiko Aoyagi
15-12 Imagawa 3 Suginami-Ku Tokyo, Japan

J.S. Bhandari
Dept. of Anthropology, Delhi University, Delhi, India

Sarita Bhowmick
Dept. of Anthropology, Ranchi University, Ranchi, India

Bhabesh Chakraborty
Cultural Research Officer, Government of West Bengal Scheduled Castes and Tribes Welfare Department, Calcutta, India

B.B. Goswami
Indian Institute of Advanced Study, Rashtrapati Niwas, Simla, India

Stephen Inglis
Dept. of Anthropology, Museum of Anthropology, University of British Columbia, Canada

Sumita Kundu
Cultural Research Officer, Government of West Bengal Scheduled Castes and Tribes Welfare Department, Calcutta, India

Almut W. Mey
Seesenerstr 17, 1 Berlin 31, Germany

Ali Nawaz
Head of the Dept. of Bangla, Bangladesh Agricultural University, Mymensingh, Bangladesh

G.T. Nurse
Papua New Guinea Institute of Medical Research, Coroka, F.H.P., Papua New Guinea

Pavla Strukelj
Slovenski Etnografski Muzej, Dept. of Noneuropean Cultures, Ljubljana, Yugoslavia

Maheshwari Prasad
Reader in Tribal Geography, Ranchi University, Ranchi

P.C. Ray
Ex. Senior Psychologist Head of the Sec. of Psychology, Anthropological Survey of India, Calcutta, India

Sachchidananda
Director A.N.S. Institute of Social Studies, Patna, India

Satish Kumar
Post-Graduate Dept. of Sociology, Patna University, Patna, India

Bhupinder Singh
Joint Secretary, Ministry of Home Affairs, New Delhi, India

J.P. Singh
Centre for the Study of Social Systems, Jawaharlal Nehru University, New Delhi, India

Ramesh Sinha
Fellow A.N. Sinha Institute of Social Studies, Patna, India

B.J. Terwiel
Dept. of Asian Civilization, Australian National University, Canberra Act

K.K. Verma
Fellow, A.N. Sinha Institute of Social Studies, Patna, India

ONE

K. K. Verma and Ramesh Sinha

SOCIO-POLITICAL MOVEMENTS AMONG THE MUNDA AND THE ORAON

RECENT social-anthropological literature has witnessed a plethora of empirical investigation into the problems of socio-political movements of the tribals. However, scholars have failed to arrive at a satisfactory or agreed explanation of these social phenomena. Ours is a modest attempt at understanding the social situation among the Munda and the Oraon which is designated as "movement".

The Munda and the Oraon, the two numerically preponderant tribes of Bihar, have a hoary antiquity which may be dated to the beginning of the first century A.D. The Munda and the Oraon, inhabiting the south-eastern and the north-western parts of Ranchi district, have always depended upon agriculture, mainly rice cultivation, for their subsistence. They have an almost akin culture, economy and social characteristics in terms of social structure. As such the two tribes witnessed, experienced and suffered together the torment of exploitation which they were subjected to, and the consequent aftermath of socio-political movements.

Tribal History

The Munda are said to be the earlier known settlers of the region (Roy 1912 : 62-82; Vidyarthi and Sahay 1978 : 30) followed by the Oraon who migrated to the region around the first century A.D. (Roy 1915 : 30). These two tribes had been in contact with each other for centuries and they cleared the virgin forest for cultivation. They were said to have their own religion and indigenous system of administration through their *hatu* or village panchayat or the council of elders. These bodies enforced the customary laws of kinship, marriage and inheritance. They evolved the *Parha* (confederacy of several villages) for the settlement of inter-village disputes and regulation of customary tribal laws. The legal authority was vested in the Parha panchayat.

The Munda Parha head was known as *Manki* while his Oraon counterpart was called Parha Raja. They came under the suzerainty of Nagbansi Raja, Phani Mukut Roy. It is said that the Raja was the chosen leader of his people (Roy 1912). In course of time the Raja established a hereditary kingdom over the Munda and the Oraon. The Raja was not the sovereign of the land, but was only a *primus inter pares* in times of defence operation (Ekka 1972 : 425). But this status, too, underwent a change when Durga Sal, the 42nd Raja, was subjugated by the Mughals in 1585 and reduced to the status of a tribute-paying chief under the Mughal *Subedar* (governor) of Bihar. Initially, the Raja accepted small periodic presents in the form of grain and jungle produce but later, under changed circumstances, he eventually converted voluntary presents into fixed tribute and thus rent began to be realized from each village. The Munda and the Oraon vehemently resisted this newly introduced system, and their resistance created difficulties for the Raja to raise the amount of tribute which he required for his maintenance (Sahay 1966 : 923). The Munda preferred to migrate to the hilly east leaving their villages in the south in the hands of the Oraon. All these villages turned into Oraon villages and a few Munda families who remained there continued to act as *Pahan* (priest) (Vidyarthi and Sahay 1978 : 38).

In course of time the royal family expanded and marital relations with other Hindu ruling houses were established. The Raja, who had become gradually Hinduised, brought people from the Gangetic plain, made them priests, artisans and soldiers and granted them Munda and Oraon village overlordship for their services. There also existed a system of granting jagirs to the members of royal families as maintenance grants. These jagirdars and tenure-holders brought in *thikadars*. They not only began extracting taxes and *begari* (free service) from their tribal tenants, but also introduced land rent in cash. The tribals opposed it as a result of which they were forcibly ousted from their *Khutkati* or *Bhuinhari* land. This clash of interests converged into an open conflict between the tribals and the jagirdars. As a result more outsiders of different ethnic groups were brought in by successive Rajas and jagirdars not only to suppress the tribals to the extent of submission but also to consolidate strength against the neighbouring kings (Davidson 1839 : 234-5). The situation thus characterised the beginning of agrarian disturbances in the region.

The movement of non-tribals into the region was accelerated by the establishment of Pax Britannica in the region. The extension of the British Raj to the Chota Nagpur plateau was followed by the advent of European missionaries. The Munda and the Oraon revolted (1831-32) against the new class of alien jagirdars and thikadars called *Dikus*. This compelled the British administration to initiate agrarian reform and to shift the administrative headquarters to the heart of the plateau. A court of justice was also set up in the region in 1834, which however, could not help the tribals but which unintentionally helped the jagirdars and thikadars by obliterating the Khutkati rights (Reid n.d. 81-3). The *modus operandi* of the Dikus consisted of the use of force and legal action in expelling the owner of the land, imposition of rent and illegal enhancement of *praedial* conditions and forced labour on their *raiyats* (Singh 1966 : 2). Consequently the original settlers lost their proprietorship over the villages and were reduced to ordinary raiyats or tenants (Roy 1912 : 219-26).

The repercussions which followed knew no bounds. A large number of tribals migrated to Assam in the second half of the nineteenth century to work there as coolies in tea gardens. The *Arakaits* (labour agents) in collusion with local officials played havoc with the social and moral order of the Munda.

The spread of Christianity (four Oraon in 1850 and two Munda in 1851 embraced Christianity through the efforts of the Gossner Evangelical Lutheran Mission) gave a new dimension to the agrarian question. The converts became more conscious, organised and defiant. The *sardars* (leaders of the Sardar movement) heeded the advice of the missionaries and thus tried to retrieve their lost rights over the land with the help of the law. Accordingly, a number of legal petitions were filed before various authorities of the British administration during the period i.e. 1858-80 for the return of alienated Khutkati and Bhuinhari lands, thus marking the onset of the Sardar movement or *Mulkui-larai*. Most of these petitions were rejected which caused distrust among the new tribal Christians against the administration and prepared the ground for the Birsa movement.

The advent of alien jagirdars, thikadars and other non-tribals and the introduction of the British administration in the region gave a jolt to the traditional form of the Munda by reversing the role of the Pahan and the Munda. The Munda was taken as landlord and the Pahan receded to the background. The Munda, who was merely a *primus inter pares* in the community and nothing more than that, sought to arrogate more authority to himself with disastrous consequences to the community. In some cases, they were tempted by alien zamindars and acted against their own people.

Evidence of the prevalence of Hinduism and its cults of the sun and mother goddess in the region dates back to the early medieval age. Hindu Vaishnavism had influenced the Munda and Oraon. The Gossain, Manjhi. Tanti, Swansi and Adhikari communities played an important role in spreading Vaishnavism among the tribals. The impact of Hindusm resulted in the acceptance by the tribals of Siva as Mahadeva *Bonga* and Parvati as Chandi *Bonga*. Many Munda and Oraon festivals had distinct Hindu overtones. Kabirpanthi also influenced these tribes. However, the converts among the Munda were not as numerous as among the Oraon. Sachchidananda (1964) and Vidyarthi (1968) have referred to the Bhagti cult among the Oraon. Roy (1928 : 227 : 1972 ed.) has enumerated as many as five religious movements. They are (i) Nemha Bhagat or Bhuiphut Bhagat; (ii) Hinduised or Bachi-dan Bhagat, including Vishnu Bhagats; (iii) Kabirpanthi Bhagats; (iv) Tana Bhagats; (v) Hindu movements. The Bhagti cult among them is said to have originated in the latter half of the 18th century (Roy, 1928 : 230 : 1972 ed.). The major cultural impact of Christianity flowed through organised missions and their planned activities. The first such organised attempt was by the Gossner Evangelical Lutheran Mission which entered the arena in March 1845. It was able to convert four Oraon by 1851. Slowly the number went up. The Anglican Mission in 1869 was next to arrive on the scene, the Roman Catholic Mission was the last to arrive in the region in the 19th century.

It is in this historical background that a number of socio-political movements among the Munda and the Oraon took place.

The Sardar Movement

The Sardar movement or Mulkui-larai among the Munda was largely the struggle of Christian tribals against jagirdars and thikadars which began in 1859. Like the leaders of the Kol insurrection, the Sardars claimed to be descendants of the original settlers. They argued that as original settlers, the tribals had an inalienable right to the land in the region and the alien jagirdar and thikadar had no right to make any imposition on them. The goals of the movement were : (i) to regain their lost right to land ; (ii) to end the system of begari (forced labour) ; and (iii) to alleviate the condition of women and tribesmen.

To counteract dispossession of land and imposition of begari, the tribals consolidated their strength through three measures : first, by filing petitions in the court of law; secondly, by mobilising the dormant resources available in the village, including mobilisation of public opinion and fund-raising campaigns to meet the expenditure incurred on legal battles, and thirdly by refusing to pay rent or perform begari. The Sardars were loyal to the British Crown and in the beginning they were not even opposed to the Raja of Chota Nagpur.

Singh (1966 : 27) has identified three phases of the Sardar movement : the agrarian phase (1858-81), the revivalistic phase (1881-90) and the political phase (1890-95). The accentuation of the movement throughout, however, remained agrarian. The movement was stimulated by the memory of the "golden past" of the race—the period before the advent of non-tribal people in Chota Nagpur. The movement spread far and wide and engulfed both the Munda and the Oraon. However, it was more intense among the Munda.

The movement began with agrarian disturbances. The Sardars attempted to occupy such of their land which the zamindars had taken away from them in 1857. The first incident occurred in Jhagra village in October 1858, where the Christian raiyats captured the zamindar and brought him to Ranchi and lodged a complaint against him. The complaint was dismissed. This encouraged the zamindar and he became revengeful. In November 1858 there was a clash at Bela between the zamindar and his raiyats. To improve the state of affairs the government decided to define and determine Bhuinhari tenure. An enquiry in 427 villages was completed but the Munda were dissatisfied with the findings. Some lands were declared in favour of the Raja which the Sardars thought should have been classed as Bhuinhari. During 1862-88 there were occasional clashes between zamindars and their raiyats. In September 1867 a petition was filed against local officials and the Raja of Chota Nagpur. The Sardars continued to file such petitions wherein mention was made of primeval times when there was neither a Raja nor a zamindar and they lived in peace. In 1869 an Act was passed which provided for the restoration of Bhuinhari lands to the raiyats from which they had been evicted on the strength of evidence collected during the Bhuinhari survey operation. In the next eleven years, the survey was completed in 2,500 villages. The Bhuinhari settlement marked the end of the dispute centering on Bhuinhari and *majhias* tenure of land; but its overall effects fell far short of the expectations of the Sardars (Singh 1966 : 28). A number of suits were filed and cases of conflict between the zamindars and raiyats increased.

The movement soon took a political and religious turn. In 1881 some Sardars organised themselves under the leadership of John the Baptist and established their raj at Doesa, a former seat of the Raja of Chota Nagpur. The leaders were prosecuted. The Sardars wanted to create an independent Munda Christian mission. The Oraon Sardars had created a separate organisation of their own. Later, the Sardars, being frustrated with the Lutheran and the Anglican missions, turned to the Roman Catholic Mission for support. At about this time Rev. Levens began his work in Torpa. He had real sympathy with the tribals. Whenever he received news of any operation against the tribals, he attempted to settle the problem. During 1889-90 the Catholic Munda agitation assumed large proportions. The government moved quickly and missionaries were warned not to join the fray. Many of the leaders were punished.

In 1890 began the political phase of the Sardar movement. The Munda boycotted the mission and continued the agitation. They asked their followers to stop paying rent to zamindars and thikadars and to abstain from appearing in local courts when summoned. This resulted in the auction of the lands of many of the raiyats. The Sardars got trapped by Calcutta lawyers. It gave them a severe jolt. Between 1890 and 1895 all court verdicts went against the tribals. In 1892 they planned to assassinate all thikadars, local officials and missionaries, but the plan failed owing to lack of sound and adequate leadership. In 1895 they were looking for a leader. The Sardars were convinced that they had been exploited and deceived by their patrons at Calcutta and that the British officials in Chota Nagpur were in league with the alien zamindars. This collusion delayed the solution of their problems through legal measures. The character of the movement changed, which ultimately prepared the ground for the Birsa movement.

Birsa Movement

The Birsa movement was basically agrarian in character and defensive in approach. Driven by an irresistible self-defensive urge, the Munda had first sought shelter in Christianity, then broken away from the missions and turned to Calcutta lawyers, and finally clashed with the authorities. The movement was agrarian in its root, violent in its means and political in its end. Birsa in his speeches emphasised the agrarian factors and sought a political solution of the problem facing his people, that is, the establishment of Birsaite Raj under a new kingdom (himself) (Singh 1966 : 191). The agrarian and social contents were mixed up in the movement. As agrarian strife involved social consequences, it arrived at not merely a political but also at a solution of the problems confronting the race (Singh 1966 : 9). The Birsa and Sardar movements in fact sprang from the same agrarian factor. The movement was religious in the early phase and revolutionary in the later. The Sardars were primarily against the middlemen and Dikus. Birsa was against the government and aimed at complete independence, both political and religious. The most important factor responsible for the emergence of the movement was the desire for economic liberation from the yoke of the zamindars and the British administration. The movement had an organizational base with ethnicity and religiosity as the basis of mobilisation and involvement. Ekka (1972 : 429) underlined three structural conditions under which the movement emerged. They were (i) encroachment of alien zamindari on Munda khutkati lands to an intolerable extent ; (ii) migration of thousands of tribals from their native land to the tea estates of Assam on being allured by Arakaites (labour agents); and (iii) famine in Chota Nagpur. The movement sought at various times restoration of traditional rights on land, revitalisation of their religion and expulsion of British officials, missionaries and alien people.

In the early monsoon of 1895 while Birsa was in a jungle along with a friend, there was a thunderstorm. Lightning struck him and he was transfigured. Thereafter he proclaimed that he had received a revelation from Divinity relating to the deliverrance of his people. This news spread like wildfire. Soon he was attributed as possessing healing power. Suffering people began running to him for his healing touch. He asked people to worship one god, preached Hindu ideals of ritual purity, morality and asceticism and denounced the worship of priests. He even promised the deliverance of his followers through the deluge, and a Munda raj driving away the oppressors, viz. zamindars and the British. Thus politics impregnated the movement and led to violent clashes. He was called *Dharti Aba* as well as Bhagwan by his followers (Fuchs 1965 : 22-34). Birsa caused apprehension among the missionaries and they prevailed upon the government to take steps against him. He was arrested and sentenced to two and a half years in jail. The four years following the movement's first phase were marked by famines and the failure of the government to curb Birsa's activities after his release. Birsaites rose in arms against the Raja, zamindars, missionaries and the government on Christmas Eve of 1899. The revolt was suppressed by force. Birsa was arrested and died in prison pending trial. He was publicly cremated so as to convince his followers that he was not a god. The movement which Birsa initiated was the culmination of resistance to oppression, both of zamindars and the administration.

Tana Bhagat Movement

The Bhagat movement among the Oraon was first reported in 1895. The claim that the followers of the movement would secure a higher status than that of the Christians and equal to the Hindus had its special appeal (Mahapatra, 1972 : 404). Jatra Oraon in April 1914 proclaimed to his fellow tribesmen that in a dream *Dharmes* or God told him to give up the worship of *bhuts* and to do away with animal sacrifice. It was God's command that they should lead an ascetic life and give up meat, alcoholic drinks, traditional songs and dance. The Oraon ought to stop ploughing the field, paying rents to zamindars and working as labourers for non-Oraon. He also said that God can only be appeased through prayer or the Bhagti cult. Most of his tenets were similar to those of the earlier prophets of the Bhagti movement. In their hymns they came to be called Tana Bhagats. Because of the refusal to allow his followers to work for zamindars and the government, Jatra was arrested and sentenced to imprisonment. As a result he went into the background. However, the movement was kept alive by another prophet, Sibu Bhagat. Agrarian grievances appear to have generated the original impulse for their absence from cultivation, and refusal to pay rent proved to be suicidal non-cooperation with the zamindars. In 1920, most of the Tana Bhagats joined the Indian National Congress and played a prominent role in the non-cooperation movement (Roy 1928 : 247-57, 1972 ed. : Fuchs 1965 : 35-46).

Jharkhand Movement

The Sardar, the Birsa and the Tana Bhagat movements not only highlighted the immediate problems and agrarian issues of the Munda and the Oraon, but affected the tribals' awakening and politicisation. The factors which fired the movement for a separate state of Jharkhand in terms of ethnicity and its transformation into a regional movement may be summed up as the growing discontent among the tribal people on account of alienation of land, a strong antipathy towards Dikus, and political developments in the wider setting of the country (Sen 1972 : 431). In 1936, provincial autonomy came into force with the result that Orissa was separated from Bihar. This influenced the educated tribal elite to demand a separate state.

The leadership in the earlier socio-political movements was provided by the traditional leaders who were rural-bred, charismatic and religious in their approach. They worked for revitalising the tribals on the Hindu model which later suffered a setback owing to the devoted work of the missionaries. The latter's continuous effort to uplift the tribals brought about new standards for choosing the leadership. It passed into the hands of western educated urban bred Christian converts (Vidyarthi 1964 : 150).

The Jharkhand movement has three distinct phases : formation phase (1912-1938), active phase (1939 to 1963), and revival phase (1964 onward). The first phase was marked by the formation of the Christian Student Organisation in 1911-12 by J. Batholmen of the Anglican Mission. It was basically philanthrophic in objective. Later in 1928, the Chota Nagpur Unnati Samaj was organised by Anglican and Lutheran educated Christians and a few non-converts. The objectives of the Samaj were (i) to uplift Chota Nagpur from the present backward state, and (ii) to improve the social, political and economic conditions of the tribals. It sought to secure employment for educated tribals, reservation in services and legislative bodies, and formation of a sub-state, joined to Bengal and Orissa. Though it sought to spread its activities among the villages, it remained essentially an urban movement (Singh 1977 : 320).

The members of the Samaj, however, differed among themselves on some issues and could not remain united for long and a parallel organisation known as the Kisan Sabha was established to focus attention on the problem of the peasants. Till then the Catholics had kept aloof from these organisations. They formed their own organisation, the Chota Nagpur Catholic Sabha. All the three organisations set up candidates under their respective banners for the 1937 elections. The Catholic Sabha won the elections. It was visualised that unless denominational differences among the tribals were ended and they stood united on a common platform, they could not shed their social, economic and political backwardness. Consequently, the Chota Nagpur Adivasi Mahasabha was convened in 1939. It was led by professional political workers, some of them highly educated and articulate. It involved tribals other than the Munda and the Oraon and extended to both urban and rural areas. Jaipal Singh, a Munda convert, emerged as a prominent leader of the Jharkhand movement.

With the formation of the Jharkhand party in 1950, the separatist movement was transformed into a party-based movement and a new secular model emerged which symbolised the aspirations and needs of the local and regional people. It led a demonstration before the States Reorganisation Committee in 1955, for a separate state, but was reconciled on being assured by the State Government of special measures for tribal development. The party was merged with the Congress in 1963. The movement was suspended for some years. However, it gained a fresh lease of life in 1970 and came to the forefront after the 1977 elections. The demand for a separate Jharkhand state has been pressed through forming an all-party action committee, and by organising rallies and agitation.

The above-mentioned socio-political movements among the tribes are indicative of the social transformation that has beset the region. The dawn of the 18th century witnessed a series of upsurges—all initiated by the tribals themselves—which took the form of movements and which were in essence a response to the transformation of the traditional agrarian system into a feudal one. Their exposure to the outside world and receptivity to external cultural characteristics provided them with the necessary impetus to protest against the hitherto prevailing exploitation. The traditional process in the past was originally responsible for initiating changes in tribal societies. It was accelerated by the modern process. If the first process brought forth a Hindu model before the tribals, the modern process, by and large, put before the tribals the western-urban industrial democratic model for inducing transformation.

A critical appraisal of the movements reveals that the concerted endeavours of the Munda and the Oraon to emancipate themselves from the prevalent morass were characterised by (a) their perceived subjection to exploitative measures adopted by the non-tribal rural rich; (b) their persistent attempt at mobilizing indigenous resources to counteract exploitation; (c) their endeavour to evolve a leadership to direct them in ending exploitation; and (d) distinct ideologies for different movements which erupted during different periods of time.

Let us explain the above socio-political movements in terms of some theoretical consideration. The locus of these movements pivoted on the issue of deprivation relative to past or present expected or feared future status. Relative deprivation carries different connotations to different scholars. Marx and Engels recognised that dissatisfaction with the status quo was not determined by absolute conditions but by relative expectation (Marx and Engels 1973). Aberle (1966) considered relative deprivation as a negative discrepancy between legitimate expectation and actuality. Gurr (1970) defined relative deprivation not in terms of expectation but in relation to perception of the situation. Thus a critical scrutiny of the explanations of relative deprivation offered by these scholars reveals perpetual lack of unanimity in regard to conceptual explanation. Two major lines of enquiry, however, can be culled on the basis of perusal of these explanations : accentuation on situational factors or structural condition (Marx and Engels, 1973, Aberle 1966), and accentuation on perception of the situation (Gurr, 1970). One can argue that a situation conducive to relative deprivation alone will not generate a social political movement. The structural condition of relative deprivation provides only the necessary condition. Sufficient conditions are provided by the perception of the situation. The areas of relative deprivation may thus be economic, political, educational, ethnic as also religious.

A situation leading to relative deprivation cropped up in the 18th century when the agrarian prerogatives of the tribals were gradually taken away, by the zamindar who introduced the system of cash rent. A group of educated Christian Munda converts, who were the first to be exposed to egalitarian ideology, were able to radiate the feelings and subsequently sensitized the deprived tribals of their rights as a consequence of which the Sardar movement began.

The Sardars' attempt to elicit assistance from the churches for the redressal of their grievances, even by conversion of tribals into Christianity, fell flat. The Sardars thus were frustrated, both with the missions as well as with the government. Their attempt to create their own church was an attack on the monopoly of the foreign missionaries. They, however, did not have a powerful or charismatic leader and they were looking for one in 1895. Birsa Munda provided the leadership. A situation of relative deprivation was induced in the tribal culture as a result of the impact of Hinduism and Christianity. Birsa under the Hindu and Christian influence initiated the movement, first aiming at ethnic unity, purity and prosperity through a reformed religion in order to "construct a more satisfying culture" (Wallace 1956: 264-281). Wearing of the sacred thread by Birsaites, though it was traced by them to their 'golden past', was a symbolic challenge to the monopoly of caste Hindus. Tribals were treated as exterior caste groups (Majumdar 1958 : 324-332). During the later phase, the region had severe famine. This led the tribesmen to cross the critical level of deprivation and there was an armed revolt against the alien elements for the redressal of their social, economic and political problems and to have Birsa Raj. The Tana Bhagat movement among the Oraon may also be explained in the same terms. The national movement too generated among the tribals the idea of non-cooperation with the feudal lords and alien rulers.

Tribal society had been different from what it was in the late 19th century when the Jharkhand movement began. The tribals were exposed to modern forces of social change and these had considerable impact on them. The movement was initiated in response to deprivation relative to present expected and feared future. They perceived deprivation in relation to "opportunity of getting economic resources, political decision making and feeling of powerlessness" for the removal of their agrarian grievances. Activists of the Jharkhand movement sensitized the masses that they were being given less than what they should have got. They drew up an ideology on the basis of relative deprivation in the area of economic, political, civic and educational spheres of the tribal life. The ideology gave a motivational force to the movements. Modern strategies were adopted to mobilise group support.

Thus relative deprivation as conceptual explanation of the situation characterised by "movement" offers a satisfactory analysis for the genesis, motivational forces and resultant movements. The Munda and the Oraon were subjected to multiple deprivations due to multiple factors. They were deprived economically owing to the introduction of the systems e.g. rent, begari, thikadari, and zamindari, which received fresh impetus with the abolition of Khutkati and Bhuinhari rights. They were culturally and emotionally deprived because of non-redressal of their grievances despite their conversion to Christianity and experienced impact of Hindu values—the latter led even to their social ostracization. Finally, they experienced political deprivation in the sphere of decision-making, which, in the later phase, led them to agitate for a separate state. It was thus their perception of the exploitative situation which led them to launch movements and revolt against the existing social situation.

SUGGESTED READINGS

Aberle, D.F., "The Peyote Religion among the Navaho." *Viking Fund Publications in Anthropology No. 42*, New York : Wenner-Gren. Foundation, 1966.

Davidson, J., "Davidson's Report." *Journal of Bihar and Orissa Research Society 21(4), 1935.*

Ekka, P., "Revivalist Movements Among the Tribals of Chotanagpur" in K.S. Singh (ed). *Tribal Situation in India.* Simla : Indian Institute of Advanced Study, 1972.

Fuchs, Stephen, *Rebellious Prophets : A Study of Messianic Movements in Indian Religions.* Bombay : Asia Publishing House, 1965.

Gurr, T.R., *Why Man Rebels.* Princeton : Princeton University Press, 1970.

Mahapatra L.K., "Social Movements Among Tribes of India" in K.S. Singh (ed.) *Tribal Situation*. Simla: Indian Institute of Advanced Study, 1932.

Marx, Karl and Engels, Fredrick, *Selected Works*. Moscow: Progress Publishers, 1973.

Mazumdar, D.N., *Bombay*. Asia Publishing House. 1958.

Roy, S.C., 1912., *The Munda and their Country*. Bombay: Asia Publishing House, 1970.

Roy, S.C., *The Oraons of Chotanagpur*. Calcutta : The Brahma Mission, 1915.

——, 1928, *Oraon Religion and Customs*, Calcutta : S. Ghatak 1972, (reprint).

Sahay, K.N., Impact of Christianity on the Oraon of the Chainpur Belt in Chotanagpur : An Analysis of Iuts Cultmal Processes. *American Anthropologist*, Vol. 50, 921-42, 1966.

Sachchidananda, *Culture Change in Tribal Bihar—Munda and Oraon*. Calcutta : Bookland, 1964.

Singh, K.S., *The Duststorm and the Hanging Mist*. Calcutta : Firma K.L. Mukhopadhayay, 1966.

Vidyarthi, L.P., *Culture Contours of Tribal Bihar*. Calcutta : Punthi Pustak, 1964.

Vidyarthi, L.P., and Sahay K.N., *The Dynamics of Tribal Leadership in Bihar*. Allahabad : Kitab Mahal, 1978.

Wallace, A.F.C., "Revitalization Movements." *American Anthropologist*, Vol. 58 (April) pp. 264-81, 1956.

TWO

Sachchidananda

MUNDA GENIUS AND THE CHALLENGE OF MODERNISM

THE MUNDA of Chotanagpur are one of the most significant tribes of middle India not only because of their numbers but also because of their long history, distinctive culture and rich heritage. They had evolved a polity suited to their needs and environment. This helped them keep their social norms intact, promote tribal solidarity and helped utilise leadership skills at various levels. By and large, their political organization was seen at two levels : the village and *Parha*. The latter was a federation of a number of villages whose principles of affiliation differed in the two areas of Munda habitat. In one area the basis of affiliation was just contiguity; in the other it was the clan.

Each village had a council (*Hatu* panchayat) comprising village officers like the *Munda* (secular headman), the *Pahan* (religious headman), their assistants, wherever they existed, and heads of influential families. The council punished breaches of social norms, decided disputes between villagers, dealt with cases of violence and grievous hurt and fixed the dates for festivals. Only some villages had a *tola* or the ward council. This, too, dealt with the same business. But appeals from its decision could be made to the village council.

More significant was the Parha council. It consisted of the headman of each village in its jurisdiction. It had a number of office-bearers each with well-defined functions. The head of the council was known as Raja. He was assisted by a *Dewan*, *Sipahi*, *Kotwar*, *Pande*, *Dhobi*, *Pankhawas* etc. The Parha council heard appeals from village councils, decided disputes between two villages and took final decisions about excommunicating a person or readmitting him into the tribe. It also dealt with breaches of such social taboos as sexual relations inside one clan or outside the tribe.

The Parha organisation has been fairly active in the Bhuinhari area. The council is a fixed body with a permanent president and a stable staff of officers. The office-bearers are hereditary and enjoy immense prestige. Each officer is associated with a distinct village. As headman of the village he performs the tasks traditionally given to the village at the meeting of the Parha. Such villages are even known as the Raja village, Dewan village, Kotwar village etc. Elaborate procedures are laid down for the council meeting and transaction of business. The meetings of a number of such Parha are still lively. Important decisions regarding cases or problems are taken at these meetings. Such Parha are the Guria Parha, Topno Parha, Soy Parha, Bhengra Parha, Sanga Parha, etc.

The Munda in the Bhuinhari area speak of 22 original clans. The uniclan villages of that area were grouped into 22 Parha, each named after a clan. Early in this century a joint meeting of Parha heads was held at Pithoria at which Barla Parha was chosen as the chief. At the next meeting of this organisation, known as Bais Parha (after the number 22), Topno Parha was elected chief. In 1946, Guria Parha became the head and Mangra, the chief of that Parha, was styled as Parha Maharaja of Bais Parha. On his death, Paulus Guria became the acting maharaja but he has not yet been confirmed.

The last meeting of the Bais Parha Mahasabha was held at Pakra in 1974. Prabhudayal Bage was elected its chairman and Masialant Topno became the secretary. It was decided that each Parha should contribute Rs. 5 per month to the Mahasabha fund. A written constitution was adopted. The new body is known as the Munda Parha Sabha. It is to have jurisdiction over the Munda living in Chotanagpur, Assam, Bhutan, Andaman Nicobar and Thailand. Its authority is vested in the *Parha Hadri.* The traditional political organisations of the Munda, such as the Hatu Sabha or the village council and the Parha Sabha, are being modernised to suit the social, economic and political changes taking place in the tribal areas and the country at large. An effort is being made to incorporate modern democratic values so as to strengthen the existing traditional institutions to promote the welfare of the tribals.

The objectives of this organisation are all-inclusive. The former organisation was confined to settling disputes between two Parhas and taking decisions in serious cases involving excommunication from the tribe. Its function was only regulatory. It fulfilled the need of a mechanism for the preservation of the social norms of the tribe and served as an instrument of Parha solidarity. For the first time this organisation embraced the entire tribe and brought the Munda living in far-flung areas under one umbrella. The objectives set forth in the constitution are to ameliorate the social and economic conditions of the Munda in agriculture, trade and industry, to safeguard traditional monuments, relics, rights, language, etc. to make progress in the field of education, health, living standard, character, etc. and to develop friendly relations with neighbours and to follow the principle of peace, non-violence and patriotism.

The constitution not only provides for the formation and functions of the Parha Mahasabha but also for the Hatu and the Parha Sabha. It is laid down that the Hatu Sabha will be formed by the Munda, Mahto and *Pahan Khunts* (lineages) of the dominant clan in the village. The dominant clan shall comprise three-fourths of the village population. It will exercise administrative and judicial power in the village. It will be accountable to the Parha Sabha of the clan. There will be only one representative for every fifty persons or more than half of this number from each of the various lineages in the village. The head of the sabha will be chosen from the Munda lineage of the clan.

One representative from each of the Hatu Sabhas will form the Parha Sabha and elect the Parha Raja from among themselves. The Parha Sabha will look after the administration, security and progress of the villages in the Parha. It will be responsible to the Parha Mahasabha. The Parha Sabha will have a *Sabhapati* (president) and *Mantri* (secretary). These will be chosen from among the members. The tenure of the office-bearers will be five years. Members of other clans residing in that area will also have representation in the Parha Sabha.

New Features

A number of new features have been introduced at the Parha level organisation. For the first time representation has been given to the minor clans living in the Parha area. This enhances the representative character of the organisation. Formerly the office-bearers of the Parha held their office on an ex-officio basis, each being the headman of such villages which had been assigned specific duties at Parha meets, such as the Dewan, Kotwar, Sipahi, Dhobi, etc. The introduction of the elective principle and fixing a tenure for the office-bearers are distinct innovations. In the traditional system the Parha Raja and its executives were not accountable to anyone. In the new constitution they have been made responsible to the inter-Parha organisation.

The new organisation is now known as the *Parha Hadri*. It has the powers of superintendence, direction and control of different Parha Sabhas and is expected to work for the progress of the Munda tribe as a whole. The Parha Hadri will have five representatives, including the Parha Raja from each Parha. The office-bearers of the Parha Hadri will be Sabhapati (president), Mantri (secretary), *Khajanchi* (treasurer), and two members will be elected for every five thousand Hatu Sabha members. The Parha Hadri will meet twice annually. It will be elected for five years.

The Parha Hadri has the power to allow its members to establish or cut off relations with other friendly communities, organisations and institutions in the area for the welfare of Munda society. It can look into the internal administration of a member Parha Sabha if the latter does not conform to rules and regulations. It can punish the Parha Sabha by stopping monetary aid or by supersession. The Parha Hadri will hear appeals from the decisions of the Parha Sabhas. It will safeguard the social customs and norms of Munda society. It will instruct the Munda not to have relations with such people whose norms and customs are very different and who may harm the Munda way of life. The Parha Hadri will prepare the annual budget and apportion it for each Parha. It will formulate an economic policy and take the responsibility of sending poor students for higher education, digging of drinking water wells, opening of dispensaries etc. It will also arrange for the publication of books about the life and culture of the Munda. Thus we see that the functions of the Parha Hadri are more welfare oriented rather than regulatory and are designed to preserve and promote Munda culture.

The office-bearers of the Parha Hadri will be entitled to a salary as fixed by that body. The head of the Parha Mahasabha will preside over all meetings and also at the installation of other officials. Without his signature no decision will be valid. The Mantri will keep record of all proceedings and also issue notices for meetings. The *Bhandari* (accountant) will maintain the accounts and present a statement at the meeting of the Hadri. Any official not abiding by the rules and regulations can be suspended by two-third votes of the Parha Hadri members.

At the apex level there is another organisation known as the Parha Parishad. The Parha Maharaja, the Mantri and the Treasurer of the Parha Hadri also function in the same capacity in this organisation. Each Parha will send to this body one or more representatives depending on the strength of its adult population. For each 5,000 adults a Parha will send one representative, for 10,000 or less two representatives, and above 15,000 three representatives. In case a Parha sends two or more representatives to the Parishad, one of them must be the Parha Raja. This body will meet twice a year to review the working of the Parha. At the annual meeting it will present its estimated budget for the coming year to the Parha Hadri. An executive committee has also been provided for the Parha Parishad. It will have eight elected members in addition to the Parha Maharaj, Mantri and Treasurer. This executive body will decide urgent issues when the bigger body is not in session.

If there is a vacancy in the membership of the Parha Parishad by death or expulsion or continued absence, a new member will be taken from the same Parha to replace him for the unexpired period of the tenure of the Parishad. The Parha Parishad has been given overseeing powers over the Parha Sabhas. It is the duty of the Parha Parishad to see that the Parha Sabhas function according to the direction of the Parha Hadri and the Parha Parishad. It can also investigate the affairs of a Parha Sabha on a written request from that body. It has also the power to warn and caution the erring Parha Sabha.

Elaborate rules have been framed to regulate the procedure of the meetings of the Parha Hadri and the Parha Parishad. The secretary of the Parha Hadri is given the names of the representatives from the particular Parha by the Parha Raja. He cannot make a change without the permission of the concerned Parha Raja. The Maharaja, who is the head of both the organisations, prepares the annual report which is discussed at the Parha Hadri meetings. In case there is no unanimity on certain issues, the case is decided by majority vote by show of hands. The Maharaja has been given a casting vote in case of a tie. The rules and regulations of the Parha and the Hadri can be amended only by two-thirds majority of the members of these bodies.

This brief review of the transformation of Munda political institutions is an evidence of the genius of the Munda people in meeting the challenges of modern times. The existing pyramidal structure of Munda polity has been expanded to include not only the Munda living in that region but in other areas of India and outside. It may not be possible for the Munda living in other regions to participate in the newly contrived polity on account of the large distances involved. But it is a measure of the aspirations of the Munda community for embracing in its formal organisation all its widely dispersed constituents, and its longing for forging pan-Munda solidarity.

The main task of the newly formed organisations is not just regulatory or that of boundary maintenance, it is largely welfare oriented and very functional to the present situation. It is also noteworthy that at the lowest levels of the newly devised polity, Munda not belonging to the dominant clans after which the Parha has been named have also been given some representation. Earlier such Munda people were regarded as aliens and had no voice in the affairs of the Parha. The recent innovation adds to the legitimacy of the Parha organisation as such.

The apex level institutions have been set up largely to deal with education, poverty and development as also matters related to promotion of the Mundari language and culture. This latter task is considered important from the point of view of strengthening tribal identity. It is also seen that modern democratic procedures have been introduced. This gives a touch of modernity to the ancient Parha-based institutions. The hereditary character of membership has disappeared in the process of modernisation. However, old designations have been retained to provide legitimacy and traditional sanction for these institutions. A close look at the transformation, particularly in its political aspect, brings out the facts that the inspiration has been largely provided by the G.E.L. Church, which is a potent force in the Munda area. It is the church and its followers who have rediscovered the strength of the Munda political institutions and given them a new content without sacrificing the old form.

THREE

P.C. Ray

SOCIO-POLITICAL AND TECHNOLOGICAL FACTORS IN TRANSFORMATION

THIS paper deals with the ontogenetic development of socio-political movements initiated mainly by the Santal and the Munda; the overt action taken by the government to quell these uprisings, the causative factors behind these and the resulting effect of government action on the tribals' way of life.

The Santal are the most numerous of Indian tribes. They generally inhabit the hills and forests of West Bengal, Bihar and Orissa. Physically, they belong to the Proto-Australoid stock, like the Munda (Guha : 1944).

Because of the enactment of the Permanent Zamindary Settlement in 1790, the newly created zamindars (landlords), to increase their own income, engaged the Santal for clearing the forest areas. As a result, they migrated to the Rajmahal Hills and to different areas of West Bengal and Orissa. As the maximum concentration took place in Santal Parganas (*Damin-i-Koh*), it ultimately became the centre of Santal tribal life. These people paid minimal rent to the government. They were leading a peaceful life till the infiltration of Hindu traders and money-lenders, who exploited them in such a way as to make them destitute. Those who could not pay the money-lenders became their serfs; whereas the others fled out of desperation. The government did nothing to stop this exploitation. As a retaliation, the Santal who remained, revolted against the British and the traders. They raised their own militia and under the able guidance of two brothers, Sido and Kanu, these oppressed people, during the first half of 1855, began to attack government officials, traders and money-lenders. Martial law was proclaimed in the affected areas, and the revolt was ruthlessly put to an end by the close of the year. Sido lost his life and Kanu was hanged (Datta-Majumdar : 1955).

A natural after-effect of the rebellion was that the Santal were plunged into deeper poverty. Many of them were compelled to migrate to Northern Bengal, Assam and Orissa to earn their livelihood.

After the revolt, a separate district, known as Santal Parganas, comprising the territory in and around Damin-i-Koh, was created and by Act XXXVII of 1885, the district was exempted from general laws and regulations. A special law was introduced to safeguard the interest of the Santal. Unfortunately these measures could not improve their plight as they had to seek the help of the money-lenders again for sustenance. The government did nothing to improve their financial position.

Another socio-political uprising initiated by the Santal after the great rebellion was the *Kharwar* or *Sapha Hor*. It was sponsored by Bhagirath Babaji, a Hindu religious leader, in 1871. Some Hinduised forms of rituals, such as worship of Babaji and the Hindu deity Mahadeo, were introduced. The disciples did not take liquor and flesh of fowl and pig. As this spiritual movement was considered by the government a socio-political agitation under the guise of religious reform, it was soon suppressed by the government by arresting its leaders (O'Malley : 1910).

There is reason to believe that this agitation was the spiritual counterpart of the unsuccessful Santal rebellion. In other words, it provided a compensatory channel for their pent-up emotions.

Another political agitation, known as *Bisham Sendra*, came into being in or about 1950. Being oppressed by money-lenders, government officials and other aliens, the Santal took recourse to a "do-or-die" attitude. They vowed that the *Diku* (alien people) should be driven out of Santal Parganas if the Santal were to survive. So they began attacking the alien people and government officers. As a result, chaotic conditions prevailed for some time. Many Santal were arrested. To appease them, the government formed a peace council comprising prominent members from different tribal communities. Subsequently these leaders formed a political party known as Jharkhand under the leadership of the great tribal leader, Jaipal Singh. In course of time, this movement subsided considerably as some of its members joined the provincial and central governments.

It is worth mentioning that during the National movement of 1942, spearheaded by the Congress, these oppressed tribes of Santal Parganas, especially of the Bokrabandh area, participated in it under the able guidance of their leaders and of Paharia, an aggressive tribe. During this disturbance, the Bokrabandh dak bangalow was burnt down and government properties were looted (Ray : 1975).

The Munda

The Munda are an endogamous tribe with several exogamous clans. The aboriginal Munda were an honest, simple, good natured and industrious people. In spite of harassment by Brahminical invaders, they were always hale and hearty and indulged in alcoholic drinking and dancing which were part and parcel of their life (Roy : 1912). According to tradition, a change in their socio-political system was introduced by the Munda themselves during 64 to 100 A.D., which adversely affected their life later. They unwittingly sealed their fate by acknowledging the Maharaja of Chotanagpur as their overall chief. He introduced the middleman, such as the alien landlord, to look after the affairs of the Munda. These landlords initiated new agrarian measures, which broke their traditional democratic system. What happened was that in 1822, the Maharaja created a new class of landlords, comprising Sikhs, Muslims and Hindus, who were given temporary lease of the Mundari villages. Consequently, the Munda were deprived of their immemorial right of ownership of their villages and land by the alien oppressors. They were allowed to hold on to only some portion of their lands. Over and above that, these landlords began to collect rent, hitherto unknown to these people (Roy : 1912). In retaliation (Dalton : 1872), they resolved to take recourse to plunder, murder and arson. On 11 December

1831, they raided the houses of Muslims, Sikhs and landlords. Even police stations were not spared. The ruling class was not prepared for such an assault. However, after many lives were lost, the insurrection came to an end on 19 March 1832. The Munda obtained some redress of their grievances as the revolt brought about some changes in the administrative set-up of the Munda country.

In spite of these changes, these people were being reduced from "holders of the villages to holders of the plough" as they continued to be exposed to the oppression of alien landlords. It can be presumed that these landlords were indirectly supported by the British as no action was taken against them. Consequently, covert hostile feelings against the intruders were rapidly generated, resulting in overt manifestation of aggression towards the oppressors.

In 1845, these down-trodden and dejected people found in the missionaries a great ally. The missionaries not only imparted education to the Munda but also imbibed in them the spirit of self-help and self-assertion. They were made to realize that they had exclusive rights to villages and lands from which they had been dispossessed. As a natural consequence, they began to assert their right by forcibly re-occupying the lands. This infuriated the alien landlords, who viewed the spread of Christianity with displeasure, so much so that they began to beat the missionaries and the tribal Christians, and often instituted false cases against them.

Another great event that shook the Munda country and affected the way of life of the Christian Munda was the Sepoy Mutiny. Christian houses and villages were ransacked and the inhabitants had to flee to the jungle. The native Christian community was broken up, but their dispersion over the district seems to have given a considerable impetus to Christianity as the number of converts largely increased after the restoration of order (Hunter : 1877).

After the restoration of peace, the general plight of the Munda improved somewhat as different Christian missions helped the backward Munda to regenerate their socio-economic life. Education made them conscious of the injustice meted out to them by the alien people. As a result, another agrarian disturbance broke out in 1889 (Roy : 1912).

The year 1895 is an important landmark in the history of the Munda. Birsa Munda, an attractive youth of 25, who had been educated in missionary schools, began a religious movement which later assumed the shape of a socio-political uprising. Birsa, being dissatisfied with the teachings of the missionaries, who hurt the feelings of the tribals by speaking ill of their religion, left their association. For some reason, he also left his village and returned after the great devastation caused by famine and the resulting epidemic, which ravaged the Munda country in 1897-99. On his return, he dedicated himself to selfless service by engaging himself in nursing the sick and the dying. As luck would have it, his magic touch healed the sick, and his activities earned great appreciation for him from the Munda and other tribals. Stories about his miraculous powers spread throughout the country, and the Munda gathered round him and proclaimed him as Bhagwan, that is, God (Sachchidananda : 1964).

In spite of several measures taken by the government, the Munda were harassed from all sides by the money-lenders and other alien aggressors, who did not hesitate to take forcible possession of their lands when opportunity came. Moreover, the activities of the missionaries—conversions as well as preachings against their religion—created in them a feeling of distrust against the missionaries on the one hand, and hatred towards the alien people on the other. So tensional feelings, already there in the mind of the Munda, were accentuated by the teachings of Birsa and gave vent to overt aggression under his able leadership. An insurrection took place but it was quickly suppressed by the government and Birsa was arrested.

After Birsa's release, his prestige rose in the eyes of his people. He was no doubt a clever politician and able organiser who had dedicated himself to the socio-economic and political upliftment of his people. He used the opportunity of his enhanced prestige to unite the people to fight the common aggressor, that is the alien people and the missionaries. He trained them in the use of the bow and arrow and other lethal weapons. He was also a shrewd man as he fixed the timing of his attack for Christmas in 1899. Armed Munda under his leadership attacked missions, houses of landlords and police stations. Many fled and many were killed. Chaotic conditions prevailed for sometime. Troops were called to quell the revolt, and the final show down took place on the Damburi Hill on 9th January, 1900. In this encounter, many men, women and children were killed. Birsa was arrested and subsequently died of cholera in prison (Sachchidananda : 1964). His death is shrouded in mystery like similar deaths in world prisons in similar conditions.

Thus a glorious epoch in the history of the Mundari people came to an abrupt end. Birsa originally started his movement as a religious reformist. Later, the religious flavour receded to the background and the agitation was converted into a freedom struggle. The oppressed Munda found in Birsa a great patriot and a prophet with supernatural power. They sincerely believed that he was capable of freeing them from the yoke of the oppressors. He instilled in them a feeling of solidarity by uniting them to fight the aggressors who had reduced them to destitution. Birsa was a politician, a diplomat with tact and intelligence, and a religious reformer as well. Though he was unsuccessful, his movement paved the way for adoption of some agrarian measures by the government for the betterment of the Munda by promulgating the Chotanagpur Tenancy Act, 1908 (Roy : 1912). He is the main source of inspiration for initiating agitations by the tribals of Chotanagpur at present.

Birsa is adored as "Birsa Bhagwan" as well as a great national leader. Statues of him have been installed at different places in the district of Ranchi, and the tribals, especially the Munda and the Oraon, pay homage to this great leader at least once a year during his birth anniversary at Khunti. The author during his studies among the Munda in 1969 attended the anniversary meeting at Khunti. It was addressed by prominent leaders, MPs and MLAs. One of the leaders declared, "Birsa is not only honoured by us but by others as well. Like Gandhiji, he is also known to foreigners. He waged war against the British and alien oppressors. Now it is proper time to act according to Birsa's teachings." Another leader declared, "Our leaders are not guiding us properly as Birsa did. No one will grant us freedom; it will have to be acquired by force. Though India has attained freedom, we are not free. We are under bondage as we are still under the yoke of oppressors and exploiters. We must unite".

Another organisation, known as Birsa Seva Dal, headed by a prominent Munda has been functioning among these people for a pretty long time. Most of the members, who are Christians, think that the Indian people can be divided into two groups, namely Diku and non-Diku. It is interesting to note that members of this organization shun the Hindus and try to persuade the non-Christian Munda to become Christian. (The people of the Kolarian tribe use the term *Diku* or *Deko* to mean the alien people. On the other hand, some old informants told the author that this term was first coined by the missionaries to mean mainly the Hindus to imbue in the mind of the tribals the idea to look upon Hindus as exploiters).

At Khunti, the author came in contact with another organisation, called the Juba Sangha. Some young Christian and non-Christian Munda of good education had formed this organisation to fight those alien people who misbehaved with them, especially with their women. Its members did not hesitate to take the law into their hands, if need be, and to take recourse to physical violence against a Diku if he dared ill-treat their women.

As the Jharkhand movement is a pressing one for both the tribals and the government, its peaceful resolution is essential for the welfare of the country. The first political conference among the tribals of Chotanagpur took place in 1915 under the leadership of educated Christian Munda. On or about 1927, the Chotanagpur Unnati Samaj was formed for the socio-economic upliftment of the tribals. In 1938, the Adibashi Mahasava was set up to demand a separate state for the Adivasis of the region. In 1950, the Jharkhand Party comprising all scheduled tribes of Chotanagpur, was formed under the able guidance of an Oxford-educated Munda, Jaipal Singh. Though he was employed in different jobs, including the ministership of Bikaner state, he resigned that coveted post and dedicated himself to the uplift of his people. He subsequently became an MP.

In 1963, the Jharkhand Party was merged with the Congress whose leaders promised to uplift the socio-economic and political status of the tribals. As the Congress did not keep up its promise, the Jharkhand party was revived. Later, some factions comprising younger members initiated several movements in 1973-75 by introducing collective farming, schooling, banking and collective labour. Thus they were successful for the time being in reducing exploitation by money-lenders, landlords and contractors. Another "non-cooperation" movement was organised from 22 May to 14 August. Taxes were not paid; survey settlement revenue camps were rendered *inactive and work on projects* was stopped. Moreover, they boycotted the panchayat election (Arun Sinha : 1978). There has been a gradual change in the policy of the Jharkhand Party, which reflects the changing socio-political attitude of the people. It is worth mentioning that some of the Santal have joined the Naxalites—a terrorist party known as the Communist Party of India, Marxist-Leninist (CPI-ML). One Santal is a prominent leader of one of its six groups. Last but not the least, it may be mentioned that the legislators belonging to Scheduled Castes and Tribes have set up a joint front on an all-India basis to safeguard their interest.

Change in World-Outlook

The following account will reveal the nature of the impact of alien forces which caused a change in their "world- outlook" and "attitudes", leading to a gradual socio-political transformation of the Santal and the Munda as compared to their aboriginal ancestors.

Santal

The Permanent Zamindary Settlement of 1970 created new landlords who engaged the Santal in forced labour. As a result many fled. Those who remained did not put up any resistance and accepted their miserable plight as inevitable. In due course of time the Santal who did not flee revolted against the government and the alien oppressors. In this struggle, they were guided by two capable Santal brothers. This insurrection compelled the government to introduce some reforms. The Santal realised for the first time that aggression should be met by aggression. The ever-increasing exploitation by alien aggressors forced them to see that their pitiable condition was caused by human beings and not by fate. But it took nearly 100 years to change their covert attitude into an overt one.

Another socio-political movement, Sapha Hor, was initiated by a Hindu religious leader in 1871, that is 16 years after the first Santal rebellion. The government considered it an offshoot of the unsuccessful Santal revolt; so it arrested the leaders and the movement subsided.

The next mentionable agitation, known as Bisham Sendra, took place three years after independence, i.e. in 1950. This time, the Santal took a vow to drive out the alien exploiters from Santal Parganas. To achieve this aim, they began to attack government officials, money-lenders and the alien people. The national government, though it arrested some people, wisely took a compromising attitude by forming a peace council consisting of prominent tribal leaders, for finding out ways and means for their upliftment. The Santal and their leaders believed that formation of the peace council was a good gesture on the government's part. So peace was more or less restored till the formation of the Jharkhand Party.

The Santal of Santal Parganas had joined the national movement to drive out the British. The question that naturally arises : why did they join hands with an "alien" people whom they wanted to drive out from their country through the Bisham Sendra movement. The reason appears to be that these simple-minded people identified themselves with the alien people, as both were exploited by the non-Indian alien. Their attitude was : the common aggressor must be driven out. They sincerely believed in the view put forth by the Congress that both the tribals and non-tribals were exploited by the British. They knew better than the alien people the devastating effect of exploitation. So they decided to fight the common aggressor.

This attitude of the Santal may be compared with that of people of varying political colours who unite when the country is threatened with aggression. Practical necessity arising out of their struggle for existence had been gradually changing their "world-outlook", and these changed attitudes are the real cause behind their socio-political transformation. It will be of great interest to include here the observation of Martin Orans (1965). He says that though the Santal have changed their world-outlook and attitudes vis-a-vis their native values owing to contact with the alien people, yet they are not inclined to integrate themselves with Hindus and others. On the contrary, they ardently desire to establish their own great tradition. This attitude is not unnatural as "a burnt child dreads the fire."

In comparison to the Santal, the Munda were more victimized, but they fought back valiantly against the oppressors, that is, the Brahminical invaders. The foreign missionaries helped them immensely in their fight against the aggression committed by the alien people.

As to the ontogenetic development of their socio-political attitude, it may be mentioned that being oppressed by alien landlords, they attacked, murdered and plundered the houses of Hindus, Muslims and Sikhs in 1831. This agitation ended in 1832 when they obtained some redress of their grievances in the form of certain changes in the administrative set-up of the Munda country.

However, 14 years after the first agitation, they found a great ally among the missionaries. They were taught by the missionaries to assert their right over land. Having imbibed the spirit of self-help and self-reliance, they began to reoccupy the lands which had been forcibly taken away from them by landlords. As a consequence, the missionaries and the Munda were harassed on all sides by landlords. Education made the Munda aware of the injustice meted out to them by the alien people. As a result, another agrarian disturbance broke out in 1889, 44 years after the previous one.

It was the most well-organised revolt that shook the Munda country. It was initiated by Birsa Munda, who had been taught by the missionaries but who had left them as they spoke ill of his religion. It was the missionaries from whom he had learnt discipline, which helped him considerably in raising and training a big militia to fight the alien people, including the British. Another contributing factor was his enhanced prestige among the Munda, who hailed him as Birsa Bhagwan. The missionaries also imbibed in him the spirit of nationalism, which he not only applied against the alien oppressors but against the missionaries as well by attacking their houses during the revolt.

As time went on, the tribals received higher education

and found employment in government services. The first political conference of the elite tribals of Chotanagpur took place in 1915 under the leadership of the educated Christian Munda. In or around 1927, another conference was held for the socio-political upliftment of the people. However, a radical change in their political attitude took place in 1938 when Adivasi Mahasabha was set up and its leaders demanded a separate state for the tribals.

The year 1950 is an important landmark in the history of the tribals of Chotanagpur. The Jharkhand Party was formed at this time. It demanded a separate province for the tribals of that region. All the tribals were united in their demand as is evident from the fact that they won 70 per cent of the Scheduled Tribe seats in the first general election. As the leaders of the younger generation thought that a fight in the legislature would be of little avail, they started a non-cooperation movement in 1973-75. It is worth mentioning that Scheduled Tribe and Caste legislators have set up a joint front to wage a country-wide agitation for safeguarding the rights of their people.

To encapsulate, during the span of 150 years, the attitude of the Santal and the Munda has shown a gradual change which may be represented as follows : escapism or accepting the situation—slight opposition for socio-economic restoration—insurrection—socio-political organised revolt—fighting through the legislature—non-cooperation as well as fighting through the legislature—participation in the Naxalite movement.

Causative Factors

The ontogenetic development of socio-economic and political transformation of the two tribes referred to above has been caused by four principal impinging factors, namely, Hinduism, the British government, Christianity and industrialisation.

All aspects of their life, namely economic, socio-religious and linguistic, have been affected by Hinduism. However, the crucial change in their way of life has been caused by Hindu money-lenders, alien landlords and government officials, whose exploitation compelled these peace-loving people to take recourse to socio-political insurrection to improve their plight.

The impact of Christian missions has changed their way of life for their betterment when compared to other impinging factors, which acted as a deterrent to their configurational upliftment. Though these people had initiated a few insurrections before the advent of the missionaries, comparatively more or less successful rebellions took place after their arrival in this country. The reason is that the missionaries not only imbibed in them the spirit of nationalism, but also made them conscious of self-help, self-assertion and self-reliance. Education made these people aware that though they were the original settlers of the country, they had been deprived of their freedom by the alien people. These were the reasons that revolts during the days of the missionaries were comparatively more successful. As a result, the government was compelled to bring about agrarian and administrative changes through special measures.

In so far as the present-day Santal and the Munda are concerned, it may be pointed out that the spirit of nationalism, broken promises of the ruling class, the creation of autonomous tribal states in the eastern region and the exploitation still going on, have compelled them to demand a separate Jharkhand state. This demand is the natural consequence of historical sequences. Their attitude vis-a-vis the government is revealed by the following remarks of one of their leaders : "We demand a separate Jharkhand because they have made us refugees in our own land" (Arun Sinha : 1978). It may also be mentioned that since 1973, the new generation of the Adivasis has initiated several non-cooperation movements against the government to compel it to accept their demand.

Technological Factors

This paper is based on the published work of the author on the Santal (Ray : 1975). The field-work was conducted at Rupnarayanpur in Burdwan district of West Bengal. It is a town-village on the border of Bengal and Bihar. The Hindustan Cable Factory, the first of its kind in India, has been established a few years back near Rupnarayanpur railway station. The main population of this area is Santal and Scheduled castes.

About 57 families, mostly Santal, were displaced for the establishment of the factory. They were rehabilitated in 292 acres of land against 766.64 acres occupied by them prior to the displacement (Das et al : 1962). They had occupied 13.45 acres of land per family before the establishment of the factory, whereas they got 5.12 acres only after their rehabilitation. Most of the displaced persons were agriculturists. So they not only suffered psychological and social loss, but financial too. Rupnarayanpur is an industrial area, so different people like Punjabis, Sikhs, Marwaris and even the Santal and other tribals from different states have migrated there for earning their livelihood. The impact of industrialisation on the life of the local people, most of whom are Santal, has been tremendous. The ancestral social position, so long acknowledged by the people, has been replaced by a new one, as is evident from the fact that during the pre-industrial period the social position was mainly determined by caste, community and economic status, whereas in the post-industrial age economic status, service and education appear to be the key factors. Similar changes have taken place in other aspects of their way of life. To cite an example, it may be mentioned that class has now acquired a new meaning. A person belonging to any class or community having a factory job acquires a new status because of his official position. In this way a new social class has been formed.

Impact of Industrialisation

Economy : In the past, the occupation structure of the Santal was mainly agriculture. However, after industrialisation, that is, since the last decade, the shift in their occupational structure has been well marked. Though a great majority of the people (71.1 per cent) practise plough cultivation, yet 28.9 per cent are engaged in non-agricultural pursuits (Das et al : 1962). It is evident from Table 3.1 that compared to the industrial worker, their non-industrial counterparts have been living through debt. So to meet their necessities, the latter group generally borrow from money-lenders, factory workers and other sources. The shift in emphasis from traditional occupation has not only enhanced their social position but also helped them to attain financial security. Many of the Santal are naturally eager to engage themselves in factories and coal mines instead of doing agricultural work. The change in the pattern of economy resulting from industrialisation has affected their attitude to many aspects of their way of life.

TABLE 3.1

Annual Income and Expenditure of Industrial and Non-Industrial Workers

Class	Average income per family	Average expenditure per family	Balance at the end of the year
Industrial worker	Rs. 1265	Rs. 1135	plus Rs. 130
Non-industrial worker	Rs. 500	Rs. 513	minus Rs. 13

Socio-political Organisation

The village council exists but its functional status is gone. Now, in case of dispute many of the Santal complain to a person recognized as leader. If he cannot settle the dispute, the matter is either referred to the union board or to a court of law.

Industrialisation has also changed their family structure. At present most of the families are of nuclear type. The incidence of this pattern is more marked among the industrial workers (Das et al : 1962).

TABLE 3.2

Composition and Number of Families through Three Generations

Family Type	Grandfather 50-60 yrs. ago		Father 25-30 yrs. ago		Ego Present time	
	No.	per cent	No.	per cent	No.	per cent
Nuclear	9	25.7	23	65.7	25	71.7
Minimal extended	17	48.6	9	25.7	7	20.0
Extended	9	25.7	3	8.6	3	8.6

Table 3.2 shows that compared to grandfather's time, the informants' time shows an increase of 25.7 per cent to 71.7 per cent in the nuclear type of family. On the other hand, a decrease from 48.6 per cent to 20.0 per cent and 25.7 per cent to 8.6 per cent in minimal extended and extended families has been observed. This finding shows the changing pattern of family composition because of changing circumstances.

In this industrial zone, the traditional functional utility of a clan has almost become a bygone thing. Though its only function seems to lie in the regulation of marriage, marriage inside the clan and with outsiders is not uncommon. Inter-tribal, inter-community and inter-clan marriages are also taking place, though the incidence is not frequent. Although a rare occurrence before industrialisation, these unions are now recognized by society.

It is worth mentioning that the Sikhs and the Muslims from Bihar are also keeping Santal girls as concubines. It may be mentioned that the attitude of the Adivasi leaders is not favourable to industrial development. One of their leaders declared recently that "industrialisation has not helped the Biharis, and it has ruined the Adivasis. We are victims of development" (Sinha : 1978). Such comments are natural in view of the fact that since independence more than six lakh tribals have been uprooted but not properly rehabilitated. Moreover, according to nationalist tribal leaders, "they will restore the old, egalitarian tribal economy and wipe out the evils of the Hindu system, like castes, dowry and the worship of idols" (Sinha : 1978).

Child Training

No tales are now told to the children by way of imparting knowledge as was done in the days of their ancestors. The most-contact Santal, especially factory workers, have realized that without proper education they will not be able to uplift themselves to the desired position. Consequently, they are very keen to educate their children. The reason for this radical change in their outlook may be explained by the fact that in factories they come in contact with different ethnic groups from various parts of India. The natural reaction of such inter-mixing is that they are influenced by the way of life of the alien people. It not only decreases their ethnocentric attitude but enhances their level of aspiration. So they have a natural inclination to raise their social status by accepting the ego-ideal of their non-tribal co-workers, who are comparatively well-off in different spheres of life, including education. This change in the mental attitude is also applicable in case of tribal non-workers, because of their living in a cosmopolitan environment.

Santal Pantheon

These Santal rarely perform the worship of spirits or deities venerated by their ancestors. The younger generation appears to be more interested in worshipping Hindu deities of the Brahmins. This change in religious observances is the result of culture-contact and industrialisation. The causes behind this new trend may be explained as follows : first, many of them are busy in factories, coal-fields and so on from morning to night. They have neither the energy or time nor the required belief in appeasing spirits in an aboriginal way. Secondly, they live in a multi-cultural zone dominated by Hindus. So they are influenced by Hinduized forms of worship.

The Santal of this region has shown a marked departure from the way of life of their ancestors. It is not unnatural but inevitable. The economic system has undergone considerable change because of shift from agriculture to factory and office work. This change in occupation is inevitable because of its practical bearing. The reason is that most agriculturists live on a minus budget, whereas factory workers can save something in spite of their increased expenditure.

The socio-political organisation has also shown a marked change. The traditional headman and other officials have practically been ousted by influential Santal and non-Santal leaders. Industrial workers and other wage-earners have developed an egocentric attitude towards the nuclear type of family structure. On the other hand, they have developed an altruistic attitude towards marriage. The impact of industrialisation has also changed their attitude to ancestral customs, superstitions and religion. Hindu deities are worshipped and witches are no more dreaded. Magicians and witch-finders are rarely called; instead doctors are consulted.

SUGGESTED READINGS

Dalton, E.T., *Descriptive Ethnology of Bengal.* Calcutta : Superintendent, Government Printing, 1872.

Das, Amal Kumar et al, "Impact of Industrialisation on the Life of Tribals of West Bengal", *Bulletin of the Cultural Research Institute.* Special Series, No. 1, 1962, pp. 24, 32, 44, 47.

Datta-Majumdar, N., "The Santal : A Study in Culture Change", *Memoir 2. Department of Anthropology.* Government of India, 1955.

Guha, B.S., "Racial Elements in the Population", No. 22 *Oxford Pamphlets on Indian Affairs.* Bombay, Oxford University Press, 1944.

Hunter, William, *Statistical Account of Bengal*, Vol. XVI. Trubner & Co. London, 1877, p. 424.

O'Malley, L.S.S., *Bengal District Gazetteers*, Santal Parganas, (1910), pp. 106-147.

Orans, Martin., *The Santal : A Tribe in Search of a Great Tradition.* Detroit : Wayne State University Press, 1965.

Ray, P.C., "Socio-cultural Processes and Psychological Adaptation of the Santal". *Memoir 33, Anthropogical Survey of India*, 1975, pp. 1-5, 33-39.

Roy, Sarat Chandra, *The Munda and their Country.* Calcutta : City Book Society, 1912, pp. 114-200.

Sachchidananda, *Culture Change in Tribal Bihar (Munda and Oraon)*, Calcutta : Bookland (Private) Ltd., 1964.

Sinha, Arun, "Tensions Mounting in Jharkhand". *Sunday*, Vol. 6, Issue 27. Calcutta : Ananda Bazar Publication. 1978.

FOUR

Almut Mey

MODERNIZATION IN THE CHITTAGONG HILL TRACTS

THE Chittagong Hill Tracts (CHT) of Bangla Desh are inhabited by 12 different ethnic groups who are, in general, shifting cultivators in the hills and plough cultivators in the flat lands. The two largest tribes, the Chakma and Marma, live in the valleys. Each consists of more than 130,000 persons. The bulk of the Tippera lives in the Indian state of Tripura, but some 10,000 are also valley inhabitants of the CHT. The hill tribes proper, settled on the mountain slopes and tops of the hills, are the Mru (15,000), the Khumi (2,000), the Bawm (8,000), the Pangkhua (1,000), and the Mizo, formerly called Lushai (some hundred persons).

Originally classed with the valley tribes, but nowadays mostly living in the hills, too, are the Taungchengya, a sub-group of the Chakma, which split away from the main tribe long ago (12,000), the Mrung, a sub-group of the Tippera (both together 35,000) and the small groups of the Sak (2,000) and Khiang (1000). All these groups, except the Chakma and Tippera, speak Tibeto-Burman languages; the Chakma, an old form of the East Bengali dialect, and the Tippera, an idiom of ths Bodo languages.

The third large group, besides the traditionally distinguished groups of the hill and valley people, is an uncounted number of Bengali immigrants whose influence and numbers are increasing more and more. In the 1960s there were approximately 25,000 Bengali Muslims and 2000 Hindus; more came in the following decade. Chakma and Marma practise Buddhism; the Tippera are Hindus; most of the Bawm, the Mizo and a part of the Pangkhua and Khiang are Christians, and the rest of the ethnic groups animists.

As far as the people can read and write, the Marma use Burmese letters (Marma means Burman), the Bawm and Mizo since their Christianisation use Latin letters (systems of transcription were developed by Christian missionaries), administrative correspondence still is widely done in English, and the Bengali inhabitants use Bengali, just as Bengali is the medium of instruction in governmental schools of whatsoever tribe. The other ethnic groups are still mostly illiterate.

The basis of all economies in the CHT is agriculture, though there are decisive differences. The hill tribes proper practise shifting cultivation (locally known as *jhum*). The valley tribes are to a large extent plough cultivators of wet rice, many of them, however, practise shifting cultivation as well, and quite a number are shifting cultivators only.

The official government policy always considered the CHT as a backward area with primitive, reluctant tribal groups without any culture and civilisation. Modernisation, therefore, in the eyes of the Bengali administration can only result from impacts of development schemes of the plains' population.

I shall try to show how modernisation is actually working in the Hill Tracts. Until now there were no socio-economic analyses of this area, only some monographs and some short articles. Former anthropological works on the CHT drew their conclusions mainly from one or two villages only. My investigations in the CHT were the first to use a large sample of 600 households in 24 villages of eight different tribes. This does not only allow inter-ethnic comparisons but also takes into account the threefold ecological and economical division of the Hill Tracts. One of these villages was visited for a longer period in 1964 and 1968, two more in 1969, and investigations in the rest of the villages were made during the first month of 1971.

I chose five villages with plough cultivation and gardening in the northern and in the middle part of the Hill Tracts, the inhabitants being Chakma and Marma. Typical was a special type of plough cultivation, called fringe-land cultivation. Fringe-land is arable land in the Karnafuli lake area, which is submerged during the rainy season and emerges during the dry period when the water level of the lake drops. This land can be cultivated only for a very short time in the dry season. Besides that I got data from a Chakma village with mixed cultivation (fringe-land cultivation, shifting cultivation and gardening) and two Chakma and Taungchengya villages inhabited by shifting cultivators only.

The shifting cultivators of the southern part of the CHT are represented by 16 smaller villages, seven of which have taken to gardening in recent years. They were inhabited by Bawm, Khiang, Hill-Marma, Taungchengya, Mru, Khumi and Tippera.

Whatever inquiries in the post-colonial development of the CHT are made, they cannot evade the consequences of the construction of the Kaptai dam, which created the artificial Karnafuli lake, the most lasting interference in the life of the hill tribes until now. The Karnafuli Multipurpose Scheme (also known as the Kaptai Hydel Project) was considered one of the most important development projects of former East Pakistan. Actually, first of all Chittagong, and here especially the harbour, was the beneficiary of the hydro-electric power. For the tribes of that part of the Hill Tracts the project turned out to be a catastrophe.

During the first year of the 1960s, the lake inundated 253 square miles, 50,000 acres of settled cultivated land, which is about 40 per cent of the district's total cultivable area Finally, more than 100,000 persons, 90 per cent of these Chakma, were displaced and never adequately rehabilitated. About 40,000 Chakma migrated to the neighbouring Indian states of Tripura and Assam, a large proportion of them was settled later on by the Indian government in NEFA.

As to the rehabilitation, the affected Bengali plough cultivators were resettled first on the best land; the Chakma, Marma and Taungchengya had to take a backseat. No rehabilitation at all was provided to the displaced shifting cultivators of the reservoir area, who lost 113,000 acres of land. The best solution might have been to deforest land in the reserved forests which comprise one-third of the Hill Tracts' total area. But the forest officers were particularly uncompromising in holding onto the reserved forest land, which is a rich source for the production of teak, bamboo and other timber, the profits of which go into the pockets of Bengali contractors and the said department.

Accordingly there is a high rate of land scarcity not only of flat land, but also of land for shifting cultivation. Many of the not adequately rehabilitated plough cultivators had to return fully or partly to the traditional method of shifting cultivation. The displaced shifting cultivators of the reservoir area had to look for *jhum* land on the hill ridges and tops, thus pressing additionally on the land of the other shifting cultivators.

Instead of opening some of the reserved forests to jhuming, the Bengali government started two new projects in the course of "development planning", the Jhum Control Scheme and the Standard Horticultural Holding. The ultimate object of the Jhum Control Scheme was "to introduce correct form of land uses and to discourage jhuming" (Pilot Scheme: 3). The justification for the plan to abolish jhum totally at long date was derived from the fact that the rotation time in jhum had fallen down to 2-3 years, so the yield per acre is not enough to feed the population. It was never mentioned why the rotation time had come down, namely because of the pressure on the land caused by the lake. It is very easy to interchange cause and effect officially. At the time of my inquiry the scheme was only working in the rehabilitation areas and brought a lot of trouble to the shifting cultivators whose jhuming was controlled and restrained so that the yield of the over jhumed fields was permanently decreasing.

The second governmental development project planned the introduction of the so-called Standard Horticultural Holding. The aim of this project was to abandon the rice production in the CHT for the sake of horticulture, thus meeting the demands in the plains, at the same time bringing about the total dependence of the hill tribes on Bengali markets. The population resisted the administrative compulsion to cultivate fruit combinations at will, the advantages and disadvantages of which were not iuquired into and proved at all. The results of this wrong, only ethnocentric-orientated government policy, were local famines in 1964, and as a *novum* in the history of the CHT, cases of starvation.

Now let us regard the changes caused by varying reactions of the hill tribes to the exogenous impacts. With the spreading of plough cultivation in the CHT (until 1860 only jhum was practised in this area) separate developments were within sight. Before that innovation everybody had the same rights to the land, swidden land was and still is considered as communal property with the private right to usufruct only. As successor to the British, the Bengali government claims the land as state property, but this is contradictory to the traditional common law of the hills. Jhum land cannot be bought or sold. Jhum-tax is levied because the state has acquired the supreme rights to the land, but not as a rent for a particular plot. As access to land is equal and swidden fields are not subject to any financial transactions, usually everybody has the same chance in the system of shifting cultivation. Therefore the societies of the hill tribes proper who all practise jhum turn out to be rather egalitarian ones.

Plough land, on the other hand, is leased by the administration. The rent is paid according to the quality and size of the land. It can be inherited, and all potential heirs hang on to it. The problem is that the plough land was always limited, not only after the dam. The land which is nowadays still available is insufficient for the families who want to cultivate on flat land. The percentage of landless families in my sample of plough cultivators had already gone up to as much as 29 per cent in the case of one village. These people have to work as day labourers, usually finding work only during harvest time, that is for 3-4 months every year. These diverging conditions of ownership not only led to a polarization beween formerly rather equal people, but also to gradual transition to market production.

There had always been a certain surplus production which was sold in the markets. Spices, tools and luxury goods were bought in return from the plains. The traditional cash crops are cotton, rice, chillies and sesame, still cultivated for that purpose by the Mru, Khumi, Tippera, Taungchengya and the bulk of the Hill-Marma. The shifting cultivators of the reservoir area have turned to turmeric and ginger, root crops being the new, most promising cash crops besides cotton.

Most ethnic groups are still selling rice as cash crop because of their high indebtedness, with the result that they have to borrow rice, or money for rice some months later in the shops of Bengali or from the few rich tribal money-lenders.

The flat land cultivators and the Bawm in the hills (to a less extent some Bawm-influenced Khiang and government-influenced Hill-Marma) found a new response to the scarcity of land in turning to horticulture. This new branch of production has gained importance as a new method of growing cash crops to meet the increasing demands of the plains. The first to start orchards were the Bawm, who were influenced by the Lushai by whom they were christianized. The first garden was established by a Lushai in 1936 in the southern Bawm area.

The valley people, however, started horticulture not before the construction of the Kaptai dam in the context of the rehabilitation programme, but because government aid was incomplete and inappropriate. Gardening became a success only after the people took the initiative and organisation into their own hands.

Land rights in garden cultivation are similar to those of plough cultivators. Garden-land is rented on government lease, the tax at the time of my inquiry was Rs. 2 per acre. The families produce individually and are the proprietors of the fruit. Garden possession comprises the—however illegal—possibility to sublet and to come to new sources of income that way.

Bengali middlemen have monopolised the marketing facilities and they naturally pay the minimum price. Exploitation by middlemen is one of the greatest problems faced by cultivators. Ninety-eight per cent of all business and all the shops in the markets of the Hill Tracts are in the hands of people from the plain districts. As measures of self-defence against the uncontrolled reign of money-lenders, the valley people (and at my time one Bawm village too) started to establish co-operatives for credit and marketing.

A change is also conceivable in the forms of organisation of labour. The hill people still are working in voluntary groups consisting either of relatives, neighbours or friends of the same age-group. The valley people, however, widely employ hired labourers; mutual neighbourly help has lost its importance. As to horticulture, gardens are worked by family members, partly with the help of day-labourers. Gardening is organised according to the principles of private enterprise, there are no voluntary working groups.

In the course of the economic development means of transport and protection were improved : some metalled or at least jeepable roads were constructed. Siting of many new villages on the banks of the lake brought the necessity to have boats. All the boats were constructed by Bengalis, the former Marma boat-building died out; store-houses, granaries and chicken houses spread widely. Since 1964-65 the Agricultural Department has been compelling flat land farmers to buy fertilizer.

Some innovations were introduced in handicrafts. In addition to the traditional cottage industries for their own consumption, there are already tendencies among the Bawm and the valley-inhabiting Marma to produce for a market economy, still mostly on a tribal level, however.

The changed natural environment has led to an extension of fishing activities in the Karnafuli lake area.

In the years after the dam construction, some private and government aided schools (primary schools, junior high schools, middle English schools, high schools and two colleges) have come up, in some cases without employing a teacher at the same time. The number of literates grew, according to my inquiry, for the Marma to 41 per cent, for the Chakma to 36 per cent, for the Taungchengya to 9 per cent and highest of all for the Bawm to 51 per cent—14 per cent of which was in higher education. The Census of Pakistan-1961 for the whole of East Pakistan shows 17.6 per cent literates. But one should not mistake the high rate of literacy as a result of government aid. A lot of this literacy is attributed to the Pali Tole, Buddhist schools of instruction of the Chakma, Taungchengya and Marma, and in the case of Christian Bawm nearly exclusively to their missionary schools, run by Bawm teachers, never by Bengali.

As a result of the improved educational facilities, some division between hand and brain work is already noticeable.

Some men with higher education are holding offices on the lowest administrative level or are employed as teachers in government (or as mentioned in the case of Bawm in missionary) schools. The christianised Bawm have the chances of working as pastors or mission clerks.

The influx of luxury goods in the hills is increasing. Most of these then were in the hands of the Bawm, followed by the Chakma and Marma in the valleys. The other groups were too poor to acquire luxury goods. A factor mainly responsible for the leading role of the Bawm in this aspect may be the expression of norms and values of a rank-stratified society of the Chin type, in which accumulation of goods (luxury goods mainly) is highly esteemed. The fact that the standard of living of the Bawm is the highest among the hill people finds its explanation here.

Clearly we find the richest families among the plough cultivators, particularly among the Marma. The quality of ploughland varies, but with first-class land one can gain considerable results, results not only in high yield, but also by subletting the land in return for half the harvest, or money for the value of half the harvest three years in advance. Though such transactions are prohibited, they are widely practised.

Furthermore, a lot of money is earned by marketing of garden products on a large scale. Even though the middlemen are Bengali, who dictate prices, profits are still pretty high. But this is only applicable to rich individuals. Considering the general conditions of the villages the Bawm as an ethnic group are better off.

The other groups of shifting cultivators are poor, but on a rather equal level among themselves, whereas the flat land cultivators show a strong polarization between rich and poor. The tendency to capitalistic wage-labour is inevitable under the existing conditions. In that respect the shifting cultivators are still in a better position, because as long as jhum land is available they can cultivate it. Taking into account that the average harvest rate (relation between seed and yield) in jhum and plough land is nearly the same, shifting cultivation, which is still possible to improve by scientific means, together with a general development of horticulture and the provision of marketing facilities, has better prospects for the future.

Regarding modernisation in the CHT, we can see the different stages of integration of former subsistence economies into the market economy of post-colonial Bengal, resulting to a great extent in economic deprivation of the majority of the tribal people, enriching a few well-to-do hillmen and helping the Bengali businessmen in monopolising the entire trade relations between the hills and the plains.

Outsiders of the district had no access to the land of the CHT, at least officially. But recently the government has declared the tribal lands open for sale to everybody. Money-lenders found it very easy until now to acquire rights in the cultivation (this is the application of the taluk system of feudal Bengal to the land-system in the CHT); now it will take a few years only to transform money-lenders into zamindars.

SUGGESTED READING

Government of East Pakistan : Pilot Scheme for Control of Jhuming in Chittagong Hill Tracts and Rehabilitation of Tribal People. Office of the Chief Conservator of Forests, E.P.

FIVE

J.S. Bhandari

THE TRIBAL SITUATION IN INDIA
Industrialization and Urbanization

Introduction

The purpose of this paper is to briefly survey the literature published under the broad categories of industrialization and urbanization amongst the tribes of India. Thus only that literature has been taken into account which deals directly or indirectly with the tribal communities in India. No efforts have been made to sort out literature published by the anthropologist from that of other scholars.

Definitional Problem

The concepts of industrialization and urbanization are very much a part of today's academic jargon. However, the meaning assigned to them are not as uniform and precise as one would have liked. They vary from one author to another.

A study of industry and industrialization must not be confined to the factory system, economic in-puts and out-puts, but should include "the use of the industrial products by a society irrespective of its source of origin" (ibid.). Moore emphasizes the loosening of the term industrialization to include these products along with the factory system under mechanical power. This way of interpretation is different from that where "industrialization" is to be understood merely in terms of the "economic and technological" system involved in the transformation of raw goods to finished or intermediate goods.

Anthropology and the Study of Industrialization

Anthropologists were initially not interested in the phenomenon of industrialization. The reasons for this lack of interest in it are not very far to seek. Industrialization, as one of the most powerful agents of economic development was strictly confined to the western countries, and though its impact and consequences were profound, since the anthropologists traditionally confined their studies to the pre-literate societies, anthropologists of yore completely ignored this. However, some studies pertaining to this problem were conducted in Africa by anthropologists.

Anthropological interest in the process of industrialization was aroused when their traditional domain viz., the tribal societies and the peasantry of the non-western world were brought within the ambience of the industrializing process. The changing political scene in the Third World countries greatly accelerated the setting up of the industries, construction of dams, and exploration of raw material in the remote areas, for quick and planned economic development. The pace of industrial development affected the lives of the communities in these parts, which hitherto had maintained a more or less unbroken, though changing, link with the past. Thus industrialization after the Second World War became a world-wide phenomenon. This led to a change in the anthropological perspective of the study of change among the preliterate societies also. Hitherto the studies in acculturation were mainly based on contact situation, changes in the value-system due to the impact of western thoughts and ideals which were propagated among them. All in all, the agents of change were mainly non-economic in nature. This is of course not to deny the existence of interest among the anthropologists in economic development and social/cultural changes. But these were mainly the implications of the products of industries far away from the cultures under study.

Anthropological studies during the last few decades have indeed become diversified in their approach and subject matter. The problem of industrialization was undertaken by an anthropologist M. Mash only in the early 1950s, when he undertook a study of the Guatemalan Indian community, which had come under the impact of industrialization in 1876 when a cotton textile mill was opened in Contel, which has ultimately become the largest textile mill in Central America.

Nash (1958) in his study has made a descriptive analysis of the impact of the factory system right in the midst of the Indian community—and has also tried to refute the sociological generalization regarding the disorganizing impact of industrialization. The time between the setting up of the factory and the conducting of the study spans well over 7 decades and hence the study is meaningful because the structural or other types of changes have become part of the present day Contelese society. Since Nash has mentioned that his was a study based on the traditional social anthropological approach of studying a small scale society, his study of the Contelese provides one model of such studies for the anthropologists. The main focus of his study has been on the persisting pattern of social life in understanding the mechanism of adjustment to new economic form. This is a study of structure, change and continuity.

The research work available on industrialization and urbanization among the tribal societies in India is extremely limited and therefore it has not been possible to make any generalizations. The interest of the anthropologists in these fields is still in the nascent stage and most of the work is therefore of exploratory nature. This also limits the comparability of the researches done by different scholars in different areas.

The relevant literature, in spite of its meagreness, has been categorised in order to be meaningful. Such categorisation will also facilitate comparative studies. Both points of similarity as well as difference can be studied. For example, the plantation industry is different from a manufacturing industry and hence different types of consequences are expected.

The tribal population of India, specially in middle India inhabited what were traditionally supposed to be remote and physically isolated areas from the centres of administration and trade. The interests of administrators and outsiders in these areas was minimal and the farthest one could think of tribal population was in terms of their coming in contact with non-tribal societies, mainly in institutional and religious spheres.

Yet these very tribal areas, specially in the middle zone of India, proved to be the richest in their mineral and other productive wealth. Besides, the tribal societies also proved to be good sources of cheap labour. Therefore, the isolation and comparatively independent economic system of the tribal communities were broken down, albeit very slowly, by the establishment of mines and quarries in their areas, and also by employing the tribal people as unskilled labourers in these labour intensive industries. With the establishment of tea plantations in Assam, North Bengal, and East Bengal, the demand for cheap labour increased and the tribal communities became the main sources of labour recruitment. With the establishment of manufacturing industries in Bihar, the tribal people also became directly involved in the new set up, i.e. in factories and mills and came face to face with an entirely new system of production and management. After Independence, when new industries were being set up, the tribal regions, because of their great potentialities, were gradually transformed into areas of big industrial complexes.

Thus chronologically speaking, we have the plantation industry, the mining and quarrying industry and the manufacturing industry which have been operating in the tribal areas and in which tribal people have been involved.

This review of literature is thus divided into these following parts: (1) Plantation industry; (2) Mining and Quarrying industry; (3) Manufacturing industry; and (4) Tribal labour. The review of urbanization is dealt with separately. One section deals with these papers which are of general interest.

Plantation Industry

As early as 1835 an experimental tea garden was set up in Lakhimpur in Assam. Since then the tea industry has had a phenomenal growth both in North India as well as in South India. Today it is one of the biggest foreign-exchange earners employing a very large number of people. In 1964, there were 9835 registered tea gardens in India, employing more than 4,39,085 people in Assam, 1,89,968 in West Bengal and 75,475 in Madras (Tea Board of India—Tea Statistics 1965-66) the three main tea growing regions.

Though the tea-gardens are not situated in the tribal areas of any of the states, they have directly affected many tribal people because they constituted the main bulk of the labour force in the tea-plantations specially in North India.

The tea industry was mainly dependent upon immigrant labour. In Assam, when tea gardens were established, it was not very easy to maintain them because of the non-availability of labour. This was because of local conditions; for example, in Assam, there was no category of landless labour and hence no one felt induced to take tea-garden jobs. They preferred the independence and ease of their position as cultivators to the discipline and regular labour of a tea garden (Gait, p. 412). The situation was more or less the same in North Bengal also. Under these circumstances, recruitment of labour was a serious problem.

Chotanagpur became a very important centre for labour recruitment. The tribal people of this area were considered most suitable for labour. Other areas which supplied labour were Santhal Pargana of Bihar. The main reasons for recruitment of the tribal people were their extremely poor economic conditions in these areas, and the allurements of the recruiting agents. (See Bose, 1954 and Devasse, 1931). We, however, lack a detailed study of the labour recruitment and its sociological implications for both the immigrants as well as for the community of which they constituted a part.

A.K. Das and H.N. Bannerjee in their book *Impact of Tea Industry on the Life of the Tribal of West Bengal* (1964) have described the impact of the tea industry on the tribal labourers of West Bengal. This study was conducted by them among the tribal labourers in four medium sized tea estates in North Bengal. They have described their findings in this book, under "economic", "social" and "psychological" impacts of the tea industry on the tribal labourers.

In all the four tea plantations, the tribal labourers hail from Chotanagpur in Bihar. The authors point out that the tribal labourers migrated to the tea plantation because there was scarcity of land in their own area. The factories have both permanent and seasonal labourers. The seasonal labourer commutes to these gardens for a small part of the year and goes back to his native village. This practice keeps the permanent labourers in contact with the traditional values of their community.

In all these plantations, the tribal people occupy unskilled, non-technical, lower level jobs. During the plucking season the whole household barring infants and old people, may find jobs in the garden.

The authors report an increase in the "nuclear households" though it was not absent earlier. The importance of clan is much less nowadays, though it still regulates marriage of the people concerned. They still refrain from killing and damaging their totem. Marriage still retains its traditional style, but inter-tribal marriages are not ruled out.

The authours have also tried to describe the attitudes of the tribal labour towards work on plantations. Most of the labourers would prefer to work in their own fields because of the "monotony and routine type of work" in the factory. They found adultery on the increase, sexual life less harmonious, divorces more common. Moral values may be said to have decayed.

The authors also mention that tribal labour differs markedly from non-tribal labour in attitudes towards future of the well being of the members of their family. They are not interested in educating their children. They would rather spend money on food, drink and personal adornment than on saving for the future. Thus a highly generalized picture emerges from their study. The authors admit, however, that this is not an absolute representative report on the impact situation.

The Census Organization in their study *Social and Economic Processes in Tea Plantation* (1968) describe two tea plantations : one in Assam and the other in Madras. The findings of these two surveys along with intensive extracts from the reports of various commissions concerning the tea industry are presented in this report. The exploratory surveys of the two plantations describe the working conditions of the plantation workers. The report is merely a presentation of the "empirical data relating to their living and working conditions". The main points that emerge from the reports are that while in Assam, the tea plantation labour is mainly drawn from the tribal population of Bihar and Bengal, whereas in the Madras tea plantation, the labour is drawn mainly from the scheduled castes. The report, however does not deal with any changes that might have taken place among these people.

B.K. Roy-Burman in his paper "Employment of Scheduled Tribes" (1972) while discussing the general employment situation among the scheduled tribes, makes some important points concerning the plantation labourers. The tribal labour drawn from different tribes maintain distinct identities, they live in different localities or are generally clustered together. They have also been able to maintain their links with their original homes, more so recently because of better and cheaper transport facilities. The important problem which he points out is the integration of ex-tea garden labour in the local milieu and since large colonies of ex-tea garden labourers in Assam and Bengal have remained outside the local socio-cultural setup, there is a danger of their being "focal points of sub-regional sentiments" (p. 31). The exposure of tea plantation labour to politicisation and trade unionism is also pointed out by Roy-Burman and he feels that when these labourers return to their places of origin "their knowledge of organizing collective pressures through trade unions and other forums, they are sometimes serving as dynamic forces in tribal communities" (ibid). However, there is no study, on these problems of plural cultures or impact of migration on the members of a migrant community or their impact on the host community.

The Mining Industry

The mining industry is one of the oldest industries in India which has been overwhelmingly dependent upon the tribal labourers. They have been working in the coal mines particularly of Asansol-Raniganj and the Jharia belt over a very long period of time. In recent years new areas have been opened up specially for the exploration of iron ore, in Bailadala in M.P. This area is also predominantly a tribal area. But there has been no attempt to study the impact of this industry on the tribal people or the impact of industry on the society within its ambit. There is only one paper by A.M. Kurup which is based on his study of the tribal labourers in the Parasia coal mines in Madhya Pradesh.

Kurup in his paper "The Changing Phase of Tribal Economy : A Study of Parasia Coal Miners" (1961) has described the socio-cultural conditions of the Gond who constitute a major segment of the labour engaged in the coal mines. His data are based on the study of 50 Gond households out of 300 Gond families being in the coal mine area. In this study he has compared the social life of the Gond coal miners with the traditional social life of the Gond. Most of the Gond families are migrants from nearby areas. Some of these families migrated to this area about 40 years ago. The study shows a marked change specially in the economic pursuits and moral values amongst the migrants compared to their traditional system. The traditional values are least respected and honoured by the new generation of the Gond. They have also taken to many new features of non-tribals specially in external output. This is however, a very plain descriptive account and is explanatory in nature.

Industrial Set-up

In our review of the literature, we find that the maximum number of studies deal with the relationship between industrial set-up and the tribal communities. The literature falls mainly into two categories : (1) that deals with the impact of an industrial set-up upon a community and (2) that deals with the impact of the establishment of an industrial complex on the community which is being displaced on this account.

A paper by Martin Orans, "A Tribal People in an Industrial Setting" (1959) is one of the earlier publications dealing with the above mentioned fields. His paper deals mainly with the effect of Jamshedpur's urban and industrial milieu on traditional Santal culture. The theoretical aspect dealt here is relation between economic activity on the one hand and non-economic social and cultural patterns on the other.

He has described his findings in three sections: (1) recruitment and commitment of the Santal labourers to Jamshedpur industry, (2) changing beliefs and practices concerning witchcraft, and (3) qualitative changes in marriage forms. With these major foci, he deals with economic (labour), ideological (witchcraft), and social (marriage forms) factors.

His findings are that although most Santal say that they migrated to Jamshedpur for economic reasons, he feels that the basic "drive" in Santal culture being "pleasure" farming would provide more time to "enjoy" themselves; their reasons for taking up industrial jobs was for improving their lot, and quite a sizable number of Santal took up these jobs or migrated to Jamshedpur for non-economic lures.

The Santal working in Jamshedpur's steel mills live both in the Company houses as well as in Bustees (hamlets) on the outskirts of the city. The life in a Bustee is different from that in a city environment. A Bustee is more like a village and hence more permissive; however, most Santal would like to move to Company houses. The city Santal are more skilled, occupy better positions and are more committed to their environment i.e., would behave like the city dwellers.

Orans finds variation in the beliefs and their interpretation regarding the witchcraft in three sets of Santal viz., the village Santal, the Bustee Santal and the City Santal. The village Santal believes in witchcraft fully; the Bustee Santal also believes in it but they feel that with education, witchcraft might be eradicated, whereas the city Santal are not fully averse to believing in it and specially so when they visit a village. They are quite afraid of witchcraft. Orans also describes changes in the forms of marriage due to urban-industrial influences.

Orans' paper deals in fact more with the problems of urban influences on the traditional Santal culture, than on the influence of industrialization. Subsequently in *The Santal—A Tribe in Search of Great Tradition* (1965) Martin Orans has studied the problem of adjustment between a tribal group and an industrial-urban centre.

This is an important monograph dealing with the problems of adjustment of a tribal community, the Santal, to an industrial urban setting of which they have been part for the last 50 years. Unlike other studies dealing with the impact of industrialization over a short span of time which, in fact, are limited to the establishment phase of an industry, this has the distinction of being one which studies the problem when the industrial complex is well established and the industry and the urbanizing factors are fully integrated with the population.

Though the aim of the author was to study the nativistic movements of the Santal industrial worker aimed at producing a literate "great tradition", the study is also important in understanding the process of culture change under industrial urban influences. "In seeking such understanding attention has been focussed on the shifting historical pressures for and against acculturation and assimilation and on the impact of a spreading market economy, industrialization and political democracy" (p. X).

Santal at present number around 3 million and inhabit the region richest in deposits of iron, coal and other crucial industrial minerals in India.

Orans has studied the Santal from territorial regions adjacent to Jamshedpur, both living outside and within the city, thus "exceptional opportunities were available to compare separately the effects of industrial employment and living in an urban environment" (p. XIII). Most Santal live outside Jamshedpur in village-like settlements *(Bustees)*. Some of these Bustees were, traditional villages and others have come up with the influx of industrial labour.

Orans has followed the methodological procedure of constructing the base-line for change from historical accounts and contemporary observation of the villages. Reconstruction of the base line on the basis of contemporary village life is rather fraught with many doubts. However, Orans has also given the account in a chronological manner, described in "before" and "after" situations.

The Santal, originally were predominantly agriculturists, with a supplementary occupation of hunting and fishing. Though the Santal followed their own ritual and religious systems, they were very much influenced by the Hindu caste system and religious ideology. Processes of accumulation and assimilation were however limited.

With the establishment of the Jamshedpur Complex and its associated industry, the web of social relationships was weakened due to migrations for industrial employment.

In 1900, Orans states, no southern Santal were literate, but in 1957 the situation was entirely different. TISCO was the primary source for this. Since education was the only basis for rewards in TISCO, it has provided the greatest incentive for them. The city Santal have 88 per cent, Bustee Santal 42 per cent and village Santal 20 per cent literacy. "Increased education resulting from industrial development and employment may be . . . said to have increased emulation of Hinduism and decreased Santal solidarity" (p. 56). Orans through his study finds that migrations for industrial employment have an important bearing on the social and cultural change occurring in a community. There have been marked changes in the marriage system of these Santal. The reason for such changes is "that migration to industrial employment makes marriage primarily a matter of individual concern . . . it weakens bonds with extended family, local linkage and village". . . . (p. 71). Similarly there has been marked "attenuation of, and non-participation in the ceremonies".

The most important part of Orans' study is the development of political and tribal consciousness amongst the Jamshedpur Santal. The Jharkhand movement is strongest in Jamshedpur. Since it is an important aspect of the modern political system, the TISCO management has also "discretely" supported some of these movements. This tendency is clearly to resurrect the erstwhile tribal characteristics/traits. But the aim is not to relive the past. ". . . it does not recreate the traditional social basis for traditional solidarity. Instead it creates a new direct bond with all the Santal and to a somewhat lesser degree with all the tribals of the area. This new bond rests ultimately on the somewhat known opportunity for the Santal and other tribals to function as a successful interest group" (p. 119).

Among the Indian anthropologists Professor L.P. Vidyarthi has extensively studied the phenomenon of industrialization and urbanization with special reference to tribal Bihar. He has completed a Planning Commission sponsored study of the Heavy Electrical Corporation near Ranchi. This is a longitudinal study. In this study he has first studied the impact of Ranchi city on the tribal culture in the pre-industrial phase and has then undertaken a "longitudinal ethnographic study dealing with the industrial complex right from the pre-industrial setting, selection of the site for the installation of the industrial units, the acquisition of land and the problem of rehabilitation of the displaced persons, phases of cultural tiers formation in and around the industrial range and a detailed study of the slum labourers". These findings have been published by Vidyarthi in various papers.

In "Urbanization, Industrialization and Social Change in Bihar" (1970), Vidyarthi deals with the processes of urbanization and industrialization in India in general and with the tribal belt of middle India in particular.

Unprecedented urban growth in India in the last three decades has invited the attention of the social scientist to this phenomenon. The Planning Commission sponsored a number of socio-economic surveys of various towns and cities of India. Besides these sponsored studies, some studies were conducted independently by some scholars.

Vidyarthi has discussed the phases of urbanization in India and has also given a typology of various urban centres. The typology is based mainly on the dominant functional importance of the centre.

During the last three to four decades industrial, mineral, commercial and communicational towns have come into existence. New towns and cities have developed mainly in those states which have rich mineral resources and forest resources and where industries related to these raw materials have been established.

Bihar's Chota Nagpur area was very much less urbanized before World War I but has seen an unprecedented industrial and urban growth in recent times. This area being one of the richest in mineral resources was made the prime region for industrial exploration. Incidentally, this region was also overwhelmingly a tribal area and therefore the impact both in the initial stages of industrial establishment and later in the secondary impacts of industrialization on the tribal people could be observed in almost controlled situation. Vidyarthi's paper traces the development of urban centres in this area. The pace of urbanization in Chota Nagpur had only six out of 48 towns of Bihar, whereas in 1961 Chota Nagpur alone had 64 towns. The highest growth of new towns was in the decade 1951-61. Most of these townships were centred around industrial establishments and the rest developed as administrative towns. Vidyarthi's paper clearly makes out the point that in Chota Nagpur urbanization is a concomitant of industrialization.

Vidyarthi has also undertaken a study of three major industrial organizations of this area. These studies were sponsored by the Planning Commission and the reports have been published.

This paper however, gives some of the basic points in the study of the Heavy Engineering Corporation (Hatia zone), Patratu Thermal Power Complex and Bokaro Steel Plant. In the study of HEC industrial complex, Vidyarthi has given a "before" and "after" picture of the area.

This complex is established on an area of 9200 acres of land which was agricultural and fallow land of 6 villages inhabited by two major tribal groups, viz., the Oraon and the Munda, who constituted 77.5 per cent of the total population. The pre-industrial society of the region was mainly characterized by "natural landscape, folk and agricultural economy, social solidarity, group cooperation and co-partnership" (p. 14). When these villagers were uprooted from their land, though they were paid adequate compensation, they had to face a number of problems and these were not tackled with foresight and therefore they continued to lead a life of "cultural disequilibrium". This study is of an initial impact situation where the time lag for adjustment to the new situation is rather short. It is not even one generation old and therefore two cultures are not yet able to adjust themselves.

His study of the HEC, in a way, is diachronic i.e. it takes into account all the three phases viz., pre-industrial set-up, the formulatory period when land was requisitioned and villagers were resettled elsewhere, and the third phase of construction etc.

In the third phase i.e. construction phase, the area attracted a large number of workers—both skilled and unskilled, from different parts of India. In the year 1961, there were around 32,550 persons in the slum colonies which mushroomed as the construction work progressed. Vidyarthi has pointed out that these labourers move from one construction work to another and thereby create a kind of "industrial nomadism".

However, the present study does not focus on the impact of the industrialization in the region over a long period of time, since it was conducted during the construction phase itself, though it does look into immediate effects over the villoges nearby. Hatia was one such village, which became the centre of a wide variety of people and ideologies coming from varied backgrounds. Before 1958, it was an isolated, homogeneous village; now it has become part of an industrial complex. A study of other villages reveals that "impact of industrialization is more on the adjacent villages". More people in these villages are opting for industrial jobs.

Industrialization has also affected the traditional authority pattern and Vidyarthi reports that this is manifested in flouting the traditional taboos, while moral laxity has "transcended its boundary".

Industrialization initiates a chain reaction—social, cultural and economic. It is not always that the region where an industry has been set up has the maximum benefit in economic terms. In fact industrial culture can directly benefit in its productive and administrative set up only those who have the requisite skills. Otherwise the local people gain nominally and at the same time they undergo the greatest change in their socio-cultural set up. We do not have any such study where the impact of industrialization has been studied, not only in the setting up of an industry in an area, but how the forces of new technology have gradually affected the population over a longer period of time.

Industrialization involved migration of workers from different regions and thereby a new social system is created where ethnic, cultural and social factors play an important role in moulding the future of the whole community. For example, large scale migrations of Indian labour to Sri Lanka, Malaya and the Carribeans in the wake of plantation industries being set up has posed problems at the national level.

In India also, social anthropologists can take up such studies which consider these consequences of industrialization and not merely the localized problems pertaining to a few villages of tribal groups (one such study is that of Martin Orans of Jamshedpur) (loc. cit.).

A.K. Das and S.K. Bannerjee (1964) made a survey of the predominantly tribal areas in West Bengal where heavy industries were set up. These industries viz., Chittaranjan Locomotives, Hindustan Cable Factory and Durgapur Steel Plants have displaced the Santal and many scheduled caste communities.

Displacement of the tribal people and resettling them in new areas have disrupted their traditional socio-cultural life. Initially many tribals worked on the construction sites; when this was over, their services were no longer required and they were thus rendered jobless. The authors also make reference to the new wants created among the tribals due to contact with outsiders and initially also the money power to satisfy them. But even after they were unemployed the desire for newly acquired goods and things lingered, thus creating a void in their life. However, this study is mainly concerned with the direct impact on the life of the tribals due to displacement from their traditional habitat and has little to offer regarding the impact of industrialization on the community.

A similar study was undertaken by the Census Organisation dealing with the setting up of the Rourkela Steel Plant in Orissa (1968). The main emphasis of this study is on the problems arising out of the setting up of a steel plant in Rourkela whereby a very large population of the area was displaced from their age old villages. In all 30 villages inhabited by about 2500 households were affected by the requisition of land for the steel plant. The inhabitants were mainly scheduled tribes being 70 per cent of the total number of the households. Scheduled castes and others constituted 5 per cent and 25 per cent respectively.

The specific points taken up in this study are (1) what were the social processes on the eve of the displacement of the population with particular reference to the reaction of the different categories of people to the prospect of the establishment of the steel plant on the one hand and the apprehension of their displacement on the other. (2) What was the response of old institutions to the new situation and whether new types of institutions came up in the wake of the changing situation etc. (3) The relevance of the old solidarities in the context of the emerging pattern of new life.

The author primarily focusses attention on the situation on the eve of the change and the immediate reaction on the traditional set-up of the displaced villagers in their new surrounding.

Although this study would not be brought under the category of "impact of industrialization", because its main emphasis has been on the conditions prior to setting up of the plant and mainly on the displacement of the people and a short span of time that has elapsed between the pre-industrial time and the time of the study, it is nevertheless rich in data which can be used in future studies dealing with the adjustment of these people to a new industrial complex, in which they would become involved directly or indirectly.

The study reveals that the traditional society of Rourkela has been greatly disrupted. The most important change has occurred in the occupational structure of the villagers. Earlier cultivation was done by 29 per cent of the villagers whereas now it is confined to only 2 per cent and new occupations as industrial labour is considerably high i.e. 77 per cent.

Tribal Labour

Though most of the papers pertaining to the impact of industrialization on the tribal societies or tribal people, in fact, highlight the involvement of the tribal people in the industries primarily as labourers, who in most cases happen to be unskilled, there are a few papers which take up the problem of tribal labour exclusively.

Roy-Burman (1972), on the basis of 1961 census reports has brought together the data to present a rounded picture of the tribal labour engaged in various types of economic activities, including those relating to industry.

He reports that among the Scheduled Tribes 3.42 per cent of the workers are engaged in the mining and quarrying industry, whereas the percentage of scheduled castes and other workers is 1.84 per cent and 2.77 per cent respectively. The majority of the tribal labour, however, is in the primary sector (91.3 per cent), secondary sector has 5.21 per cent and the tertiary sector has 3.4 per cent. Though Roy-Burman has not confined himself to the industrial labour alone, in describing tribal labour.

Vidyarthi's paper "Aspects of Tribal Labour Force in Chotanagpur" (1969) is based on his wider study of Ranchi city and the Heavy Electrical Corporation which has also been published separately. Though Vidyarthi categorically states in this paper that the tribal labour has failed to meet the demands of Chotanagpur, he does not describe how he has reached such conclusions.

Ranchi has been a big draw for the tribal emigrant, and recently for the non-tribal also. The tribal labour migrating to Ranchi is significantly of the Christian converts who constitute 86 per cent of the total, whereas only 8 per cent and 6 per cent are non-converts and Hindu tribals respectively. Christianity, thus may be a motivating factor leading to urbanism. The total population of Ranchi was 1,39,487 in 1961 and the tribal constitute 29.7 per cent of the total.

The figures given in the paper regarding the employment of the tribal labour are not very clear. The non-converted tribal and Hindu tribal are overwhelmingly in manual labourer jobs and converted tribals are in salaried occupations and are ranked as middle class people.

Tribal women also constitute a large percentage of the labour force. They generally commute daily between their villages and the city, where they find some work.

However, Vidyarthi's survey reveals that a higher percentage of the converted tribals is unemployed as compared to the non-converted or Hindu tribals. No reasons are given.

The position of labour in the Hatia Industrial Complex is different. Prior to industrialization, there were no industrial workers in the rural area. Only the agricultural labourer existed.

In 6 villages, previously 76 per cent depended on agriculture activities, but now only 11 per cent have retained it, 88 per cent were the agricultural labourers, but now there is none. Now in industrial work alone 70.5 per cent are engaged. There has been a tremendous change in the occupational structure of the local community. The main reason for changing the occupation was obviously loss of agricultural land, rendering all agriculture-based occupations to vanish. Majority of the tribals are in unskilled labour category (20.18

per cent), skilled ones and office workers are 19.4 per cent and 0.46 per cent respectively.

Vidyarthi in this paper also describes the condition of an industrial slum in Hatia and Dhurwa.

In the study of eight villages situated from 2 to 20 miles from the factory, he finds "interesting processes of change caused due to industrialization." Though agricultural economy continues to be intact, younger people opt more for factory work. However, the chances of these villagers being absorbed in the factory work are remote because now it needs only skilled workers. This has caused frustration among the villagers.

Vidyarthi's paper deals with tribal labour in towns and therefore it does not give any idea about the conditions from which the tribal labour has been drawn and the socio-economic life in the village they inhabited.

O.R. Gallaghar in a paper "Migrant Labour from Tribal-Chotanagpur" (1973) has filled in these gaps to a certain extent and in fact he himself suggests that his paper may be taken as a supplement to Vidyarthi's study. Gallaghar describes the pattern of labour migration from one Oraon village. This survey outlines what kind of villagers migrate to work, where they go, the kind of work performed, their earnings and general life experiences of the workers while away at work. Though the survey is restricted to one single village, Gallaghar believes it may not be too dissimilar to other tribal villages in the South Bihar area.

The motives for outside village work remain today as they were in the past viz. Oraon poverty conditions. Oraon villages have become labour pools from where cheap labour can be drawn on seasonally or periodically. The duration of outside village work is usually between one to six months during the slack season. Occasionally it may be for the entire period of a year. The majority of the workers during the survey period were working in Ranchi, which is about 10 miles from the village and most of them were daily commuters. A majority of them worked as coolies and none as skilled workers.

Gallaghar finds that the Oraon live together even in their work sites and feel more comfortable in their own company. Though they learn many new habits, they are not given to keep them permanently. Only their families which have sufficient rice production back home, gain sufficiently by seasonal migrant labour system. Others can barely meet the demands of day to day existence. Whatever may be the condition Gallaghar notes, the Oraon want to come back to their village i.e. their home.

This system of migrant labour has a positive role also in industrialization on the one hand and keeping the seasonally unemployed rural people in some system of gainful activity on the other. More such studies would surely be important in finding the pattern of migration and the means to provide gainful employment to the people in various areas which are perpetually in the grip of poverty and lack of cultivable land.

Urbanization

The phenomenon of urbanization, with reference to the tribal communities, is most inadequately represented in the published literature. For the purpose of the present review, we have included all those publications (which are also not many) which deal with the phenomenon directly or indirectly that is, in terms of urbanization and urbanism whether the urban influences on the tribal people are dealt with or the growth of tribal towns is described. We have also included those studies which deal with the traditional towns with a sizable tribal population living with non-tribal citizens over a considerably long period of time. *Cultural Configuration of Ranchi—a Survey* (1969) by L.P. Vidyarthi may be regarded as one of the first studies of urbanization by a social anthropologist, pertaining to a sizable tribal population. Ranchi is a fast growing city and has become recently a centre for industrial and administrative activity in a predominantly tribal region. The population of Ranchi is composed of Hindus (48.6 per cent), Tribals (29.7 per cent) and Muslims (19.6 per cent). The study is full of statistical tables, but the descriptive part is rather scanty. Though the study does emphasize the phase of transition from tribal system to industrial urban system, it does not delineate the process of transformation.

B.K. Roy-Burman (1970) has described the process of changes in the North East Autonomous Districts of Assam,

NEFA, Nagaland and Manipur. This is predominantly a tribal area and also strategically important, lying on the international borders.

He considers the modernization process on two axes—firstly exogenous which imply all that is happening through western technology, political and social organizational aspects which are making inroads into this area; and secondly, the endogenous which occurs "through the continuous interaction of its traits and its ecology."

The most important break-through in the isolation of the region has been achieved by the opening of new roads and communicational facilities. The new modes of transport have brought many people closer to each other in terms of time.

The urban population of this region is rather small. However, there are many towns. Shillong is the most outstanding among them, which is now the state headquarters of Meghalaya and prior to which it was the capital of Assam. Its population is 1,02,398 (1961 census).

Roy-Burman points out that these towns have exerted a very uneven pull on the tribal population of their adjoining areas. "This is perhaps related to the growth history of the towns. . . Most of these towns have come into existence and developed not through the growth of the economy of the tribal population concerned but through the operation of extraneous factors like the requirement of the administration, as in the case of Shillong, Kohima etc., or the location of the social service institutions of the missionaries, as in the case of Churachandpur in Manipur" (p. 7).

Roy-Burman states that the exogenous origin of these towns is reflected in their morphology i.e. town structure.

However, today the role of these towns is very important, "They have become focal points of endogenous growth and spread of new ferment in the region".

He has also given some salient features of these towns, as follows :

(1) In these towns the tribal and non-tribal hardly share a common life. Their contacts are few and formal, and hence these communities tend to form cysts of incommunicability

around themselves. This however brings the people of different tribal groups together against the non-tribal.

(2) The dilemma of reference group. The confrontation of the tribals and non-tribals leads the former to harp on "tribalism" but at the same time they must look beyond it for their survival.

(3) The tribals live in two worlds, the modern and their own. They share modern technology but possess the emotions of the tribal world.

The above generalizations put forward by Roy-Burman need not be accepted as such. These questions can be answered more cogently by empirical studies which are sadly lacking. We have no study of a tribal town, though there are a number of towns in the tribal belts. Many new towns are coming up in NEFA also which are of an entirely different nature as compared to the towns of middle India. In NEFA, urbanization is an effect of administration and development whereas in Bihar and M.P. it is industrialization which is leading to urbanization.

G.S. Aurora in his book *Tribe-Caste-Class Encounters* (1972) addresses himself to a different problem. The book discusses, besides other things, influences of urban centres on the social-cultural, economic and political processes of the tribal people who are not exactly part and parcel of the dominant culture of the region, but lie on the periphery.

The study deals mainly with the Bhilalas of Alirajpur Tehsil (Jhabua District), M.P. Bhilalas, a part of the "Bhils and related tribes", are the numerically dominant community of the region. They are essentially a rural community with interaction with other rural communities. But they also participate in the socio-political processes emanating from the regional headquarters, the town of Alirajpur. The dominant community of the region is the Rajputs, who also ruled the erstwhile princely state of Alirajpur. Bhilalas constitute 56.3 per cent of the total population of Alirajpur Tehsil. Alirajpur is the sub-divisional headquarters of the revenue department. District and Sessions Court and Block Development offices are also situated here. It is also an important market of the region.

Here the most important link of the Adivasis are with the Rajputs, which were in terms of tradition, ritual and power, relations.

The Patels (Bhilala) are closest to the Rajput jagirdars in terms of culture. Patels were headmen of ryotwari villages. The Patels have helped in spreading urban traits to the tribals. The Patel, a part of the urban-based administrative set up, acts as model for his adivasi community and the Patel himself tries to follow more and more the urban pattern of life, depending upon his closeness to the urban-based institutions.

Aurora's study deals with the relationship of tribal villages with the urban society. His study is analytically made at two levels—(1) at the rural level, it deals with the inter-tribal relations and tribe-caste relations, and (2) at the urban level it deals with the differing influences on the various tribal communities as exerted by urban and socio-political forces. But the main emphasis is on the dominant Bhilalas. (Alirajpur Town population is 10,161, its tribal population is 1283 or 12.6 per cent of the total).

Since the Rajas of Alirajpur had affinal ties with the Bhilalas, owing to common law unions between them, these ties were symbolized at many occasions.

The author conceptualizes the town not merely as a centre of economic and political power, but also a crucible of ideas, values and skill. The links of the tribal people with the townsmen have many repercussions on his values. He comes in contact with the Vanya (trader), politician, administrator and his own fellow tribals. Through constant touch he imbibes certain urban culture idioms, such as purity, pollution, caste and class consciousness.

Aurora points that "in case of Alirajpur tribals, we are forcefully struck by the fact that the tribals have such significant relations with the non-tribal commercial and administrative centres that their social life cannot be fully grasped. Unless the role of these urban foci are also discussed . . . . Practically all the significant developments within the tribal system can be traced to specific processes originating or passing through urban centres" (p. 267).

In a different setting B. Chauhan (1970) has studied two towns and 4 villages in the district of Banswara, Rajasthan, to find out the extension of the urban frontiers to the hinter land which is populated primarily by the scheduled tribes (71.15 per cent). The towns also have significant percentage of schedule tribes households. His study provides the basis for understanding the social processes of tribal urban contact operating in the areas where the towns are small. It further discusses the nature of the hinterland and the channels of diffusion along with the roles of large villages and the small towns. But the towns, in spite of their being in the urban sector, are not able to provide substantial support to the villages in every aspect viz., lack of occupations in secondary sector, lack of interaction through official relations and lack of industry which acts as a pull factor. However, certain urbanizing influences were noticeable among the tribals like in the fields of education, medical care and material goods.

Conclusion

The phenomenon of industrialization and urbanization in the tribal sector in India is both old and new. It was the tribal belt which provided the basic raw materials—iron ore and coal—as well as cheap labour which were exploited by the early industrial set up. The first steel plant at Jamshedpur is already more than 50 years old and the tea plantation industry of Bengal and Assam drew heavily on the tribal labour from middle India. This however, did not attract the attention of the anthropologists in the earlier years who were mainly interested in the tribal ethnography and thereby their studies ignored the factors of socio-cultural changes which emanated through the external factors of industrialization. This of course, does not mean that the studies of acculturation were completely neglected by the earlier ethnography.

The present survey makes it clear that most of the papers pertaining to these areas are basically directed to studying the phenomena of tribal villages that were uprooted for making room for the establishment of industries and the consequences of this upon these uprooted people. The industrial set-up, in fact, is incidental to many of these studies. This is of course due to circumstances, where a certain industrial unit has been functioning only for a short period of time, its impact may not be easily perceptible in the social structure of a society and therefore the obvious factor of "disintegration" of social structure may be more highlighted. The study done by Orans (1965) is the only one where the tribesmen have already been living in an industrial urban complex for over 50 years and therefore have overcome the initial forces of "disintegration".

Most of these studies are focussed on the problems resulting from localization of an industry in a particular area and the concomitant changes in the communities living within its ambit. Thus, locus of an industry and the participation of the local inhabitants in the industry are the basic problems. However, in the tea plantation industry the locus of the industry and the immigrant labour force fall in a separate category i.e. the labourers come from places other than where the plantations are situated and therefore the impact of industry upon the tribal labourers is highlighted.

Majority of the studies compare "before" and "after" situation. The "before" situation is presented on the basis of constructing the traditional social system and the "after" situation is presented on the basis of what it was found to be by the researcher at the time of his investigations. The main conclusions drawn by these studies are that the traditional structures are "disintegrating", which in fact, imply that the institutional patterns are changing like larger families making way for the smaller families; marriage rules are being relaxed; there is an increase in pre-and extra-marital sex relations; and the changes in the occupational structures of the people under study.

The process of urbanization, especially in predominantly tribal areas, have also accelerated recently. Urban growth in these areas may be traced on two axes—(1) industrialization, (2) administrative-cum-developmental work. Industrialization has spurted the growth of urban centres in middle India and administrative-developmental activity has spurted it in north-eastern India. Besides these newly developed urban centres, there has been an orthogenetic growth of towns in some tribal areas, mainly in Rajasthan and Madhya Pradesh. Industrial-urban centres of middle India are still in the process of shaping their growth and therefore the urban pattern of living is not very well crystallized in most of the immigrants except in case of Jamshedpur which has already passed through this process over a period of five decades. But, then, Jamshedpur has a small tribal population. On the other hand, towns in Rajasthan and Madhya Pradesh fall in a different category. These are traditional towns with administrative, educational and commercial activities. The impact of urbanizing factors in these towns is neither radical nor sudden. The growth of towns in north-eastern India is a recent phenomenon and as such an entirely different type of "pre factors" are expected in this area. The most important thing about the towns in north eastern India is their population composition. They are overwhelmingly tribal in their population composition.

Needed Research

The future researches on these twin problems need to be formulated on clear perspectives in terms of methodology, hypotheses and concepts. The existing literature points out clearly that it is primarily explanatory in nature and is mainly done with the help of interviews and schedules.

Anthropological studies are by and large micro-level studies. Therefore, the question arises can we have micro-level studies of industrialization and urbanization and if so in what manner and with what techniques. Confining ourselves at this stage to the tribal communities alone, we are already delimiting the area of investigation. Micro-level studies conducted in depth with single-factor focus can be extremely useful in understanding the dynamics of change. Such studies may not be useful in generalization applicable at macro-level but they can surely add to our understanding at that level as well. Further, the traditional anthropological techniques can still be utilized fruitfully in macro-level studies. In fact one might be tempted to say that at this stage macro-level studies of industrialization in the tribal sector do not really need to be taken up.

Industrialization is both a process and product and this distinction needs to be kept in mind. Industrialization as a process would imply encircling the people in its productive and organizational activity and thereby influencing the structure of the community. On the other hand industrialization as an agent of change through its resultant product would be to study the changes brought about by the products in socio-cultural system of a community. This is meant to indicate that the studies dealing with the industrialization can be of the following types :

(1) Study of communities where the industry/industries is located within their tradional habitat.

(2) Study of those communities which are not directly within the locale of the industries and have not been disturbed from their initial habitat but are participating in industrial complexes. It would be extremely useful to study the impact of industrialization of various communities both tribal and non-tribal being in the same region. Except in few exclusively tribal areas, most of the regions which have come under industrial complexes contain a mixed population and these communities have different social structures. Such a comparative description of the impact of industrialization on the different groups living in an area will highlight the degree of response to changing situations. Even within the tribal segment of the population, various tribal groups may respond variously due to different cultural and structural elements.

It may be appropriate to mention here that the processes of change generated by industrialization and urbanization cannot overlook the traditional structural goals which provided an analytical perception for understanding change. Therefore, the factors of caste and religion may remain important parameters. Bose (1962) while discussing the impact of industrialization on the tribal life contrasts it with the impact of Hindu social organization on the tribal communities. In relation to Hindu society they retained "their group identity" but became part of the traditional economic and social system. As a group they carved out a place in the caste system (p. 6). Under the impact of industrialization, the tribal individual goes alone as a "wage earner" and his old ties are more or less dissolved and the individual is released as an emanicipated unit to take his place in competitive productive organisation (ibid). Thus Bose has shown group-status change to individual-status change due to different impacts. Such generalizations though important, need more empirical studies.

Industrial development generates many ideological changes also. One such important field is of politics. In those industries which are labour intensive and have a sizable tribal population, it may be worthwhile to study the role of trade-unions, participation of tribal labourers in it and the consequent changes they (the tribal labourers) bring about in political ideology into their own traditional habitat. This "feed-back process" has a special value because most of the industries are also located in politically volatile regions viz., West Bengal and Bihar.

In the field of urbanization, we notice two distinct types of urban centres: (1) created and developed exclusively by industrialisation, and (2) traditional towns which developed because of local needs of administration and development. In those towns whose growth is sudden and where tribal people have migrated for jobs—industrial or otherwise—effect them through the agencies of a purely urban nature. This may result in the tribal population adopting themselves to processes of modernization. But in the traditional towns (like those of Rajasthan and Madhya Pradesh) where tribal peoples have been living side by side the caste Hindus and Muslims for a considerable period of time, a type of structural adjustment grows which has a consonance with the traditional value system and this in turn reinforces the traditional institutions like the caste and occupational specialization. An entirely new type of situation may be hypothesized regarding those urban centres which are developing in exclusively tribal areas (like Nagaland, Meghalaya and Arunachal and Mizoram). In such cases the over riding forces are of modernization without any traditional group providing any alternative.

SUGGESTED READINGS

Aurora, G.S., *Tribe-Caste-Class Encounters*. Administrative Staff College of India, Hyderabad, 1972.

Bose, N.K., "Some Observations on Industrialisation and its Effect on Tribal Life". *Men in India*, 1962, 42 : 1 : 5-10.

Census of India, Volume 1, Part XI E. 1968, *Social Processes in the Industrialization of Rourkela*. Monograph No. 1. Office of the Registrar General of India, New Delhi, (Ed. by B.K. Roy-Burman), 1961.

Census of India, Vol. I, Part VII-A. 1968. *Social and Economic Processes in Tea Plantations with Special Reference to Tribal Labourers.* Office of the Registrar General of India, New Delhi., (Ed. by B.K. Roy-Burman), 1961.

Chauhan, B.R., *Towns in Tribal Setting*, National Publishing House, Delhi, 1970.

Das, A.K., and S.K. Bannerjee, *Impact of Industrialisation on the Life of the Tribals of West Bengal.* Tribal Welfare Department, W.B., Calcutta, 1962.

Das, A.K. and H.M. Banerjee, *Impact of Tea Industry on the Life of the Tribals of West Bengal*, Tribal Welfare Department, W.B., Calcutta, 1964.

Das, A.K., Special Problems in Tribal Transformation. Industrialization as a means of such Transformation. *Bulletin of Cultural Research Institute*, 1966. VI. 122. pp. 5-10.

Das Gupta, P.K., Impact of Industrialisation on Tribal Life, *Bulletin Anthropological Survey of India*, 1964. 1 and 2, pp. 13.

Gallaghar, D.R., 1973. "Migrant Labour from Chotanagpur," *Indian Anthropologist*, 3 : 1. 22-44.

Gould, H.A., "Some Preliminary Observations Concerning the Anthropology of Industrialization, *The Eastern Anthropologist*, 14. 1. 1961. pp. 30-44.

Kurup, A.M., Changing Phase of Tribal Economy. A Study of Parasia Coal Mines. In *Changing Tribes of Madhya Pradesh*, Tribal Research Institute Chindwara, Indore, 1961.

Moore, W., *The Impact of Industry*, Englewood Cliffs, N.J. Prentice-Hall, Incop. 1965.

——Impact of Industrialization on Tribal Life. *Vanyajati*, XI, 2. 1963.

Nash, M., *Machine Age Maya : The Industrialization of a Guatemalan Community*. Chicago, The University of Chicago Press 1958, (Phoenix Book, 1967).

Orans, Martin, A Tribal People in an Industrial Setting, *American Journal of Folklore* 71 : 281, 1958. pp. 422-45.

Orans, Martin, *The Santal—A Tribe in Search of Great Trachain*, Detroit, 1965.

Roy-Burman, B.K., Cultural Factors in Economic Development and Technological Change in Tribal India, *Journal of Social Research.* 8 : 1 : 1965. 21-32.

Roy-Burman, B.K., Modernization Processes in the Hills of North East India, *Journal of the Institute of Defence Strategy* (January) 1970.

Roy-Burman, B.K., Employment of Scheduled Tribes, Mimeograph, 1972.

Sharma, T.R., A Tribal Community in an Industrial Context, *Journal of Social Research* V. 1; 1962. 114-23.

Vidyarthi, L.P., Historical Process of Urbanization of Ranchi. *Journal of Historical Research*, 1964. VII, pp. 2.

Vidyarthi, L.P., (a). Social Implications of Industrialization in Tribal Bihar. *The Anthropologist*, Special Volume II. 1969, 37-52.

Vidyarthi, L.P. (b). Aspects of Tribal Labour Force in Chhotanagpur. *Tribe*. VI : 3 : 1969, 1-9.

Vidyarthi, L.P., Urbanization, Industrialization and Social Change in Tribal Bihar. *Journal of Ranchi University*. VI & VII : 1969-70. 1-38.

Vidyarthi, L.P., *Cultural Configuration of Ranchi—A Survey*, Calcutta Bookland Private Limited, 1969.

Vidyarthi, L.P., *Socio-Cultural Implications of Industrialization in India : A Case Study*. Council of Social Cultural Research, Department of Anthropology, Ranchi University, Ranchi, 1970.

SIX

Maheshwari Prasad

IMPACT OF URBANISATION ON A TRIBAL VILLAGE

A Case Study of Tusmu in Chotanagpur

THE SOCIO-CULTURAL transformation of primitive societies has occurred rather rapidly in recent history of mankind. Tribal societies have not remained immune to the changes. The transformation has been generally chanellised through the phenomenon of urbanisation, although the impact of non-urban agencies, as for example missionaries, has not been less spectacular. But more often than not they have also operated from urban bases. In fact, entirely new elements are introduced by urbanisation in the socio-cultural set-up of a region; the urban centres function as foci of diffusion of innovations.

With increasing urbanisation contacts with a stronger culture (a substitute for the term superior culture) are established and gradually these become firm. Developed technology slowly but steadily penetrates the region surrounding an urban centre. Under the impact of contact and diffusion of innovations, metamorphosis of the economic and socio-cultural fabric of traditional society follows. Money economy gradually tends to replace subsistence economy with all its attendant corollaries. A new hybrid culture, characterising the transition phase of urbanised transformation, begins to take shape. Ultimately the process of cultural liquidation runs its full course and the age-old cultural set-up of a region is completely eroded.

The dynamics of socio-cultural adaptation and transformation have been well documented by social scientists, notably anthropologists and sociologists. Geographers have not lagged much behind. Sterling,[1] Cole,[2] Dozeir,[3] Hoffman,[4] Crist,[5] Hunter,[6] Lentenek[7] and Gowing,[8] to name only some in the forefront, have discussed the themes of the changing face of the socio-cultural landscape, transformation of traditional economies and communities, economic transition from traditional to commercial agriculture and acculturation of primitive folk. However, the transformation of tribal societies under the impact of urbanisation has, by and large, remained a neglected area of enquiry. The process of transformation and the interaction of tribal culture with it offer a fascinating field of enquiry to social scientists. Perhaps, a comparative study of socio-cultural transformation of tribal and non-tribal societies with identical environmental conditions and under similar urban impacts, may provide a key to ascertain the role of differential cultural background in this process.

Our object is to study the impact of urbanisation on economic condition and socio-cultural values of tribal society, as also to make an assessment of the bearings of variant socio-cultural backgrounds on the process of adaptation and change. The observations recorded are based on one week of field-work in a tribal village—Tusmu—of Chotanagpur in December 1977 during a socio-economic survey camp sponsored by the Department of Geography, Ranchi College, Ranchi University.

Before studying the socio-cultural impact of urbanisation it is desirable to have an idea of the physical environment and social condition of Tusmu because the stage for human interactions is set by these factors. Tusmu shares the habitat with thousands of tribal villages of Chotanagpur. Yet, in detail there is a remarkable variation with respect to them: Nature has not made the mistake of creating any two completely identical spatial units. It is the physical environment which imparts to a unit the tinge of individuality. Likewise, social conditions are pregnant with variations. Together these control the human response to cultural adaptation and transformation.

Physical Milieu

Tusmu lies at an elevation of about 2,250 feet from mean sea level, on the Ranchi Plateau—a rejuvenated peneplain of the Chotanagpur region. It is nearly 11 km to the west of Ranchi—the second largest city (1971: 210 882) in the region.

The village environs present a markedly dissected surface which is impressively reflected in the density of drainage in the area. The village is quietly seated on the bank of a lean tributary of the river North Koel. The topography is punctuated with subdued hillocks, rocky exposures, debris of boulders, pebbles and iron nodules. It is remarkably undulating. The village occupies the edge of a low-water divide from where the headstreams of North Koel and Subarnarekha rivers originate and spread out in opposite directions. It is an overdrained area.

The topography compromises a series of lowlands (*Dons*) and uplands (*Tands*). As it is bounded by the North Koel on almost two sides, the lowland occurs in a crescent shape covering the southern, western and northern sections. The upland covers the central and most of the eastern part of the village. The upland boundary is marked by an abrupt drop in the slope of 4 to 5 feet. Gully erosion is conspicuous in the northern part along the riparian tract. The lowland lies just above the bed of the North Koel. It is undoubtedly the most fertile tract, as it is covered with soil having a high proportion of silt and clay. The upland soil is poor in fertility; it has a high proportion of sand.

Moisture is the key factor determining the soil's agricultural character. It is soft and capable of growing different crops when wet; it becomes almost hard mortar when dry, perhaps on account of high proportion of iron in the soil. The topography, climate and soil do not favour an easy use of river water for irrigation. The steep slope and undulation, the seasonal character of the river and rapid percolation and evaporation of moisture from the soil with a high proportion of sand result in moisture deficiency throughout the non-monsoon months. The underground water resource is also poor on account of rapid run-off, paucity of permanent water bodies contributing to replenishment of underground water, and impervious and crystalline sub-surface rocks.

Most surface wells occur on the upland, in fact, its edge is marked by a chain of such wells. The upland soil, with a relatively high proportion of sand in comparison to lowland soil, lends itself remarkably to vegetable cultivation. Moreover, the scattered vegetable fields owned by individual farmers can be easily taken care of from near the settlements against damage by stray cattle and theft. The physical milieu, in fact, has nothing very remarkable to recommend itself for switching over to commercial peasant agriculture based on adoption of modern techniques. Yet, the village people have responded, in no small measure, to agricultural facilities made available through urbanisation. But unless we have examined the social aspects we may leave the question 'why' unanswered at this point.

The capacity of cultural adaptation and change of a society depends on the social background of people. We will, therefore, turn our attention to some aspects of social and economic conditions of the people inhabiting the village.

Community Structure

In a sense, the community structure of Tusmu may be said to be representative of tribal villages of Chotanagpur. There is a very clear dominance of a specific group of population, the tribe, i.e., the Oraon. This is not surprising in view of its location in what may be designated as the Oraon belt of the region. The population is composed of two broad groups: (i) tribes, and (ii) non-tribes. The latter may be further classified into two sub-groups : non-tribal Hindus and non-tribal Muslims. The relative position of the different communities is given below :

TABLE 6.1

Community Structure of Tusmu

Name of Community	Number of families	Total population.	Number of persons employed	% of persons employed to total population of community
Tribe: 1 Oraon	24	209	135	64.59
Non-Tribe Hindu :				
1. Koiry	16	155	101	65.16
2. Gope	11	70	44	62.85
3. Brahmin	1	12	5	41.66
Non-Tribe Mohammedan	3	21	14	66.69
Total	55	467	299	64.02

Source : Field-work, December 1977.

Tusmu is basically an Oraon village. There are altogether 47 houses occupied by 55 families, 24 of which are Oraon. They account for nearly 45 per cent of its total population. In the non-tribal group, Koiry is the most dominant caste; it is followed by Gope. The community structure of this village is essentially not attuned to the requirements of the most dominant group of the Oraon. The functional base is not diversified among this tribe. A member of this tribe, in the absence of that of the Munda tribe, performs the functions of the village priest (*Pahan*).

The primitive, purely subsistence economy, based initially on agriculture, did not leave much scope for development of an intricate functional structure of society. The tribes did most of the work by themselves except perhaps that of blacksmithy and weaving. Bamboo basketry, however, has been a traditional occupation of the Mahalis. There are three Oraon families of this group but at present only two stick to this traditional work. The third family has taken over the function of Gorait—the village messenger—over the years.

The community structure of the non-tribal Hindu group reflects a stronger orientation to the functional basis of population. The two dominant castes of this group—the Koiry and the Gope—are celebrated cultivators and cattle keepers. In all probability the extension of agricultural land by reclamation owes much to these people who have definitely settled in this village long after the Oraons. In Hindu society the Brahmin has a key position; so there is a Brahmin family in the village. The Mohammedan families by engaging in weaving performed the function required by the whole society, though now all have given up this traditional occupation.

The spatial pattern of community structure is an important feature in the cultural landscape of the village. The Oraon, being the original settlers, occupy the centre of the settlement and their place of worship (*sarna*) is very close to it. The sites of subsequent settlements, occupied by different non-tribal communities, fringe the core of the built-up area. Consequently hamleting is a striking feature of the village.

Caste hierarchy has evidently not only survived but persisted in successive settlements in the village. The spatially detached location of the Brahmin house virtually commands the main entrance to the village from the east, i.e., towards the city of Ranchi. The small worshipping place of Goddess Durga (*mandap*) is a salient cultural feature and the most significant social religious institution for the non-tribal population of the village. The locations of *sarna* and *mandap* attest to the dualism of social make-up of the village.

Employment Pattern

The employment pattern varies appreciably among the different communities of Tusmu. For the village as a whole, only 64 per cent of the population is gainfully employed, i.e., 36 per cent has no employment of any sort. In the case of the Oraon, the picture is the same. In the case of the non-tribal Hindu community the percentage of employed is 65.16, 62.85 and 41.66 for Koiry, Gope and Brahmin castes respectively. The percentage of employed to total population is the highest (66.69) in the Mohammedan community, and the lowest in the Brahmin family. It appears that under the impact of Ranchi city, members of the Koiry caste and the Mohammedan community have changed over to intensive vegetable cultivation, which has provided them with means of education and consequent outside employment. In contrast, the question of participation of females in works does not arise in the case of the tradition-bound Brahmin family. Moreover, the number of persons in the younger age group is much greater in the latter case. It is an interesting theme for investigation whether the non-agricultural Hindu castes can take full advantage of urban impacts to improve their economic conditions.

Size of Family

The size of the family is of great relevance to cultural adaptation and change. The larger agricultural families are economically sound and have greater capacity for responding to innovations. They have greater mobility with respect to such a process, although socially they are generally steeped in tradition. The smaller rural families are economically handicapped and are more prone to social disintegration.

The size structure of families in different communities is shown in Table 6.2. The maximum number of families (31) of all communities occurs in the class of 5 to 10 persons, nearly one-fourth in the smallest class of less than five persons. The two most dominant communities of Oraon and Koiry are characterised by the persistence of some large families. Perhaps, a numerically stronger group is more capable of supporting large families. There are two families of 16 to 20 persons and one of above 20 persons, all belonging to the Oraon and Koiry communities. Large agricultural families appear to have greater strength to resist disintegration under urbanisation.

TABLE 6.2

Size Structure of Families in Different Communities

Community	Number of families	Number of Persons in Family				
		Less than 5	5—10	11—15	16—20	Above 20
1. Oraon	24	5	15	1	2	1
2. Koiry	16	3	8	2	2	1
3. Gope	11	5	5	1	—	—
4. Brahmin	1	—	—	1	—	—
5. Mohammedan	3	—	3	—	—	—
Total	55	13	31	5	4	2

Source : Field-work, December 1977.

Land Ownership Pattern

The economic impact of urbanisation on different communities in an agricultural village depends to a large degree on the productivity of land. A community has stronger motivation for adopting innovations if the land is productive because the expectation of return from investment is more realistic. The land ownership pattern assumes significance in this context. The pattern between the tribal and the non-tribal population of Tusmu is shown in Table 6.3.

Some interesting socio-economic aspects are revealed by the land ownership pattern. The tribes own maximum land in case of second class lowland (*Don*) and third class upland (*Tand*). In case of first class lowland the acreage owned by tribes exceeds that owned by the non-tribes. In terms of productivity, the maximum area owned by the tribes is that portion of the lowland which is the best and also that of the upland which is not the least productive. Thus there is a strong economic basis for motivation for adopting farm innovations under urban impacts.

TABLE 6.3

Land Ownership Pattern

(*Figure in acres*)

Type of Land	Total Area	Owned by tribes	Owned by non-tribes
Lowland : Don I	31.40	17.50	13.90
Don II	123.03	38.00	85.03
Don III	18.30	6.60	11.70
Upland : Tand I	17.65	7.15	10.50
Tand II	70.71	29.51	41.20
Tand III	243.45	71.75	171.70
Homestead (cultivated)	1.75	1.25	0.50
Total	506.29	171.76	334.53

Source : Field-work, December 1977.

The land ownership pattern among the non-tribes is different in some respect. The maximum land owned by them constitutes the portions of class two lowland (*Don*) and class three upland (*Tand*). Considering again the productivity of land, the least productive area is mostly owned by the non-tribes—a fact which attests to their much later settlement in the village. The first and second classes of lowland are excellently suitable for paddy cultivation whereas the same classes of upland are remarkably good for market gardening, particularly vegetable cultivation. Most applications of innovations are limited to this aspect of agriculture. The traditional importance of vegetable cultivation on homestead land among the tribes is reflected in such area being in excess of that of the non-tribes.

Facets of Urbanisation

Urbanisation has been variously defined by social scientists. Smailes defines it as follows :

> Urbanisation is the process whereby land and inhabitants become urban. It refers to a change in both place and

> people . . . Urbanisation means that an increasing proportion of human society becomes townsfolk, and as this happens towns grow in population, spread in area, and make an ever-increasing impact upon the countryside, both upon its appearance and upon the life of its inhabitants. More and more of the landscape becomes townscape, and people come to live in an environment that is both physically and socially urban.[9]

The latter part of this definition of urbanisation, concerning its impact on the countryside and life of the inhabitants, has greater relevance to our study. Changes in its agricultural landscape and the life of the people are attuned to urban impacts of Ranchi city. Therefore, we would investigate economic impacts as constituting the background for socio-cultural changes in the village.

Economic Impacts

Agriculture is the main occupation of both tribal and non-tribal communities. Culturable land accounts for nearly 94 per cent of its total area of 296.87 acres. Of the total population 74 per cent is engaged in agriculture. In the case of tribes, it is 74 per cent. There are twenty-eight marginal farmers in this village, 11 of whom belong to the tribal community. The number of wage earners is 23, ten of whom belong to the tribes. There are 32 families which possess less than 2.5 acres of land. The two landless families belong one each to tribal and non-tribal communities; the number of persons in the former is 10 and in the latter 8. The landless families are relatively of large size.

The economic impacts of Ranchi city are more perceptible than socio-cultural ones. Adaptation of agricultural innovations has been the key feature of economic transformation.

Pumping sets have been provided to cultivators on loan basis. The communitywise break-up of the ownership of pumps is presented in Table 6.4.

Some salient points emerge from this table. The tribal community has responded to the use of pumping sets but most sets are owned by cultivators of one caste, i.e. Koiry. The Brahmin family owns two pumping sets, one each of diesel and electric.

TABLE 6.4

Communitywise Distribution of Pumping Sets

Serial No.	Community	Horse Power	Pumping Set	
			Diesel	Electric
	Tribe			
1.	Bandhna Oraon (Group leader)	5	D	—
2.	Gandura Oraon	3	—	E
	Non-Tribe			
3.	Koiry : Gopal Mahato	3	D	—
4.	Bhola Mahto	3	D	—
5.	Sohrai Mahto	3	—	E
6.	Dhaneshwar Mahto	3	—	E
7.	Parwal Mahto	5	D	—
8.	Gope : Shiv Nath Gope	4	D	—
9.	Brahmin : Bihari Ram Pandey	3	—	E
10.	-do-	5	D	—

Source : Field-work, December 1977.

It appears that consciousness and capacity for taking benefits of government schemes are basically confined to the dominant communities. Again, social status has apparently influenced the ownership pattern of pumping sets among different communities.

A group lift irrigation scheme has been completed in June 1974 with the assistance of the Bank of India. This scheme has almost revolutionised agricultural practices as well as the cropping pattern of not only the beneficiaries but also of other cultivators.

The following is the communitywise break-up of the beneficiaries of the scheme in 1974-75.

The majority of the beneficiaries of this scheme belong to the tribal community. The group leader, who executed the loan agreement with the bank, is an Oraon. The scheme has certainly benefited small tribal cultivators who individually were not able to afford the cost of assured pump-irrigation of their crops. Under this scheme an intake well has been constructed, cemented pipe laid through the fields, cemented water channels made and a 5 H.P. electric irrigation pump installed.

TABLE 6.5

Communitywise Break-up of the Beneficiaries of Group Lift Irrigation Scheme 1974-1975

	Name of Community	Number of Beneficiaries
	Tribe	
1.	Oraon	10
	Non-Tribe	
2.	Gope	2
3.	Mohammedan	1
	Total	13

Source : Field-work, December 1977.

The scheme covers 30 acres in *Kharif* (winter paddy etc.), 20 acres in *Rabi* (spring wheat etc.) and 0.15 acres in *Garma* crops (summer vegetables etc.). Besides there is one big diameter, 26 short purpose and 82 surface wells to irrigate crops, particularly those for the urban market. It is not surprising that cultivation of vegetables and hybrid maize (for supply as corn-cob to Ranchi city) has become an important activity in this village. The vegetables grown include cauli-flower, cabbage, cucumber, head cabbage, bell pepper, potato, pumpkin, peas, radish, string beans, sweet potato, tomato, garlic, onion and a host of others. Vegetable seeds and plants are sold in the Chutia locality of Ranchi city. Farmers of the Chutia have given up cultivation of vegetables and are specialising in developing seeds and plants.

TABLE 6.6

Acreage Under Vegetables, Maize and Sweet Potato

Crops	Acreage
1. Potato (rainy season)	80
2. Potato (winter)	32
3. Sweet potato	5
4. Vegetable (summer)	31
5. Vegetable (winter)	52
6. Hybrid maize	20

Source: Field-work, December 1977.

The economic impact of urbanisation is also reflected in the use of seeds of high-yielding varieties of paddy and wheat. The area under HYV paddy is about 145 acres in this village. Prescribed doses of fertiliser and pesticides, available in Ranchi city, are being applied. Soil acidity tests have been carried out and application of basic slag, which is available in abundance at Jamshedpur, has been recommended for raising the productivity of upland *Tand* soils.

Triple cropping has become possible, intensive vegetable cultivation is more popular and scientific cultivation is taking shape. Cowdung fertiliser from Ranchi city is brought for application to vegetable fields in the village. Each tractor load costs nearly Rs. 100. This exemplifies a situation in which a strong link of exchange tends to be established between an urban centre and the surrounding region. There is a ruralward flow of capital, technology and other forms of inputs and urbanward flow of products of intensive cultivation, particularly perishable commodities.

Purely subsistence peasant farming is in the process of getting commercial orientation. The urban impact is visible in increase of income, improvement of the standard of living, penetration of an element of homogeneity and change in the attitude pattern of the villagers.

What is most interesting is the conflict in Tusmu between the traditional ways perpetuated in the backwaters and outside influences. Proximity of Ranchi city is the key factor underlying the wave of socio-cultural changes in the village. It has set forth not only economic but other inducements of transformation.

On account of its location close to an all-weather metalled road from the city of Ranchi to the steel-town of Rourkela, it was taken over by the government in 1975 for being developed as a model tribal village. Subsequently, several agencies became active in its overall development. The Junior Chamber of Commerce, for example, is educating people to avoid drinking during daytime. A community hall is functioning as the nucleus of social activities. Banking organisations, particularly the Bank of India, have shown interest in reducing the incidence of exploitation by unlicensed money-lenders.

The impact of urbanisation on the village cultural fabric is clearly evident. The advent of electricity and communication facilities (transistor, radios) has exposed the village folk to the outside world. The youth dormitory (*Dhumkuria*), which was the pivot for sustaining traditional socio-cultural values, has become functionally defunct; although physically it does exist in a dilapidated condition. Previously, the economy was based on subsistence. The whole system of customs and habits, communal ceremonies, dances, beliefs and religious observations revolved around agriculture. Now urban impacts have made life busy and complex, extended modern technology and amenities but created a situation in which clash of individual interest is frequent, group rivalries common and frustrations rampant.

Urbanisation has introduced some alien elements in the traditional culture of the village: the western dress, an aggressive attitude towards inter-group harmonies, and a sense of belonging to a different society. Certainly it is a hybrid culture, it cannot take root in the village but neither can it flourish in the urban environment. Nevertheless, it has upset the socio-cultural conditions by alluring the villagers to towns. The large-scale urbanward migration of tribal youths from the region as a whole is a phenomenon of great social consequence. A contributing factor has been the growth of population which has created a rural proletariat of part-time farmers, most of whom can derive neither complete subsistence nor full-time employment from their tiny holdings because of inadequate financial resources, generally poor quality of arable land and persistence of primitiveness in agriculture. Youths in the most vigorous age-group tend to migrate outside for employment, social-cultural institutions have been left to be cared for by persons of either minor or overage groups. The weakening of the middle link as a consequence of the migration of youth lies at the root of the decadence of these institutions.

The impact of Ranchi city on the culture of Tusmu is quite perceptible. Although the most fundamental culture traits have undergone little change, one cannot fail to be impressed by the outward metamorphosis of certain aspects of way of life of the people. At least the impact has contributed to partial removal of the seals of cultural blindness and motivated the population, thoroughly steeped in tradition, for sustained economic and social progress.

Conclusion

The process of urbanisation is essentially linked with machine civilisation—a civilisation of consumption—which swallows up and destroys all those cultures which stand in the way of its expansion. Many less-resistant cultures, such as those of Andean or American Indians, have been swallowed up by this civilization. Such a process is commonly regarded as progress. But its price is a society improved in cultural terms, yet marked by an increasing destruction of human values and human potential.

Mass society swallows up minority cultures. The economic forces generated by urbanisation work against the survival of the minority culture of tribes. The greater the proximity of a city, the stronger its impact on a society. Buchanan has drawn attention to the steadily mounting and pervasive pressures of the mass media which are powerful agents of change of minority cultures.[10] In fact what we consider acculturation is the gradual erosion of cultures basically enshrined in the languages of minority groups; for example, the tribes in the present case. But it is the process of deculturation and not of progress and acculturation. An inevitable side-effect of urbanisation—industrialisation, the key to economic growth—is the genesis of the process of cultural liquidation which Tusmu seems to be undergoing at the present time.

NOTES

1. Henry S. Sterling, "The Changing Face of Rural Mexico : A Review, *Geographical Review* : Vol. XXXIX. No. 1 (Jan., 1949), 139-143.
2. Monica Cole, "The Rhodesian Economy in Transition and the Role of Kariba," *Geography*, Vol. 47 (1962), 15-40.
3. Craig L., Dozier, "Mexico's Transformed Northwest : The Yaqui, Mayo and Fuerte Examples," *Geographical Review*, Vol. LIII, No. 4, (Oct. 1963), 548-571.
4. George W., Hoffman, "Transformation of Rural Settlement in Bulgaria," *Geographical Review*, Vol. LIV, No. 1 (Jan. 1964), 45-64.
5. Raymond, E., Crist, "Traditional Agriculture : Diagnosis and Prognosis," Geographical Record, *Geographical Review*, Vol. LV, No. 3 (July, 1965), 434-437.

6. John M., Hunter, "Transformation of Rural Communities in Africa," Geographical Record, *Geographical Review*, Vol. LVIII, No.4 (Oct. 1967), 565-567.
7. Barry, Lentnek, "Economic Transition from Tradition to Commercial Agriculture, The Case of El Llano, Mexico," *Annals Assn. Amer. Geogrs.*; Vol. 59, No. 1 (March, 1959), 65-89.
8. P.G. Gowing and W.H. Scott, eds. *Acculturation in the Philippine : Essays in Changing Societies*, Quezon City : New Day Publishers, (1971).
9. A.E. Smailes, "The Definition and Measurement of Urbanisation, *Essays on World Urbanisation*, Edited by Ronald Jones, George Philip and Son Ltd. (London : 1975), 1-18.
10. Keith, Buchanan, "Economic Growth and Cultural Liquidation : The Case of the Celtic Nations," *Radical Geography : Alternative Viewpoints on Contemporary Social Issues*, Edited by Richard Peet; Methuen & Co. Ltd. (London : 1917); 125-142.

SEVEN

G. T. Nurse

LABOUR MIGRATION AS AGENT OF CHANGE
African and Melanesian Societies

TWO MAIN traditional patterns of labour migration, the permanent and the temporary, are apparent from history. Though permanent labour migration has sometimes involved the migration of persons who wished simply to engage in labouring pursuits in foreign parts, the majority of voluntary permanent migrants aim rather at more prosperous life-styles and higher prestige. The most typical form of permanent migration designed to provide simple physical labour is slavery. The slave labourer is removed, most often without reference to his own wishes but occasionaly willingly, from his place of origin and hardly ever returns to it. His status is sealed by his becoming property. His experiences and fate depend on the conduct of his owner.

Slavery has a well-defined part in the traditional social structure of many African peoples, but in Melanesia it represented the result of incursions from outside and its full-blown form never affected more than the coastal areas of what is now called Irian Jaya and the islands lying to the west of it. The claims to hegemony over these regions made by the Sultanates of Ternate and Tidore were maintained by the kidnapping and export of Papuans to the dominions of those potentates. The violence of traditional New Guinea society was such that enslavement seems often to have been life-saving, and in general was not accompanied by overmuch hardship (Rowley 1965). Nor was the domestic slavery of Africa arduous (Douglas 1964); it was only when the demand for slaves rose abroad that particular cruelties of procurement and transhipment became associated with the institution, though it must be admitted that in traditionally despotic societies like those of Dahomey or Buganda the lot of the slave was no better, and may even have been much worse, than it was in the plantations of the New World.

Neither the African nor the Melanesian slave was often given the opportunity to return to his homeland. The consequences of the slave trade to the populations of origin of these people lay principally in some degree of population depletion and through that in random fluctuations in genetic structure. The consequences of temporary labour migration are necessarily vastly otherwise. It is almost invariably voluntary, practised more considerably by males than females and by adults and adolescents to the exclusion of children, and generally terminates with the repatriation of the labourer. It affects population genetic structure only by the loss of reproductive potential during absence and perhaps by the occasional acquisition of a marriage partner from the area of labour. Its principal results are not biological but social and economic.

We are concerned not with the whole of Africa and the whole of Melanesia, but with those regions of either most familiar to the writer, namely east-central Africa and particularly Malawi and Mozambique, and the central Highlands of Papua New Guinea. Both of these regions have furnished since World War Two a number of labour recruits for work in places remote from them. On both labour migration has operated as an agent of change; but the nature and direction of change, though in many ways similar, have presented a number of contrasts.

Common Factors in Migration

At first sight it appears that the circumstances of labour migration in Africa and Melanesia have a great deal in common. In both instances the sale of labour service has represented the entry into a cash economy of societies based traditionally on subsistence agriculture. Where primary production is concerned solely with the growing of crops for local consumption, importation of goods can only become systematic when a consistent surplus is available of crops suitable for export. Neither demand nor quantity is sufficient to make this possible for either type of tribal society. In both, however, there is a labour surplus composed principally of relatively unoccupied men.

The intensely seasonal rainfall of east-central Africa dictates a limitation of agricultural activity to two fairly short periods of the year. Men assist women in preparation of the land before the rain, and usually also in the final harvest a few months later. Otherwise, their principal pursuits are hunting during part of dry season and repair and construction of houses. Neither of these are full-time occupations, and the force available for their pursuit is far in excess of what is needed. The livestock is tended by prepubescent boys. In the New Guinea Highlands there is somewhat more energy expended in clearing land, and the seasonality of rainfall is less marked, but the men are on the whole no busier than they are in Africa. The principal domestic labours, including care of the pigs, are performed by the women (Rappaport 1968). As a result numbers of men, other than those who carry out specific communal functions, well marked in African chiefs and headmen but less precise in the "big men" of Melanesian communities, are often quite dispensable.

There is more often an awareness in African tribal society than in Melanesian that labour is a marketable commodity. This probably derives from the unself-conscious attitude to slavery. Slavery was, however, unknown in the New Guinea Highlands, but institutionalized reciprocity extended to services, and the idea that services might similarly be exchanged for specie and that converted into cargo was quickly grasped, once the opportunity for employment was extended. An even more pressing need emerged as the colonial governments were established and cash became necessary to pay taxes. The poll-tax was demanded in all colonial territories from fit adult males; women, even when they were heads of households, were almost invariably exempt. The men, as hunters, were charged in their societal roles already with the procurement of everything that was not produced by village industry; it was inevitable that as goods from outside were brought into tribal consciousness, it should be the men whose responsibility it should be to obtain the means of gaining them. For all these reasons it had to come about that men would leave the villages to exchange their principal asset, their physical strength, for money.

This was not, all the same, quite as inevitable or as smoothly effected as circumstances might seem to demand. The penalty for non-payment of taxes was compulsory labour, but, that could be done locally, on roads or other public works, without the need to go very far from the village. Traditional trade needs were satisfied by the barter of artefacts, hunting trophies and sometimes, when that was in abundance, food, and the need for trade goods additional to the traditional ones was sometimes long in being felt. The needs of the employer, in fact, very frequently, at the onset of colonialism, were more pressing than those of the potential employee, and coercive or deceptive means were often employed. These were not curbed by analogous government measures, in both areas, involving the imposition, albeit temporary, of the *corvée*.

Though everywhere colonial governments were in theory strongly opposed to the use of forced labour for private expatriate ends, it was generally not easy for the untutored villager to distinguish among white men all claiming to wield authority. Such lack of sophistication was often exploited quite unscrupulously by labour recruiters. There is room to suspect that in parts of Africa, though happily no longer in Papua New Guinea, it still is. To my personal knowledge it was still happening as recently as eight years ago, and there is no reason to believe that it has ceased. Labourers did not always go willingly; often did not understand the terms of the indentures to which their legal consent was secured; were prevented from returning home when they were due to do so; were subjected to hazards and harshness for which their village experience had little prepared them.

Nevertheless, when the abuses were removed, or those who suffered them had learnt to discount them, the economic motives still operated strongly, and were reinforced by cultural pressures which were in either instance generated by the nature of the traditional society. It is in these cultural pressures and their feedback that the differences between African and Melanesian migrant labour may be seen mainly to lie.

Migration Contrasts

Central African societies at the time of the earliest effective European contact fell either into Group A of the two main categories of African political system described by Fortes and Evans-Pritchard (1940), or were in the process of realignment into it following a period of disintegration owing to military interventions by stronger Group A states. That is, they either had, or had lost and were reacquiring, the apparatus of government: centralised authority, administrative machinery, and judicial institutions. Even the most afflicted, impoverished or isolated village, functioning to all intents and purposes autonomously, either acknowledged some link with a larger and more powerful entity or was in the process of assimilation by one. No matter how devastating the wars which had passed across it, a hierarchy of authority was retained within the village and was exercised, and internal disputes were settled by consensus rather than conflict. There was, as there still is, an acute sense of history and ready acknowledgement of either intrinsic or extrinsic permanent unilateral descent groups constituting corporate units and possessing political functions. In short, even where the state was not overtly in existence, it was recognised as an ideal.

On the other hand, Melanesian society is essentially without a centre, atomistic, individualist, and receptive of change. Hierarchies are evanescent and histories are rarely retained in detail. Groups form, disintegrate and reassociate without any pattern beyond the needs and desires of the individual and his kindred. There is no set and definable universal social unit beyond the household; the proliferation of terms used by anthropologists for different types of aggregation of households, clans, phratries, parishes, villages, demes, wards and so on, attests the indefinition of political units. Rituals celebrate not solidarity but competition; they are media for self-assertion and aggrandisement, not for corporate emotion or dedication. Material wealth is the touchstone of status, and is acquired by industry and astuteness rather than by due tribute.

From one angle emigration to remote places from both of these milieus can be seen as flight from aspects of traditional society which are distasteful to the individual. Competition within the New Guinea village naturally leaves a number of the less capable competing men disadvantaged. Before contact, such men could have no recourse except to acquiescence or change of allegiance. Migrant labour has opened the way to success in village terms without deliberate disturbance of village stability as well as enabling men who dislike conflict to withdraw from it (Brown 1973). When they return to the village they are sustained by the wealth they have acquired in the remote places, and are able to re-enter the village system at a level of power and prestige they could hardly have attained had they remained within it.

In central Africa the motives are generally rather different. Conflict within the group certainly may play a part, and I have known village courts prescribe a period of labour migration for an individual who had committed offences which traditionally would have called for expulsion or execution. But such instances are unusual, and the more usually operative style of conflict, particularly in matrilineal societies, is that between affines. In an uxorilocal situation husbands oppressed by their affines may form bonds among themselves, as has happened in the development of the *nyau* ritual among the Maravi (Rita-Ferreira 1966). Since the bonds, to be effective, must be sustained by some secrecy of ritual, such devices tend to be regarded with great suspicion and disapproval by the political authorities. A compromise given the *nyau* brotherhood partial control over funeral rites was worked out among the Maravi, but with the arrival of European hegemony and the consequent growth in the influence of Christian missions this became ineffective. As a result, the temporary suppression of *nyau* during the colonial period, when it was regarded as potentially politically menacing, left many men with no means of relieving societal tensions except by labour migration.

In the patrilineal societies of central Africa the position was somewhat different, but it produced similar effects. Political intervention by the colonial government here took the form of suppression of raiding and warfare. Warfare was by no means integral to the cultural pattern, as it was in New Guinea, though at least among the Ngoni a military form was given to age-set initiations; but during the period of upheavals of the late eighteenth and nineteenth centuries battle had come to be informally accepted as part of the *passage* of a young man towards becoming a householder, as a mechanism involved in enacting a change of role. When this no longer became possible the substitution of labour migration occurred very smoothly.

It is in this context that the contrasting cultural significance of labour migration in Africa and Melanesia is perhaps most clearly seen. In Melanesia it afforded an escape from, and in Africa an alternative to, conflict and violence. Paradoxically, in societies of which warfare was an integral part the opportunity to avoid it was welcomed, whereas in those in which conflict was regarded as essentially contrary to right living it was nevertheless deemed necessary to find a substitute for it. Deeper currents can perhaps be descried here, differences of social psychology more profound than the economic superficies of the two cultures can reveal.

Without any firm tradition of political stability or inherited framework on which to build one, Melanesian societies are intensely receptive of novelty and find it easy to reject large segments of what appear at first to be their most fundamental components. For the central African the problem is rather the integration of novelty by means of carefully worked out social equations into a pattern which is regarded as in itself immutable. These contrasts play with great intensity on the degree and nature of the changes which migrant labour accomplishes in either society.

External Stimulus

Any broadening of the knowledge of the outside world in a traditionalist society is first brought about by the intrusion into that society of non-members. Even where a single member leaves and then returns, the stimulus for him to leave in the first place is provided by human agencies external to his own society. Such a stimulus may be as tenuous as a rumour brought by a traveller or as surprising as the arrival of a government patrol; but until some sort of concept of the exterior is mediated by human experience there is no valid reason for wishing to explore it.

The first information is naturally interpreted in terms of the familiar. The range of material concepts available to a traditionalist society is generally narrow, and the political concepts are limited by what is known locally to be politically possible. Where the intervention of non-members clashes too incompatibly with the values of society, it becomes necessary that new means of interpretation must be sought. This can happen in two phases : one within society itself and the other through the partial integration of members into the system represented by the intervention. It is in the latter context particularly that labour migration become an agent of change.

In central African society labour migration confers material advantages on the migrant and his lineage. These are of special importance when it happens repeatedly. Most men among the Ntumba and Ngoni, and a very large proportion among the Cewa, make at least one journey to the South African, Rhodesian or Zambian mines or to the tobacco or sugar plantations of Rhodesia. This first journey constitutes the ritual surrogate; but many continue to present themselves, again and again, for re-engagement, and such men accumulate wealth for themselves and their lineage and secure some resources backing against time of lessened agricultural productivity. Except in terms of manufactured goods and novelties, and the payment of bride-prices among the Ngoni, wealth is of little real social importance. The prestige of a man continues to rest mainly on his position within his descent group, and though wealth can buy some improvement of this it does not substantially alter it.

I have known of hereditary slaves among the Yao who as returned labour migrants have improved the prospects of their children by distributing gifts as if they themselves were not slaves but lesser members of the lineage of their proprietors, and this is an acceptable form of social manipulation; but they themselves have gained prestige by the simple fact of having been away, and what is important is less the value or quantity of the gifts than the manner and direction of their giving. As labour migrants they have associated on terms of approximate equality with persons of higher local standing and undergone with them part of their *rites de passage*, and this in itself helps to elevate their status. Legal slavery has, of course, been abolished, but even if it had not it is doubtful whether their owners would have prevented their going; an accretion of prestige to a client elevates his patron in these societies.

But it is not only, or particularly, the men of lowly status who engage as labour migrants in Africa. An aristocracy which needs cash and wishes for wider acquaintance with the external world has been quick to avail itself of the opportunities presented by labour migration. It is well-known that one African Head of State has passed through the mines and thereby, though with quite extraordinary determination, gone on to universities in the United States and Britain and established himself as an authority on the history and culture of his people as well as having successfully practised abroad as a physician. The African migrant labourer can come from any point in the social hierarchy.

On the other hand the New Guinea highlander has no incentive to migrate if he has prospects of success in his own society. Since such success is measured in terms of wealth, his motives for migration, where they were not simply refuge from conflict, would be exclusively the acquisition of cash and manufactured goods for display. Knowledge and experience would be valued by the migrant as sources of advantage, but in themselves they would mean much less to the traditionalist Melanesian society than they would to the African. The effects of migration on the traditional societies would, therefore, appear to differ quite radically, but I, nevertheless, propose to show that fundamentally they are similar in at least one important respect.

Migration as Agent of Change

That labour migration should operate as an agent of change in traditional societies is inevitable. Where slave trade was involved, there were the loss of persons of both sexes and their genetic potential, and the gain in material wealth which generally accrued to society by their sale; but there was also the presence of traders, outsiders, with different customs and different values, to exert an influence on society. Temporary la bour migration, on the other hand, removes mainly the most dispensable men and introduces new ideas acquired by the returning migrant as well as a wider range of, and consequently demand for, manufactured goods. The scope of village life is broadened by an increased awareness of its area of reference and by an increased range of implements and other commodities available for use by its members. There is some cushioning of the possible effects of failure of primary produce. There is perhaps some questioning by the now experienced labourer of the values of the society in which he grew up.

To this extent the African and Melanesian situations are similar. They differ in the position of the men who actually leave the village in the traditional hierarchy, and the use made of the goods and experiences acquired. The Melanesian will adopt an unfamiliar apparatus or technique readily; the African, more closely bound to the practices of his ancestors, will not. The Melanesian benefits individually from migration by an accretion of personal wealth and prestige; the African gains both, but much of the gain is redistributed to his kinship group or other corporate body to which he owes allegiance. It might be expected that the greater flexibility and receptivity of Melanesian society would promote a more ready adoption and exploitation of new ideas and techniques, while the rigid African system would offer more resistance. Both the common factors and the contrasts can nevertheless be held to be superficial. A far more fundamental situation is discerned when the migrant labourer is seen not as the passive transporter of change but as one of its components; in short, if we extend to labour migration the type of insight which La Fontaine (1977) has brought to the subject of *rites de passage*.

La Fontaine stresses that the acknowledged purpose of initiation rites is to change individuals, and that the ritual constitutes an experience which supports the authority of traditional values by the successful endurance of ordeals which are accepted as proofs that a change has been effected in those particular individuals. The ritual thus becomes self-validating by being the medium of transition of the initiant from one state to the next. Once *passage* has been undergone, its details are unimportant provided that its nature is acknowledged. Even where the ritual comprised a highly ordered sequence of events which have to be correctly performed, there is scope for change in detail provided the structure remains recognisable. Labour migration engagement and discharge fulfil the requirements for such a ritual, and can easily be conceived of as such; and that change has taken place in the returning migrant is readily apparent. The acceptance of migrant labour as *passage* within the range of traditional values is consequently simple.

There has been little determined corporate opposition to labour migration in either Melanesian or African traditional society, whereas if it had been seen to be radically disruptive a fairly strong resistance might have been expected, at least in Africa. The adaptive facility of Melanesia might make resistance less probable, but in Melanesia labour migration has been accepted without even the minimum of aggressive demonstration which many innovations seem very temporarily to provoke. The clue to this curious passivity might lie in the status of the men involved in migrant labour. In Melanesia they would tend to be those of least social prominence, *ol rabes man*, whose gain in status on their return could most effectively be demonstrated not by rejecting traditional values but by enacting an estimable role within them. In Africa the motives of migration for men of the whole status range would be to consolidate high status or non-competitively to secure advancement. In neither case is it to the advantage of the returned migrant to disturb the value system of his society. Thus labour migration would seem to operate most fundamentally to preserve the *status quo*, and only superficially and stealthily to erode those aspects of it which are least essential to its continuance.

SUGGESTED READINGS

Brown, Paula, *The Chimbu : A Study of Change in the New Guinea Highlands*, London : Routledge and Kegan Paul, 1973.

Douglas, M., 1964, "Matriliny and Pawnship in Central Africa." *Africa 341*, 1964, pp. 301-313.

Fortes, M.E. and Evans-Pritchard, E.E., *Introduction to African Political Systems*. Oxford : Oxford University Press for the International African Institute, 1940.

La Fontaine, Jean, "The Power of Rights." *Man 12*, 1977. pp. 421-437.

Rappaport, Roy, *Pigs for the Ancestors*. New Haven : Yale University Press, 1968.

Rita-Ferreira, A., "The Nyau Brotherhood Among the Mozambique Cewa" *South African Journal of Science 64*, 1966, pp. 20-24.

Rowley, C.D., *The New Guinea Villager*. Melbourne : Cheshire, 1965.

Van Velsen, J., "Labour Migration as a Positive Factor in the Continuity of Tonga Tribal Society", in *Social Change in Modern Africa*. Edited by A. Southall, London: Oxford University Press, 1961.

EIGHT

Ali Nuwaz

THE GARO HILL TRIBES OF BANGLADESH

THE GARO are not the autochthons of Bangladesh but an aboriginal hill tribe dominated by ancient customary laws within their own culture area. They are of Mongoloid origin. "Their faces are round and short. The forehead is not receding but projects very little beyond the eye, which is small, on a level with the face, very dark and obliquely set. The want of prominence in the nose is remarkable. The whole face has appearance of being flattened, the mouth staring in the compressed prognathos.[1]

The Garo are a non-literate, matriarchal and matrilineal society. A sort of cross cousin marriage is prevalent. The husband stays in the house of the wife almost as a non-salaried worker. "Property descends from generation to generation through motherhood".[2] The male never inherits property. After the death of the wife, the father can even be driven out of the house by the children. Children are known by the mother. Women are predominant in the family.

A peculiar type of horticulture, locally termed as *jhum chash*, on the slopes of the hills and hunting are the principal means of the livelihood of these people. The population is approximately one lakh.

The dwelling places of the Garo are the historic Modhupur jungle, about thirty miles west of Mymensingh town by the side of the Mymensingh-Tangail-Dacca road, and places on and around the Garo hills situated along the frontier between Mymensingh district of Bangladesh and Meghalaya state of India. Hills and forests, streams and torrents, springs etc. are the common environment of the Garo area.

Originally, according to the lore of the tribe, the Garo were a nomadic people who emigrated from Tibet. Others trace their origin to north-west China, probably to pre-historic days. No dependable evidence is available about their origin excepting these lores.

The Garo tongue possibly belongs to the Sino-Tibetan language group. Primitive characteristics are found in this language. Ethnolinguistic studies may provide a more exact picture. The language of this tribal group is called A Chik Katha in their own term, meaning hill language.

The Garo are divided into two groups : A "chik and Mandai or Mandi", meaning hill Garo and plain Garo respectively. The latter dwell on plain land in the foothills and have frequent contact with nearabout non-Garo villagers. So, some cultural infiltration has taken place in them, which includes religion too. Christian missionaries have been preaching among the Garo. Now, most plain Garo have accepted Christianity. This is the result of dedicated work of the missionaries for about a century. Poverty was the main pass for the access of outside culture into Garo society.

Mandai, Mandi and Mande are synonymous, meaning man. In Chinese, "min" means the same. Probably, these words come from a common stock. The Garos on the plain land were termed as Mandi or Mandai, i.e., man, which possibly suggests that the hill Garo was not accepted as man.

The Garo, as a whole, are extremely conservative maintaining their indigenous cultural traits, but the plain Garo, specially those who have accepted Christianity, have become susceptible to modern culture. The Garo were untouched by outside cultural influence till the Muslim rule in Bengal. During the reign of Moghul Emperor Jehangir, a military expedition was sent to Assam, headed by Mirza Nathan, who marched to the foot of the Garo hills and pitched his camp there. He has left a very brief account about these hill people, saying : "They eat all sorts of things except iron, which is the hardest of all, and cannot be chewed with teeth. They eat ass and pigs and make no exception of any other things."[3] This suggests that these hill people were previously unknown to the then rulers, not to speak of exerting cultural influence on them. Cultural infiltration into Garo society started during the mid-British period through Christian missionaries and officials, who first lured two young Garo cowboys of the plains by offering them beautiful dresses, palatable food and valuable gifts. Thus, the two boys began secretly receiving education from Christian teachers without the knowledge of their parents and notice of the chiefs of the tribe. By and by, preaching of Christianity began and the process still continues, resulting now in a large Christian Garo population.

There are some Garo who are third generation Christians. Some among them have received higher education and are economically well-off. Many Christian Garo young women are now found serving as nurses in hospitals in and outside Bangladesh. We do not know of any case of conversion of a Garo to Hinduism or Islam. Of course, a few local Muslims have married some wealthy Garo women. Hindus generally did not do so because of their strong social taboos.

The inferior social position of males in Garo society has encouraged them to accept Christianity more than the females.

There is another hill tribe, named Hajong, in the same area which is superficially influenced by Hinduism but the infra-structure of their culture is deeply rooted in their own ancient social system.

Though Christian Garos have been culturally very much influenced by modern civilization, the process has not helped them much to bring about a change in their society at large. Garo society as a whole is still inclined to maintain its indigenous customs and traditions. The modern educated Garo hate the traditionalists and criticise them as extremist but in vain.

The Garo are not idol worshippers. They do not have religious books. Of course, Garo lore tells us that originally they had religious literature written on buffalo skin. On their emigration from Tibet to their present abode, hungry Garo ate up their religious books for want of food. Thus, they lost their religious scripture for good, leaving behind only some confusing lore and verbal stories, traditional customs and practices for the coming generations. Garo religion is nothing but a jumble of indistinct and indefinite ideas which are more social and cultural than spiritual. Their belief-system is based on fear.

The Garo are unconcerned about the happiness of heaven and punishment of hell; rather, they are more terrified by the harmful actions of ghosts and evil spirits in their everyday life. They do not give a good name to the new-born because of the fear that ghosts and spirits may cause its death. The Garo do not move about freely everywhere as they fear evil spirits. The Anangwari bridge on the Ildak river in the Garo area is a danger spot for them. They believe that ghosts and spirits live there in the guise of snakes. The Garo are afraid of the Bugarig bridge, too, because, they believe, it swallows up human beings. They believe that there are places where specific ghosts dwell. So, they try to avoid those places. They believe that tigers are nothing but evil spirits; sometimes they move in human society as human beings in daytime, but at night they transform themselves into tigers. Double personality of this type is termed in the Garo language as *Matsadu Matsaved.* A Garo changes his original name if attacked by a tiger in the belief that the new name will confuse the tiger. They believe that if a Garo is killed by a tiger or an animal, he will definitely be reborn as an animal. About the cat also, the Garo have some supernatural beliefs. For that reason, the Garo do not eat cat though they are habituated to eating almost all kinds of animals.

There are trees, stones and hillocks which they think to be the abode of ghosts and they are afraid of these. They believe that danger, disease and death occur on account of the harmful influence of evil spirits who are their eternal enemies. It is their belief that Nature is a conscious living object and ever antagonistic to them. The Garo developed this belief out of their experience of natural calamities befalling them, which they explained in terms of animism. Thus, they attribute personality to inanimate objects.

So, the Garo are afraid of ghosts, spirits and angry Nature. But what is the remedy against them ? The Garo believe that they can protect themselves from ghosts and spirits by magical practices, sorcery, by appeasement of Nature or by offering sacrificial meals to them. There is a class of medicine men among the Garo named *Khamal* who can punish or pacify ghosts and spirits by resort to magical practices. These people are honoured in Garo society. It is also believed that they possess a double personality since they can appease or punish the evil spirits.

When an epidemic breaks out in a locality, the Khamal orders the spirit of the epidemic to leave the locality. In a ritual, they build a horse-figure with bamboo and place it in a central place. They then trap animals like the monkey, a big-size rat or the dog, tie them by the neck and drag them through the village. Afterwards they kill them by strokes of a special type of knife and cut them into pieces which are thrown all over the village. Further, they rub the blood of the animals on the doors of every house, and then hang the skeleton of the animals penetrated by a long bamboo, by the side of the bamboo-horse or in a public place. This, the Garo believe, frightens the evil spirits away. There are many other rituals like this for the same purpose.

To guard a new-born baby against spirits, the Khamal passes the little baby through the hole of an extinguished earthen furnace to make the baby fireproof. The bamboo-fenced cottage of the mother and the baby is protected by thorn and folded strings all around, with a net on the door and a big fire inside. The net and strings are to threaten the spirits that they will be caught if they come to harm the baby. The Garo believe that the Khamal can detain the ghosts and spirits by his magical powers. They also treat diseases by charms and talisman.

The Garo fear the return of the dead in ghost form, but they look to the reincarnation after a period of penance.[4] In the Garo religion, the idea of the next world is very indistinct. They believe in soul-matter and life-essence.[5] If the soul flees the cage of the body, death occurs. This idea coincides with that of a great Bengali mystic folk-poet, Lalan Fakir. To quote him :

Khachar majhe achin pakhi
Kemne ase jai,
Dharte parle monoberi
Ditam pakhir pai

(In the cage, an unknown bird, in every breath, comes and goes. I wish, I could catch it and with strings of mind, bind it by the leg).

The Garo believe that life is nothing but a manikin situated in the head.[6] If it leaves, the cage of the body falls lifeless and dead. This idea may have some relation with the Tantric idea.

However, according to the Garo belief after death the soul first rests on the Chikmang, the highest peak of the Garo hills, and, then for some time, travels hither and thither in unknown places of an unknown world until it returns to the earthly environment either as a ghost or as man or animal in rebirth.

After the funeral, the living family members offer for consecutive few days boiled rice for the soul of the dead. It is both out of affection and fear. If the soul of the dead is dissatisfied and displeased, it may come back as a ghost to harm them. Of course, the soul may be born again in the world as a human being or as an animal. The physical resemblance and behavioral similarity of the children with ancestors probably make them believe that ancestors are again born to the clan. The Garo worship their ancestors not as an act of piety but out of a mixed feeling of a fear, affection and earthly gain.

Though there is no clear concept of sin and piety in Garo religion, it is believed that a bad soul is reborn as an animal. The idea of being born as an animal probably gave rise to the belief in totemism. Each clan of the tribal group believes that a particular animal was their ancestor. So the clan never harms that particular species.

The sacrificial meals for ghosts and spirits are called "Rogala" in Garo tongue. The sun is one of the strongest *manas* of the tribe. To appease it, the Garo offer some horticultural crop, blood and intestines of poultry, and wine. The moon, the stars, the earth, rain, thunder, crops, river, hills, mountains, wind, death etc. are also considered to be *manas*, and the Garo try to appease them by sacrificial meals.

According to an ancient lore of the Garo, named "Duramunga San-dumunga Dakgrika", the river Brahmaputra gave his son, Singra, in marriage to Simera, the daughter of the mountain, Tura. In accordance with the custom of the matriarchal society, Singra went to live in Simera's mountain house, but died of hunger as the young wife could not cook the food of his choice. It resulted in a serious quarrel between Brahmaputra and Tura. With the help of torrential rain, the river swelled higher and higher until the mountain was about to drown. Then, Tura appeased the sun and wind which dried up the flood in seven days and saved Tura. The moral of the story is : Appease Nature in time of need. The Garo practise it deligently. Secondly, a newly married Garo girl takes special care to cook food for her husband. A similar story of non-stop rain and swelling of water submerging the highest mountain is found in ancient Chinese folklore.

The Garo sacrifice animals to feed mother earth so that the life-essence of their lands may increase to give them more crops.

At the death of a person, the Garo sacrifice as many lives as possible, which formerly included human beings too, to increase the life-essence of the dead so that the soul may climb the highest peak of the mountain where it is to rest. After the death of an ancient Chinese king, his servants and attendants were also buried alive in the palatial royal tomb. Probably the object more or less, was the same.

The Garo spread a portion of the funeral ashes in their land to infuse the life-essence of the dead into it so that the land becomes fertile and productive. In ancient China, the dead were buried in agricultural land to increase its fertility.

According to Garo lore a woman named Nastu Nupantu created the earth, rather land, out of a handful of sand taken from the fathomless bottom of the sea when nothing existed save water. A similar story is also found in ancient Chinese folklore. The similarities between Chinese and Garo lores possibly provide some anthropological testimony that the Garo came from China. According to Chinese folklore, a goddess went to the seashore, took handfuls of wet sand one after another, made various shape of animals with each handful and breathed into each to make it a living creature. Thus, creation began. Such an idea is found in some formal religions too. May be the idea was originally borrowed from the primitive people.

One of the greatest compulsory religious functions of the tribe is *Mimangkham*, which literally means ceremony for a departed soul. Pre- and post- funeral rituals, meant for the salvation of the soul, are as follows :

The dead body is bathed by a female first with water, then with oil, while other womenfolk sing the traditional wailing song. Then, the body is worshipped with valuable materials the family can afford. Next, the corpse is dressed traditionally by males, laid on the pyre with the face towards east or north. The dress differs according to the sex of the departed. Before the body is carried to the pyre by a particular set of people, every relative of the dead is required to place a piece of cloth or a garment on the corpse. After the cremation, persons appointed for the purpose, take bath to purify themselves, offer boiled rice and an egg for the soul, take a small half-burnt bone, put it underground in the courtyard of the house where the dead person used to reside. A square platform is raised on the spot wherefrom, after a few days, the soul goes up to rest on the highest peak of the Garo mountain.

After the funeral, the family members take only vegetarian diet for seven consecutive days and also offer the same as sacrificial meal to the soul. After that period is over, the family members eat a particular kind of small fish for the first time. Next day, a feast is arranged with fowls, pigs, rice and wine. Self-brewed wine is a must in every religious and social function of the Garo. On the eve of the feast, a small portion of the meal cooked is put on a banana leaf and offered to the departed soul at the place where the half-burnt bone has been kept. The place is called *Khatik.* It is enclosed with four flags on the four corners. Every day, a small quantity of food is served to the departed soul for a certain period of time. The food must be that which was liked by the person while alive.

A dummy corpse is also kept inside the Khatik. The dress of the dummy differs according to sex. If the corpse is of a woman, the dummy is adorned with the usual ornaments of the lady while she was living. This practice is generally not followed nowadays in apprehension of theft.

Last of all, one night, a procession starts with the dummy moving from house to house where wine is served in honour of the departed soul. This continues throughout the night. After the procession, the dummy is again kept in its original position. Feasting, drinking, dancing and singing with accompanying musical instruments go on. Sacrificial food is served to the departed soul for the last time.

This is a brief account of the ceremony for the departed soul but, in actual practice, it is a lengthy process.

As already observed Garo religion is an agro-based religion. The following facts will bear it out :

The Garo divide the year in twelve months. In each month, in accordance with the position of their crops, they hold a number of festivals and perform rites and rituals for the protection of their life as well as of their crops. It has already been said that the hill Garo are habituated to a type of horticulture locally named "Jhum chash", in dense forest full of ferocious animals, like tigers, bears and elephants and poisonous snakes. Over and above they live in a constant fear of ghosts and spirits. While going to the place of work away from home, they move in bands, singing in chorus and blowing buffalo-horns. All adult males and females work in such dangerous places from sunrise to sunset and then return home in the same manner. At night some males go to guard their fields and stay there on bamboo *machans* built on high branches of big trees.

The Garo also believe that some evil spirits can take away their grain from the fields as well as from their stores. To remedy these, they hold festivals and perform rituals every month.

In the first month of their year, which falls nearabout the last month of the Bengali year, the Garo celebrate new year's day. It is not only a festival but also a religious function for their safety and welfare throughout the whole year. In this month, they clean the jungle for agriculture. Next month, they sow rice. Before that, they perform a festival named "Asiroka" to check the evil influence on their paddy. The following month, they weed the land, and in this connection, they observe the "Jakrakari" festival. In the fourth month, the Garo harvest maize and hold the festival of "Abrengdanga". Next month, they harvest some crops and prepare the land for the second rotation. In this month, they worship the goddess of crops by celebrating a similar festival. At the end of the first-half of the year, they harvest tropical crops and celebrate about half a dozen such festivals.

At the beginning of the next half of the year, the greatest and most thrilling festival of the Garo takes place in which the entire tribe is in a joyous mood. In this festival, they consume a major portion of the wine set apart for the whole year. Young boys and girls madly dance together. They drink wine without measure and select their future partners by gesture and posture of mutual understanding. In this festival buffalo horns are continuously blown alongwith playing of tribal musical instruments, including big-sized drums. The dancers loudly sing in chorus; sometimes they hoop together. Some of the stronger boys dance with swords and shields to threaten evil spirits. The dancers wear a special dress and paint their face and body with hand-impression. On the whole, a wild atmosphere prevails.

Many such monthly festivals, all centering on crops, take place. Not a single month passes without one or more festivals of this kind.

It has already been said that these festivals are observed not as an act of piety but for protecting crops from evil spirits, which are about a dozen in number and among which "Rakkasi" is the worst.

Coming to the relation of sex-life with religion, it may briefly be mentioned that ante-nuptial unchastity, incest or promiscuity are prohibited in Garo society, not from religious point of view but from that of social relationship. But at one time, there used to be group marriages with no restriction on sex-life. Later, restriction was imposed. Now, if an incident of ante-nuptial unchastity takes place, any of the two persons involved is fined. In controversial cases, the guilty is detected by any of the following means:

(1) An egg is dropped into boiling water. If the egg does not get boiled, the person concerned is considered not guilty. (2) The involved parties appoint a Khamal (priest) each to represent them. The appointed Khamals enter chest-deep water and recite some magic words. Afterwards, both submerge simultaneously. The representative of the guilty person cannot remain under water for a longer period on account of the severe attack by aquatic animals. Garo society accepts the verdict of either means not only in such cases but in all other cases. However, if a fine is paid, the person concerned is absolved of the crime.

If a married man or a woman is found guilty of a sex-crime, similar punishment is imposed on the man. In the case of the woman, her inheritance is confiscated as punishment.

Marriage among the Garo is a complicated affair. In special cases, a man can marry a girl and her mother too at the same time and they have a normal sex relationship accepted by society. Such marriage takes place to keep the ancestral property intact. With the same purpose, a young man may sometimes marry a minor girl and keep having normal and regular sex-relation with his mother-in-law till his wife attains adulthood.

It is a brief description of the Garo way of life. The name of the religion is *Sangsarek*. Of the many Garos interviewed in course of the present study, some were found educated, but none could explain the meaning of the word Sangsarek. Probably, it is not a Garo word. The Bengali word, Sangsarek, meaning worldly or domestic, might have entered the language of the Garos at some later period. If so, the name of the religion itself indicates that the Garo religion does not have any spiritual concept, rather it is a religion for conducting only the mundane or domestic life in their own way.

The above is a brief description of the findings of a survey work covering about six months in 1978. Further intensive survey is recommended to reveal the many mysteries that the Garo society abounds in.

NOTES

1. Col. Dalton, *Descriptive Ethnology of Bengal.*
2. Major A. Playfair, *The Garos.*
3. Nathan Mirza, *Baharistan-i-Gayabi.*
4. Major A. Playfair, *The Garos.*
5. This belief is probably widespread in many South-East Asian countries.
6. A similar idea in not uncommon among the tribes of South-East Asian countries.

SUGGESTED READINGS

Amal Das Gupta, *Manusher Thikana*. Calcutta, 1971.

District Census Report, Mymensingh, part 1-IV.

Garo Sanskriti. Dacca : Ministry of Information and Broadcasting, People's Republic of Bangladesh, 1978.

Janira, A Journal of Virisiri Cultural Academy, Vol. 1, Mymensingh, 1978.

Karim, Nazmul, *Samaj Vijnan Samikshan*, Dacca : Naoroj Kitavistan, 1973.

Maimansingher Sahiti-o-Sanskriti, Mymensingh District Council, 1978, pp 572-603.

Nathan, Mirza, *Baharistan-i-Ghayabi, Vol. 2*, Gauhati : 1936, pp. 528-529.

Pakistaner Upajati, Dacca : Pakistan Publications, 1963, pp 25-36.

Shilpakala, A Journal of Bangladesh Shilpakala Academy, Vol. 1, 1977, pp 24-37.

Samad, Ebne Golam, *Nritatva*. Dacca: Bangla Academy, 1973.

NINE

B. B. Goswami

HILL TRIBESMEN OF NORTH-EAST INDIA
The Impact of Christianity

ALONG with many other forces of change, the impact of Christianity in North-East India has brought about drastic changes in the life-style of those who have embraced the religion. The positive undertones are many. Because of Christianization the colourful tribes of North-East India are utilising the best of the developmental programmes for materialistic benefits, and interacting and adapting the ideational values of the 'higher' religions. Some of the earlier British ethnographers have also referred tangentially to the negative consequences (Parry 1932 : 21-24). The ethnographic picture drawn by them is of the time when the British administration held sway. But the cultures are constantly changing. In the field of politics I have shown the changes in my book, *Mizo Unrest* (1978). Some of the radical political movements are the results of politicisation of culture.

The impact of Christianity has set in motion many new religious movements and cults which are looked down upon by Christian tribesmen. These cults and institutions can be seen as the by-products of cultural and ideational confrontation. A few of these merit systematic research study. The anthropological usefulness of such a study will be :

(a) to observe some of the living values and institutions ;
(b) to interpret internal confusion and dilemmas of societies ; and
(c) to understand the perception to live one's own way of life in the face of the threat from a superior ideology.

Mizoram

The area comprising the erstwhile Mizo Hills District of Assam, formerly known as the Lushai Hills, acquired the status of a Union territory with a new name, Mizoram. The first Christian missionary reached Mizoram in 1891. Since then most of the people who call themselves Mizo have embraced Christianity. In the process new cults have come into existence among the Mizos. (A few of the movements are mentioned in my book on *Mizo Unrest*). I mentioned here only two. Certain institutional aspects and historical incidents of the hill people's life are instanced to show the areas for further probing.

1. Zakia Pawl

Pentecostalism throughout the world is becoming a popular denomination among the followers of Christianity. In Mizoram it has a very interesting history. Following the conflict between the rules of the Presbyterian Church and the personal convictions of a few Mizos, the United Pentecostal Church (UPC) managed to enter Mizoram. Christianity in Mizoram spread through the Welsh mode of periodic revivals.

The revivals helped spread Christianity. They also gave birth to new cults. When in 1935 revivals broke out in Mizoram, Zakamlova, a trained pharmacist of the Aizwal Welsh Mission Veng Church, was the deacon and the leader of those who believed in the manifestation of Holy Spirit through possession (Goswami 1966). During the Christian revival, while being possessed the Mizos had the church's permission to speak in an unknown tongue. Many heard the "Voice", and many were endowed with the gift of prophecy. Subsequently the situation went beyond the control of church leaders. As such the standing committee of the Welsh Presbyterian Church on 26th September, 1935, issued a fiat saying that listening to the Voice, prophesying, speaking an unknown tongue and all other signs of revival should be discouraged.

It may be noted that *zawlnei* (Shakespear 1912 : 110), *puithiam* (priest) and *dawithiam* under the traditional Mizo religion also had been using these techniques while performing their rituals. In 1937, at the Durtlang Assembly, Zakamlova, who was one of the Welsh Mission delegates, took up the case of the Mizo revivalists for discussion, but the Assembly endorsed the instructions of 1935. Zakamlova and his group of revivalists argued that "tongues are not devilish and primitive resurgence." He, however, could not prevail over the Welsh Mission decision.

On 26 August 1937, he went to Calcutta to join hands with another foreign Christian mission. He was prohibited from doing so by the Superintendent of Lushai Hills. Incidentaly this was the time when revivals broke out in Kelkang village near Champhai (1949) about which McCall has written a detailed account. As the revivalists were not allowed to attend church meetings, Zakamlova organised meetings at his residence. He continued to do so in spite of the Superintendent's threats. He was summoned to court on 29 April, 1938, and fined Rs. 100 on 6th June. The fine was, however, not realized on technical grounds. In June 1948, he formed a Committee of Revivalists. The Pentecostal movement took roots in an organised form in 1953.

The movement became so popular that the Presbyterian Church had to ignore the performance of possession dances and "tongues", which used to be the usual phenomena during church meetings. As stated earlier, these had deep roots in the traditional religion of the Mizos. The movement gave birth to a very important sect (*pawl*) known as Zakia pawl. The theological dimension of the pawl is that it is neither possible to worship God in the Presbyterian Church nor in the Pentecostal Church. As Jesus has saved humanity by shedding His own blood, there is no point in singing unnecessary songs except those of joy. The followers of the sect believe that all should be merry in praise of God. The merrymaking idea filters down to the level of the traditional way of living to a certain extent (marriage and family) and the social experimentation level in others (sex). The followers of this *pawl* live in the eastern part of Mizoram and in Aizawl town.

2. Khuangtua Pawl

This cult is named after the late Khuangtua. It is also popularly called *thiangzau* (The word is always used in the singular). Before the regrouping of Mizo villages in

1966, the followers of Khuangtua pawl were scattered in a number of places, but most of them were from Mawngkawn village. Khuangtua used to live in that village. Khuangtua's followers believe in Christ, but they say that this should not debar them from leading a way of life which they think is best.

They are not averse to polygamy and believe in cooperative/collective work. They have faith in their leader ; his order is considered to be final. In contrast to Christian Mizos, they love their traditional past. Their songs, dances and sacrifices have many similarities with the past. After regrouping, they are mostly (120 houses) concentrated in Baktawng villlage under the leadership of Chana, brother of the late Khuangtua. At the time of my field-work, Chana was living in a big house with his six wives. He had a total of 21 members in his family. His eldest son was living in a separate house with three wives. The total number of members in his family was 19. The rest of the families were monogamous.

It is said that pre- and post-marital sex relationship is common among them. Only the head wife of the head of the house can sleep on the *Khumpui*, the main bed in house. Otherwise the head of the family visits them by turns. The whole house is divided into small cabins where each wife and her children sleep.

The followers of Khuangtua are considered by Christian Mizos as perverts and spoiled. They are neither Christian nor traditionalist. In Baktawng, the Christian look down upon them. They are being persuaded to discard their way of life and adopt Christianity as preached by the Mizo Synod.

As regards sex laxities, the late Khuangtua was arrested many a time by the Superintendent for alleged immoral activities as averred by Christian Mizos, but never a charge was proved. The fact is this that Khuangtua's followers and Chana tried their best to keep aloof from Christians and led an uninhibited life of their own. The taking of rice-beer, which is detested by Christian churches, is common among the sect. Yet a Christian won't deny that as carpenters, smiths or even as agricultural labourers, Khuangtua's followers are better and more hard working than Christian Mizos.

My observations show that Khuangtua's followers look at sex in a more relaxed manner than the Mizo Christians and the many stories told about them and their leaders are exaggerated. I quote from my field notes an evening's experience among the followers of this sect :

> "I went to attend a meeting without giving them previous notice. At the right corner of the hall, a large traditional pot of *zu* (rice-beer) with three siphons to sip the liquor, was kept. There were about 14 people. When I entered the hall I found the people drinking and dancing. The meeting was specially arranged because a young man (parallel cousin of the head of the house) had killed four wild animals about a fortnight back (which was quite a significant number for his age). They collected all the skulls and kept them in the centre of the main hall of the house. The head of the house offered zu as a token of praise. In the gathering there was a tremendous longing for their traditional customs, music and dance. Everybody was happy drinking, singing and dancing with occasional chanting (*hlado* in Pawi dialect), accompanied with drum beating. The songs either concerned bravery or war. To me the music was undeniably good and completely different from the Mizo hymns which I am used to hearing every day. The whole atmosphere was vibrating with joy, and occasional *hlados* reinforced the atmosphere of appreciation of bravery of the young man . . . there was the pretty-looking daughter of the head of the house, who was being fondled by young boys by holding her cheeks, pushing, dragging, pressing her mildly during singing. It appeared to me that it was slightly more than what I am used to see. But that is all. The dances were very rhythmic with exclamations of joy like "Chihieu", "Chihieu" etc. People were helping each other to take more of zu with courteous gestures. . . ."

The thiangzau have also had links with Welsh presbytry. According to Christians, a very negligible section of the *hmilims* (revivalists) got perverted and became thiangzau.

But then there are individual Christians who without joining a sect can become a thiangzau. The final stage, according to Christian informants, for a thiangzau is when a man and a woman start living together or occasionally meeting for sexual intercourse. These intercourses are explained by the thiangzau as the destined call and instruction of God. "Man and woman intentionally never do so (sexual intercourse); it is God who directs them to do so". If due to their intimacy a child is born it is called *thlrau sawn* (issue of the spirit). The couple living together under the spell of Spirit or God, without going through marriage, are designated as *Khurbing*.

Nagaland

Nagaland became a full-fledged state in 1963 when it was separated from Assam, of which it was a distinct part during British rule. As in Mizoram, in Nagaland, too, revivalism has given birth to many by-products of Christianity. However, it is comparatively a recent phenomenon there—a post-independence event. Many villages of the Ao Naga area have been influenced by the Revival Movement of the Dehra Dun Pentecostal Centre, resulting in a lot of psychological problems and neurotic patterns of behaviour. Healing through prayer, dreams, cure through salt taking, flying neurosis etc. are common. In this and other such matters, tension among the pastors to hold senior posts and romantic intrusion of non-Nagas have both played their part. In 1957, an Ao pastor, who could not pass the qualifying training course, was refused a post. He threatened to revive the traditional Ao culture. Before he could muster a good following, he was given the post. In 1960, a United Pentecostal preacher from Kerala, who fell in love with a Naga woman, was asked to leave Nagaland. He, however, managed to organise a big philanthropic-cum-religious centre in collaboration with a rich American.

Shihanani School

The most important sect in Nagaland is one organised by Rev. Shihoto of the Sema tribe. He differed with the Nagaland Baptist Church on 15th March, 1954, on the issue of his promotion to a higher post. At first he secluded himself. Then after twelve years, he organised a new school at

Aghathashi village. He blended traditional religion with Christianity and claimed that his sect had a social work purpose only. He named it the Suffering Party. He became almost a hermit, divorced his first wife and took another married woman and called her his spiritual wife. To begin with he could muster 20 families, but now only 12 families are left as his followers. They do not go by the Christian code of conduct and values as preached by the American Baptist Mission of Nagaland.

Many more such by-products and marginal religious movements can be observed in the hill areas of North-East India. A thorough appraisal of these will be useful to highlight the many hitherto unknown psychological and ethnographic issues. Regarding the origin of many of these schools, I feel Keesing's (1958) observation is pertinent. He believes that when authoritarian systems of dogma and practices are shaken, any individual who claims to have some new revelation of truth can secure a following. Apart from the deprivation conflict and frustration, which may be reasoned as the causes, the urge to carve out a social identity different from the Christian identity cannot be ruled out. A thorough study is called for before the people who are holding on to some of the values of the traditional culture are swamped.

SUGGESTED READINGS

Goswami, B.B., "Note on the Lushai Family", *The Eastern Anthropologist*, Vol XVI, No 3, 1963.

Goswami, B.B., "Spirit Possession in a Hill Tribe of Assam". (In) Proceedings of the Summer School in Anthropology (Ed) N.C. Choudhury, Calcutta : Anthropological Survey of India, 1966.

Goswami, B.B., *Mizo Unrest : A Study in Politicisation of Culture*, Jaipur, Alekh Publisher, (forthcoming).

Keesing, F.M., *Cultural Anthropology : The Science of Custom*. New York : Holt, Rinehart and Winston, 1958.

Lloyd, J.M., *On Every High Hills*, Liverpool : Foreign Mission Office.

McCall, A.G., *Lushai Chryslis*, London : Luzae and Co. Ltd., 1949 London.

Parry, N.E., *The Lakhers*, London : Macmillan & Co. Ltd., 1932 London.

Shakespear, J.(Lt. Col.), *The Lushai Kuki Clans*, London : Macmillan & Co. Ltd., 1912.

TEN

Machiko Aoyagi

TRANSFORMATION OF TRADITIONAL RELIGION

The Influence of Christianity

THIS IS a case study of the transformation of a traditional religion under Christian influence in Palau, Western Caroline Islands, Micronesia. Micronesia has successively been under Spanish, German, Japanese and American administrations. Soon after the first encounter of Palauans with the white people, the village of Melekiok, one of the principal villages in Palau, was attacked by an English warship in the latter half of the nineteenth century. Thereafter, the dominant foreign powers one after another tried to control the islands with new rules to which the Palauans could hardly adapt themselves. Catholic missionaries from Spain came at the end of the nineteenth century, and their efforts resulted in the decay of traditional Palauan customs which were against Christian teachings. During the German occupation, there appeared several Palauan prophets who foretold their people that the foreigners would soon leave their land. Modekngei, a religious movement, has to be understood in the context of these nativistic trends.

Modekngei has become a mixture of traditional Palauan religion and Christianity. On the one hand it is an example of an old religion which has been transformed into a new one under Christian influence, and on the other it is an example of Christianity infused with traditional religious customs. This raises two important questions: (1) How was the old traditional religion transformed by Christianity? and (2) What impact did the movement have on the traditional Palauan social structure?

Palauan Traditional Religion

In old days there were many gods in Palau. Some were village gods and some lineage gods. Generally speaking, the former were concerned with public matters, such as war, construction of the meeting house, communal fishing and so on, while the latter were concerned with personal matters. Villagers went to see a man or a woman who could communicate with his or her lineage god to ask the reason for their illness, or if they would return safely from their journey or wage-earning trip to the phosphorite mines in Angaur island. Some lineage gods were feared because they were believed to harm people who displeased them.

Except in a few instances, each village had its own god. Although the names of such gods differed from village to village, they seemed to have some common features throughout Palau.

The common features were:

1. Village gods were male and often appeared as war gods. Some of them were particularly celebrated for their predictions about the outcome of inter-village battles.

2. Every Palauan village had a village council consisting of ten titled men, from the first to the tenth rank. One of them, frequently the title man of the fifth rank, worked as an intermediary between the god and the villagers.

3. There were two ways to intermediate between the god and the villagers. One was completely shamanistic. An intermediary—we may call him shaman in this case—chewed betelnuts ceaselessly, making his gum bloody, till he fell into a trance. Then the god came down from above into his body and gave prophecy or revelation to the villagers through his tongue. Those around the shaman could easily understand it because it was spoken in the Palauan language. After the god left the shaman's body, saying "I am going to heaven", the shaman was utterly worn out. When he woke up, he remembered nothing of what had happened during the trance.

The other way was not essentially shamanistic and an intermediary in this case might be called a medium. To invoke the god, the medium sat alone in a special place separated by a curtain of coconut leaves and repeatedly called the god's name without chewing the betel-nut. After a while the god came down and gave certain prophecy or revelation. In this case the voice of the god was like a whistle which no one could understand save the medium.

4. Gods put the taboo on various foods, such as fish, turtle and crab. Eating any of these foods made the person sick or crippled.

5. Certain gods were said to force people to bring money to them under the pretext of producing a satisfactory result.

As for the lineage god, who might be either male or female, similar methods were employed in invoking gods, but observance of the food taboo was required of only the lineage members in question.

What is Modekngei ?

About 1915, soon after the beginning of Japanese rule, a man called Tamadad was reported to be divinely possessed in Choll, a small village on the northern tip of Babeldaop island. Because he was a medium of the village god, it was his duty to invoke the god upon the villagers' request. On one occasion, however, he behaved abnormally. He kept crying "Ohi, ohi!" all day long. People wondered if he had gone crazy. A little later a friend of his named Ongesi joined him in raising the cry. The village chief ordered other villagers to prepare hot water with medicinal herbs and to place it in the meeting house. Tamadad and Ongesi came there on their own and cleaned their bodies with it though nobody had told them about the medicinal hot water. The people realized that the two were truly possessed by the god.

They became known all over Palau after they revived with their medicine a woman who was thought to be dead. They gradually won followers by healing and prophecy. Accordingly Ngiraomkuul, the village god of Choll, began to take precedence over other gods.

After abolishing the food taboo on the banana in Choll village, they made a village-to-village tour with the some purpose. They were welcomed in every village. People were willing not only to give up the food taboo, but also their own gods. Rejecting the medical care of a Japanese hospital, many of the sick gathered in Choll village. Ongesi was especially active in curing sick women. He forced them to have sexual intercourse with him, making them believe that they could not recover from sickness without it. Besides it would please the gods.

Later another of their friends, Runguul joined Tamadad and Ongesi. The three became leaders of a religious movement in the early days which was named Modekngei by them—it means all together in the Palauan language—Runguul outlived the other two exerting a great influence upon the movement.

Modekngei has become a mixture of old Palauan religion and Christianity in belief and rite. Both Tamadad and Runguul were trained as soldiers in the German military at Yap. It is quite likely that they were familiar with Christianity. In 1926 they erected a big cross eight meters high and two meters wide on the top of a mountain for Ngiraomkuul the village god of Choll.

According to Modekngei myth, centuries ago Palau had a god who one day left the islands for Europe where he was born as Jesus Christ and founded Christianity. After many years the god, all of a sudden, remembered his home country and returned there. In Palau of those days, false gods were distressing people by putting the taboo on various foods. Knowing that, the god ordered Tamadad to chase them away. From Modekngei's point of view, Modekngei and Christianity are one and the same religion. But there is one big difference: the followers of Modekngei never killed their god; so that they are not sinful like the Europeans who crucified Christ.

There are several characteristics in Modekngei which reflect traditional Palauan religious customs. They are:

1. To invoke the god for prophecy or revelation, a leader calls the name of the god without chewing betel-nuts. The voice of the god sounds like whistling, which no one can understand except the leader. But it is said that the present leader is not able to communicate with god and a woman, Ongesi's adopted daughter, plays the role in his place.

2. To cure illness several plants are used. Most of these have been used as medicine in traditional Palauan medical treatment. But Modekngei believe that the most effective medicine is water and particular stones. Water is taken from

a stream in Choll by the title man or medium. The stones have been handed down from Tamadad to the present leader. The water and stones are believed to be good for every disease.

3. The Modekngei church service comprises prayer, hymn and *osruch*. On special occasions *oldars* is added to them. Osruch is an act of the church attendants to clean their bodies with hot water boiled with medicinal herbs. Such water has been used in traditional medical treatment for curing the sick and by women in childbirth. At the same time the attendants eat a piece of burnt and crushed coconut. It looks like Holy Communion, but it is also believed that the former Palauan gods loved the smell of burnt coconut. It made it easier for them to come down. Oldars is the act of offering food to the god. The food is arranged like a heart in front of the altar. The shape symbolizes the cluster of particular stars by which Palauans used to judge the time for planting and fishing.

4. The church altar has spears and a small box-chair with red cloth atop it. The spears are said to have been used by the gods glorified in hymns. They are cleaned with medicinal hot water at every service. The box-chair is for the god to sit on when he comes down to the human world. The red cloth may have a special meaning because it was used to chase false gods away. Incidentally the early leaders always wore a red loin cloth.

5. Prayers in the church are divided into two sides, right and left, according to the order of their birth. Division into two halves is one of the basic principles of traditional Palauan social organisation.

On the other hand, Christian influences may be found in the following practices.

1. On the altar of the Modekngei church in Peleliu island, there is a cross among several spears, all of which are cleaned with medicinal hot water at service time. And at Ibobang Modekngei church a big picture of Christ with three angels is put up at the rear of the altar.

2. The most important days for Modekngei followers are Christmas and the New Year. They have a church service on Saturday, Sunday, Tuesday and Thursday, among which

Saturday is the most important. On Thursday they offer foods to the god.

3. Drinking, smoking and eating red pepper are forbidden. The reason: when Christ was suffering from thirst on the cross, wrongdoers gave him a glass of water with some liquor, cigarette and red pepper in it to add to his distress.

4. They adopt the idea of the Father and the Son from Christianity, but not of the Holy Spirit. This is because dualism is in accord with the Palauan traditional principle found in every level of social organisation, but trinity is not. The god of the right side is called the Father and the god of the left side the Son. In hymn, Ngiraomkuul is always glorified in the name of Ngiraomkuul *es krist.*

5. Although traditional Palauan religion had little relation with morals of people, Modekngei is concerned with them. The followers are taught not to steal, not to quarrel, not to drink, and not to smoke. If they displease their god, they will be punished by the god who will sicken their beloved ones. Modekngei, however, has nothing to do with weddings and funerals in which Christianity plays an important role.

Modekngei Tactics to Gain Followers

The reasons why people readily gave up their traditional village and lineage gods to become Modekngei might be explained by the following:

Palauan did not consider Modekngei a new or strange religion. In Palau, especially in Peleliu island, there was a belief of "the Second Advent of the God". It is said that one day Wodul, the highest god in Peleliu, ascended to the heaven, leaving word that he would be back again. A woman of high-ranking lineage of Peleliu told me that when Spanish missionaries came there to propagate Christianity, Peleliu islanders welcomed their Christian god, misconceiving that it was the Second Advent of Wodul. However, knowing more about Christianity, they gradually became doubtful of adoring the god who was brought by foreigners. When they heard that a god had descended to Tamadad in Choll, they were well grounded in accepting readily the teaching of Tamadad.

Moreover Tamadad, Ongesi and Runguul were all regarded as excellent medicine men as well as prophets. The fame they gained by their success in healing and prophecy spread day by day. A number of stories of their successful prophecy are told by Modekngei followers till today. With regard to the food taboo they let the villagers of Choll try to eat a tabood food, banana, with the guarantee that no one would get sick or be crippled. The result was as they foretold. Nothing happened to villagers who ate it. This enhanced their reputation. When they visited other villagers, people awaited their coming and chased the village and lineage gods away, shouting "Wrong gods, wrong gods; get away from here!"

In addition, the Modekngei god has been considered to have something to do with money making. Money has always been a matter of primary concern to the Palauans. It is no exaggeration to say that the Palauan social and political structure has been constructed with focus on money making. A woman showed me the coins blessed by Runguul to bring more money. She had kept them carefully with her.

Runguul also organised a mutual financing association or lottery. Its members received in turn the money collected monthly from the rest of the members. The mutual financing association proved to be effective in uniting the Modekngei members as well as in giving them the joy of possessing money blessed by the god. The association is continuing and at the end of every month the members gather for a big feast in Ibobang, the present centre of Modekngei.

Modekngei leaders seem to have adopted skilful tactics, perhaps unintentionally, of retaining old Palauan beliefs and customs in their religion while giving up those which they felt were inexpedient, such as the food taboo and monetary contribution to gods. On the other hand, adoption of Christian elements has been effective in giving their religion a fresh look and also in giving Ngiraomkuul, the village god of Choll, an advantage in overcoming the gods of other villages. Although the religious dogma has not been neatly prescribed, the story that Ngiraomkuul was born in Europe as Jesus Christ is only a rationale to explain the elements of Christianity in their religion. And the Christian elements have seemingly increased in course of time.

It is said that in the early period of Modekngei, Choll was full of people who came from all over Palau. During the Second World War, while Modekngei was prohibited by the Japanese many Palauans, including Catholic believers, secretly visited Runguul to ask for amulets, which were believed to protect them from bombing by the U.S. Air Force.

Impact on the Traditional Organization

The Japanese Government repressed the Modekngei movement soon after Tamadad and Ongesi started to engage in prophetic and medicinal activities. The leaders were put in jail several times and their followers were questioned at Japanese police stations. Modekngei was described as an anti-Japanese movement by an American anthropologist, Arthur Vidich, who made a research right after the Second World War. But neither Modekngei nor anti-Modekngei Palauans recognize their religion as anti-Japanese. The reasons why the Japanese prohibited Modekngei have been differently understood by the two opposing groups. Anti-Modekngei Palauans, some of whom as assistant policemen under the Japanese arrested Modekngei leaders, gave the following reasons:

1. Modekngei leaders prohibited the sick from going to hospital. As a result, many of the sick died.

2. The leaders defrauded their followers of a lot of money which they had collected on the pretext of contribution to their god.

3. Ongesi was especially notorious, for he sexually exploited sick women under the guise of healing.

4. As Modekngei means altogether, its leaders claimed that all the followers were not only brothers and sisters but also husbands and wives who could have free sexual relations among them. By claiming so, the leaders forced female followers to serve them sexually.

On the other hand, the Modekngei insist that anti-Modekngei Palauans instigated the Japanese government to take punitive action against them. According to them anti-Modekngei were mostly Catholic and high-ranking chiefs who were envious of the powerful growth of the Modekngei.

Choll is a small village on the northern part of Babeldaob island, which has been established by refugees from Peleliu island who brought their village god with them. Choll (new village) had not been a high-ranking nor principal village at all and its god had not been powerful either. Moreover, there were a few informants who stated that the god of Modekngei was taken from Yap, or Tamadad himself was a Yapese, one of the drifters to the Choll shore on their voyage from Yap to Palau for getting stone money. There is no doubt that the rapid growth of the power of the Choll god and villagers had some impact on the traditional Palauan social organization, and it may be true that higher ranking chiefs took offence at the movement. Modekngei followers came to hate those Palauans who sided with the Japanese in repressive actions. Although the ban on their movement was removed right after the war and they became openly active again, the emotional disagreement between Modekngei and anti-Modekngei Palauans continued and is evident even today.

In 1974, Modekngei established the Belau Modekngei School at Ibobang on Babeldaob island. The followers contributed money and gave their labour free. Men constructed the school building and dormitories while women culivated land to grow crops for the pupils. They built a splendid church on the campus. Instead of Choll, Ibobang is now the centre of Modekngei where the present leader and his assistant—a woman who acts as medium—reside. Along with religious teachings, the school emphasises the Palauan identity, particularly under the special "study and work" curriculum. Half a week is for study and the other half for work, such as farming, fishing, basket weaving, wood carving, and so on. Since the school lays emphasis on the Palauan identity, the response of the Palauans has apparently been cool.

According to the present leader, the number of Modekngei followers today is about 700 or 800. The number has been gradually decreasing in recent years. That is mainly because many of the younger generation have stopped believing in the Modekngei god. Indeed Modekngei might be considered one of nativistic movements, but it is unlikely to become a core of Palauan nationalism.

ELEVEN

Satish Kumar

THE GOND OF RANCHI
A Study in Acculturation

CENTURIES of close living between the tribal communities and the caste-ridden Hindu community has revealed the impossibility of complete isolation on the operational level. Social anthropologists feel that it is neither possible nor desirable (Sachchidananda, 1968) to study tribal cultures in India as isolated entities.

In the recent past a number of studies have been made focusing attention on some of the tribal groups aspiring for caste Hindu status. Changes in the tribal communities on this line have been variously explained. Bailey (1960) explains such changes, occurring among the Gond, through the continuum approach in which tribe and caste stand at the opposite ends of the pole. Srivastava (1966) applied the concept of cultural approximation to cover such changes. Mandelbaum (1972) cites the example of two groups of the Kotas of Nilgiri Hills —one trying to retain and preserve the tribal heritage and the other consciously identifying itself with caste Hindus. Surjit Sinha (1959), while examining the case of the Bhumij, says that most of them have gone far towards becoming Kshatriyas.

There are many more such studies. All stress the fact that the institution of caste is gradually taking hold of tribal social structure as has been the case with Indian Muslims and Christians. But the institution of caste is not the whole of Hinduism. To have a picture of Hindu influence on the tribals, one has to look deep into it. The various ceremonies connected with life-crisis occasions, the various terms they use to signify these, observance of festivals, mode of worship and things like that have to be examined in detail in relation to the prevailing norms and institutional practices among local Hindus. Only then one can assess the extent of Hindu influence on the life-pattern of the tribals.

The Gond, who are concentrated in Ranchi district, are possibly the only tribe in the area which tries to identify itself fully with the Hindus. In some of the Gond villages there are a few households of Oraon who have become Christian converts. In the same villages, the missionary has not been successful with the Gond in spite of the fact that there is no organized body of Hindus to draw them to their own fold. It is, however, interesting to see how they are becoming, as Elwin (1942) puts it "Hinduized without being Hindus".

The 1961 census puts the number of the Gond in Ranchi at 13,160. They are also found in Singhbhum (14,734). A sprinkling of their population is found in the districts of Palamau, Hazaribagh, and Santal Parganas also.

The Gond of Ranchi have not attracted as much attention of social anthropologists as the other tribes of Chotanagpur. Except for a solitary study by Sachchidananda (1970), no other authentic account is found on Ranchi Gonds. L.P. Vidyarthi (1964), dealing with various changes in the tribal scene of the Chotanagpur region, has left this community from the purview of his study.

The Gond of this area speak the Sadari dialect. They are a patrilineal and patrilocal community with a distinctive social organisation of their own.

The Gond living in the Simdega sub-division of Ranchi district do not have any written records to enlighten us on their origin and migration pattern. They have, however, their myths and legends to corroborate what they say about their migration pattern. They claim that the Gond originally came from Gondwana in Madhya Pradesh via Orissa. A number of my respondents claimed to be direct descendants of the Kshatriyas who once ruled the kingdom of Bundelkhand. They still negotiate the marriages of their sons and daughters in Madhya Pradesh. Though the other Gond of the area dispute the claim, they, however, do not object to marrying with the Gond living in the same area.

The Gond of Ranchi are divided into six clans, namely Bhay, Pradhana, Manjhi, Besra, Neti and Dhurwa. All are associated with living creatures, i.e. with tortoise, cobra, buffalo, bird, tiger and fish respectively. These creatures are not to be harmed and are held in respect and honour by the clans concerned.

The Life-crises

As in most tribal communities and Hindu households, the life-crises among the Gonds are marked by a number of elaborate rituals. Those connected with birth, marriage, and death speak of the Hindu influence on them.

Among the Gond of Ranchi "Jamain", popularly known as "Dagrin", is a Chamar or Dom woman called to attend to women in labour. It is she who cuts the umbilical cord at birth. Usually the first issue is welcome in the family, more so if it is a male child. Six days after the birth, both the mother and the child take a purificatory bath, known as *chhathi* or *nahan*. Among the local Hindus too this is known as Nahan, but Chhathi is a different occasion among them. It signifies a birth feast at which relatives and friends gather. After the ritual or purificatory bath the washerman takes away all the clothes of the family members for washing. The male members are shaved and their nails pared. The women, however, have only nail-paring. After that the *Mundan* or head-shaving of the child takes place.

Compared with the Gond, it is obligatory for women in a Hindu family to have nail-paring at Nahan but the male members are not obliged to shave or pare nails. The Mundan ceremony normally takes place a few years after the birth and usually at some sacred place and not necessarily at home, as among the Gond. On the same day, the process of divination takes place through which they try to find out the ancestor whose soul has entered the body of the newly born. Divination is a common practice among the tribes of the Chotanagpur area. On the 12th day of the birth, known as *Barahi*, the child is given the name of that ancestor whose soul has entered his body. A feast is organised on that day.

The pollution period for other members of the family ends on the day of Nahan, but the mother can enter the kitchen for cooking only after three months. Till this period, no one takes anything to eat from her hands.

Ear-boring and sacred-thread ceremonies are also observed by the Gond of Ranchi, but there is no time fixed for it. Usually, the sacred thread is given before marriage either by a Brahmin or by a Gosain. Ear-boring is also done normally by a Brahmin or Gosain, but in case one is not readily available, anyone in the community knowing the art, can do it, provided his clan and that of the child is not the same. A feast is organized after it.

Marriage

Marriage is a religious sacrament for the Gond. Usually it takes place when the boy and the girl attain puberty. The age of marriage varies from 15 to 20 for a boy and from 10 to 12 for a girl. A few cases of child marriage were found but it is becoming unpopular as was evident from the 17 marriages observed during the field-work. There were only four cases of child marriage.

Invariably, it is the father of the boy who is on the lookout for a suitable match. The negotiation is finalised when what they call the *rashis* of both partners tally, for which purpose a Brahmin is usually consulted. The negotiations may be broken if the boy or the girl is found otherwise unfit. After the match is finalised, elder women of the groom's family go to see the bride and she is presented with a sari, bangles, and some cash. Sometimes cheap ornaments are also presented. Marriage takes place usually after a year of the finalisation of the negotiation. Till then the groom's side has to send one sari, bangles, comb, mirror, rice, etc. to the bride on every Ekadashi of the Bhadon month.

The bride price is fixed at Rs. 2.50, which is known as *kanyadam*. Of this amount, the boy and the girl take Re. 1 each and the respective parties are given 25 paise each. The date of marriage is fixed after consulting the almanac, for which a Brahmin is called. Application of vermilion, signifying the actual marital rite, is first done by the groom from the nose to the forehead of the bride. The bride repeats the same on the groom. This is not done by Hindu women. A

Gond woman never applies vermilion in her life again. This is also unlike the Hindu practice.

Instances were found of *kajal* (lampsoot), dust of the groom's feet and oil being used in place of vermilion. The Gond are divided on this also. Families using vermilion are known as Sinduria; those using *kajal* are known as Kajalia; those using the dust of the groom's feet are known as Dhurwa, and those who use oil are known as Teliya. A Sinduria family occupies the highest status among the four and can enter the kitchen of the three, while the other three cannot do so. This may be because the vermilion users are nearer to the Hindus.

Apart from arranged marriage, marriage by mutual consent of partners also takes place. The boy applies vermilion on the forehead of the girl at the weekly market or village fair. This is known as *Dhukku* marriage and is prevalent among the other tribes of the Chotanagpur area. Marriage by intrusion may also take place if the girl feels that the boy's love for her is waning. In such cases, the girl simply goes to the boy's house and starts living there as the bride. The boy's family allow her after initial hesitation.

In the areas covered, the percentage of such marriage is not more than five. Such cases, though not formally forbidden, are not encouraged. Polygyny is allowed, but a second wife can be taken only when the first wife is childless and the husband is economically well off. Only one or two such cases were found.

Unlike the Hindus, the Gond allow divorce. It takes place when (a) the wife is barren. But this is seldom a case for separation. In most cases, the husband brings another wife without deserting the first one; (b) there are indications that either the husband or the wife is having extra-marital relation; and (c) the wife is quarrelsome.

Widow remarriage is also found, but in most cases the widow is remarried to the younger brother of the deceased.

Death

Under the ostensible influence of Hindus, the Ranchi Gond are, ideally, supposed to put Ganga water along with some *tulsi* leaves into the mouth of a Gond on his death-bed.

As Ganga water is not available in the area, they put water from any well or stream.

Only old people are cremated. The eldest son of the deceased lights the funeral pyre first. After that other male members of the family follow.

Children are buried at a fixed place in the village.

Three days after the death, the male members of the family shave their heads. It is repeated after ten days. This is known as *Dasvan*. Shaving takes place on the bank of the river where the cremation took place. This is followed by a bath in the river after which the male members change their sacred-thread. The family-barber gets all the clothes worn by the man who first lighted the pyre. At night, the primary kin of the deceased cook food themselves and eat it together.

The same day the Pargania and the Brahmin are given customary gifts. Thus the pollution period occasioned by death ends and any auspicious celebration can take place now.

Beliefs and Rituals

The Gond are emphatic in their claim that they are Hindus. They offer worship to Mahadev, Ram and Krishna. The literate among them were found reciting from Hindu scriptures like the *Ramayan* and the *Mahabharat*. Though there is no temple in the area, they are aware of its functions. They honour the cow and abstain from harming it. There are strict sanctions against those who unknowingly kill a cow. They have to expiate the sin. They do not accept water at the hands of Harijans and Christian converts.

Besides Hindu deities, they worship local deities too. Graha, Marila Jaughadev or Bardev, is the supreme deity. It is worshipped by all clans every three years.

When the crop is harvested, they offer worship to the Ropakhani deity. At the outbreak of any epidemic, they offer worship through Baiga at the *sarana*.

Among the Hindu festivals they observe are Holi, Dussehra, Diwali, Ram Navami, Rath Yatra, Raksha Bandhan, Jitiya Tirethiya, and among the tribal festivals they observe are Karam and Sarhul.

Political Organisation

In Ranchi, all the Gond were found owing allegiance to a political organisation called the Raj Gond Kshatriya Mahasabha. Its office-bearers are elected every three years. At its meeting, the people express their support for any proposal by raising their hands. The main function of the Sabha is to chalk out plans for the betterment of the people. It encourages parents to send their children to school and also advises them to abstain from intoxicants. The Sabha holds an annual meeting to which members from Orissa and Madhya Pradesh are also invited.

The second session of the organisation passed several resolutions to motivate people for reforms and to induce them to accept more of Hindu styles of life. Some of the resolutions are :

1. The killer of a cow should be punished and asked to expiate the sin.
2. *Satya Narain Katha* should be periodically held in each family.
3. The sacred thread ceremony should be a must for a Gond and no Gond should be permitted to marry without that.

The Ranchi Gond do not live in separate villages clanwise as do the Munda and Oraon. In their village a few households of Munda, Oraon, Dom and Ghasi are also found. The Gond in this area, therefore, have to adjust with the multi-ethnic communities of the village. It is because of this, probably, that there is no clan-head or priest.

Dom and Ghasi have some functional roles in the lives of the Gond. At the time of marriage they are called to play the drum locally known as the *Mandar*.

Dance

Dance is an inseparable part of tribal life. Among the Gonds, the Domkach dance is very popular. Both men and women participate in it. It is held daily after a marriage is confirmed and continues till the marriage takes place. It is held in both the bride's and groom's houses.

In certain Hindu families also, Domkach is performed but only by the female members of the groom's side, and that, too, only on the night the marriage party leaves for the bride's place. It is a type of stage drama in which only rustic women participate.

Conclusions

From the above three important points emerge : (a) That there is positive evidence of the Gond inclination towards the Hindu way of living; (b) that in their enthusiasm to identify themselves with the Hindus, there has been partial adoption of Hindu traits; and (c) there are still some practices which owe their origin to various ethnic groups with which they live.

The various socio-religious practices among the Gond of Ranchi highlight their strong inclination towards the Hindu way of living. They keep the pigtail, abstain from harming the cow, and wear the sacred thread. They observe almost all Hindu festivals and worship various Hindu gods. The Raj Gond Kshatriya Mahasabha is also acting as a mechanism to make them conform more to Hindu norms and values, as is evident from its resolutions quoted earlier.

They observe the pollution period at childbirth and have specific rituals to mark the end of such a period. Acceptance of the Brahmin on almost all sacred occasions like birth and marriage, further confirm their inclination towards the Hindu way of living. Tallying of Rashis in marriage, awareness of the functions of temples, importance of the Ganga water and Tulsi leaves, shaving at the time of Dasvan, and giving of *dan* (gifts) to the Brahmin suggest that Hindu values act as reference points for the Gond.

All the socio-religious practices found among them do not resemble the Hindu way exactly. Equating Nahan with Chhathi, the mode of performing Domkach, shaving the head three days after a death in the family to be followed by the same on Dasvan indicate partial adoption of the traits. When the eldest son lights the pyre of his father, he is followed by other members of the family. This too is an example of partial adoption.

Regional colour on socio-religious practices is bound to show in inter-personal relations which are, in turn, manifested in various rituals as institutionalised way of living. The Gond of Ranchi are not exception to it. They have forgotten their original Gondi language and have adopted the Sadari dialect used by the Munda and Oraon. They observe the Sarhul and Karma festivals and accept Baiga for the worship at Sarna. Process of divination at child-birth and marriage by intrusion etc. are typical tribal practices of the Chotanagpur region.

One can say, therefore, that the case of the Gond of Ranchi is an illustration of their gradual process of acculturation which may lead them to their assimilation into the Hindu way of living.

SUGGESTED READINGS

Bailey, F.G., *Tribe, Caste and Nation.* Oxford : Oxford University Press, 1960.

Mandelbaum, David G., *Society in India.* New Delhi : Popular Prakashan, 1972.

Sachchidananda, *The Tribal Village in Bihar : A Study in Unity and Extension.* Munshi Ram Manohar Lal, 1968.

Ibid., "Tribe-caste Continuum : A Case Study of the Gond of Bihar." *Anthropos*, vol. 65, 1970.

Sinha, Surjit, "Bhomij-Kshatriya Social Movement in South Manbhum" *Bulletin of the Deptr. of Anthropology*, Government of India.

Srivastava, R.P., *Tribe-caste Mobility in India and the Case of Kumaon Bhotia*, in Haimendorf (edit).

TWELVE

B. J. Terwiel

THE TAIS AND THEIR BELIEF IN KHWANS
Towards Establishing an Aspect of "Proto-Tai" Culture

TYLOR was one of the first anthropologists to point out that in any culture there may be found archaic aspects, or "survivals" which could be systematically studied and he wrote that "collections of such facts are to be worked as mines of historic knowledge".[1] These ideas were further developed in various ethnological schools. To some evolutionists, such survivals were traces of an earlier, less developed stage in the history of mankind. To some diffusionists, they demonstrated the spread of certain customs in the dim past. Such evidence was at times brought forward in a rather uncritical manner and this is probably the reason why the study of survivals has become discredited and has received but little attention in modern ethnology.

Nevertheless, in our opinion, the study of survivals can be helpful and relevant, not so much as an independent method to establish links between different peoples, but as an aid to deepen historical knowledge. The collection of survivals appears most promising when dealing with a range of related cultures which have been separated from each other for some time, and which have developed independently since their separation.

The Tai people[2] are particularly suited to such an exercise. They are widely distributed over mainland Southeast Asia. Tais can be found as far west as Assam and northern Burma; they form the dominant groups of Thailand and Laos; they constitute the most numerous group of the ethnic minorities in northern Vietnam and there are many millions of them in the Chinese provinces of Kweichow, Kwangtung and Yunnan.

Though each Tai-speaking group may be aware of the fact that there are ethnically related peoples in other parts of Southeast Asia, there is no sign of a pan-Tai movement. Various groups have been independent from other Tais for many centuries.

Yet all Tai languages are so closely related as to be almost mutually intelligible. This may be regarded as evidence for the idea that in the past the Tais formed a close-knit community. Linguists refer to the parent-language of all modern Tai languages as "Proto-Tai", but as yet no firm date has been assigned to this ancestor of Tai language.[3] It is clear, however, that between one and two thousand years ago the Tais formed a relatively homogeneous group and that since that time they have been effectively separated into many societies and that these have developed under differing sets of circumstances.

Several anthropologists have been tempted to compare ethnographic records and to establish which aspects of modern Tai cultures are likely to have formed part of a "Proto-Tai culture".[4] Usually these comparisons have dealt only with the relatively broad questions such as the general characteristics of the religion, the basic mode of production and the size of the elementary polity. Uptill the present, one of the richest fields for such goal-directed comparison has been largely neglected. This concerns the study of ceremonial details. It is especially in rituals that actions are performed generation after generation in much the same form (whilst the form remains the same, over time shifts in the assigned meanings may be recorded).

In this essay, an example is given of the technique of comparing ritual details of related but distinct ethnic groups. It is part of a series comparing such components, and a survey of Tai funeral customs as well as an overview of the beliefs surrounding the city pillar have already been completed. Ultimately they will form part of a broad study which intends to describe aspects of Tai culture before the dispersion.

The method is simple and straightforward. First, all ethnographic sources have been scanned for information on a particular aspect of Tai ritual and religion, in this case the ceremony of summoning a kind of "life-force" (*khwan*), and related beliefs. This survey is presented in the order Lebar (et al) have followed: beginning with the western groups (Ahoms and Shans) through to the southern groups (Siamese Tai, Khorat group and

Pak Tai group), the central Mekong river groups (Nüa, Lü, Yuan and Laotian Tai), the central upland groups (Black, White and Red Tai and the Neua) and the eastern groups (Tho and Trung-cha).[5]

The second part consists of placing the results of the ethnographic overview in a wider perspective by scanning the occurrence of similar beliefs amongst neighbouring peoples, such as the Burmese, Chinese, Vietnamese and Cambodians. Subsequently it is possible to assess the likelihood of intercultural borrowing.

Western groups

There is little known of the Ahom culture. Traditionally it was Tai but it appears to have been submerged into the Hindu traditions prevailing in Assam. Talish, who described the Ahom kingdom of the latter part of the seventeenth century,[6] does not mention the perception of the human body, nor does he mention the summoning of khwans. The only source of information on this subject is the *Ahom-Buranji*,[7] the annals of the Ahom people from the time of the creation to the end of their rule in the nineteenth century.

In the *Ahom Buranji* many ceremonies are mentioned, and one of these, Rikkhvan,[8] appears to be none other than the ceremony of the summoning of vitality. The identification of this ceremony rests not only upon linguistic evidence, *rik* meaning "to call" in the Ahom language,[9] and *Khwan* is apparently related to the "proto-Tai" *xwan*,[10] and which will be called *Khwan* from here onward.[11] This identification is also facilitated by the translator's short description of the Rikkhwan ceremony. He calls it "a religious ceremony performed to get new life, and later in the annals it is "a religious ceremony performed for longevity of life".[12]

Altogether, the ceremony is mentioned at least fourteen times in the *Ahom-Buranji* and these occasions occur at fairly regular intervals throughout the book, with the first falling in the mythological past, the last one in 1783. The events which lead to the holding of a Rikkhvan ceremony vary greatly. Rikkhvan can be part of a purification ritual,[13] a burial,[14] a celebration of a victory,[15] a solemn oath[16] and a ceremony to avert bad luck.[17] An interesting paragraph deals with a specific kingly ceremony called "Rik-Khanmungkhanban", according to Barua: "a ceremony in which Lengdan, the Lord of Heaven is worshipped by offering sacrifices to grant long life and prosperity to the king and the country."[18] The Ahom text leaves no doubt that this is yet another variant of Rikkhvan, namely summoning the life force of the country and the towns. All these references make it clear that throughout the centuries Rikkhvan, the ceremony of summoning the khwan, was performed by the Ahom kings, and at least on one occasion[19] some of his chief advisers held the ritual.

With regard to the Shans, only two references to their concept of "vitality" have been found. Seidenfaden states: "Like the Laos, the Shans believe in a plurality of souls or khwans. They divide the soul in 32 khwans."[20] Phya Anuman Rajadhon lists the Shans as one of the groups of Tai speakers believing that a khwan can take flight and thus cause a person to become ill.[21]

Southern Groups

Whilst there is but scanty information on our topic for the western groups, there is a wealth of literature on the Siamese Tai and their belief in khwan. Researchers are not all in agreement as to the translation of the concept khwan. Wales calls it a guardian spirit in the head, who easily takes offence, with disastrous effects on the welfare of the individual.[22] In different context I have called it "ego", "soul", "morale", "grace" and "prosperity".[23] Phya Anuman Rajadhon, closely following the standard dictionary,[24] calls the khwan an unsubstantial thing supposed to reside in the physical body of a person. If it leaves the body the person will be ill or experience some undesirable effects.[25] The fact that the Thais use the concept in a wider sense for various animals and substances which possess guardian spirits, such as the khwan of a buffalo, of rice, of a bullock cart, of tools, of musical instruments,[26] of a ship, of a house post and of a *mya* or city state[27] has tended to favour a translation of "spirit".

Wright has, however, pointed out that the khwan does not seem to haunt like a ghost and that the khwan may not be regarded as a separate soul, temporarily inhabiting a body.[28] With an insult, an accident or a severe fright to the host body the khwan suffers in that it fades. Many of the educated Siamese Tai make a clear distinction between "ghost" (*phii*) "soul," (*winjaan*), "consciousness" (*ceedtaphuud*), "mind" (*cid*) and "khwan", though there are some areas of overlap for ordinary people.[29] The meaning of khwan, especially when seen in the context of medicinal practices seems to be no other than "animation", or "vitality". When a person is lethargic, depressed or dejected, some of the life force seems to have disappeared (khwan *haaj*).

The khwan of a person denotes a specific general quality, but specific parts of the body can also be assigned that characteristic. Thus a Thai can speak of the khwan of the eyes, of the mouth, and of the hands. This does not mean that these can be assigned separate individual "souls." Instead, such expressions simply refer to the liveliness, to the animation of that particular part of the body. In traditional medicine, it could be that a certain part of the body, say the kidneys, the ears, the intestines or the heart was found to have insufficient vitality, and a ceremony to remedy the situation was prescribed.

Efforts by scholars to obtain an exhaustive list of parts of the body which can be assigned a khwan in central Thailand have proved fruitless. Individuals vary greatly in perceiving how detailed their bodily divisions are, but for central Thailand the number of body parts which are readily assigned a vitality of their own is relatively small.[30] Heinze's informants could not list more than six parts of the body where a khwan may reside.[31] Moreover, in the central part of the Thailand the texts used for summoning the vitality do not specify other than a person's general khwan.[32] In traditional medicine, this khwan seems to be localised in a person's head, in other words, the head contains the seat of animation.[33] The ancient word for the clavicular region of the thorax is *raag* khwan, the "khwan's foundation"[34] and this also suggests that the head may be regarded as the khwan's most important abode.

Ideally, as an individual grows up and becomes physically stronger, his khwan becomes stronger too. He becomes more able to deal with upsetting events; he will not be easily frightened out of his wits and he will not be overcome by grief or fall into a deep depression. The summoning of such a healthy person's khwan has become removed from its basic therapeutic character. During the traditional first shaving of a month-old child, and again during the top-knot ceremony, when they were young teenagers all persons underwent a formal khwan-strengthening ritual, and a similar ceremony forms part of the preparation of a young man for his ordination into the Buddhist order. Strengthening the khwans of bride and groom is also part of the elaborate wedding ritual. Rightly, Heinze regards such khwan ceremonies as "rites of passage", a ceremonial to help an individual formally enter a new stage of life.[35] These formal khwan-summoning rituals have often been described[36] and the details need not be reiterated here.

Of much more interest for our purpose is the summoning of the khwan for medicinal purposes. Women who have recently given birth and newborn children must have been considered extremely vulnerable in the days before modern hospitals and medical extension services. It is traditional to hold a khwan ceremony three days after birth. This is not an elaborate ritual, like the "rite of passage" khwan summons held when a child is one month old; it is usually held *en famille*. Devoid of elaborations, it tells us something about the core therapeutic principles involved. The third-day khwan ceremony begins with presenting a dish with offerings to the unseen powers. Appropriate gifts are, apart from the ubiquitous candles, incense and flowers, a soup made with freshwater fish,[37] a young coconut, a bunch of bananas of a specific variety[38] and some sweetmeats.[39] Three leaf-shaped candle holders, with three candles each, are taken from a bowl of white rice in which they were temporarily struck, the candles are lighted and smoke from the lighted candles is wafted towards the child. Both wrists of the infant are then loosely tied with white cotton thread, and a blessing is spoken over the child. It is believed that this ritual will strengthen the child's vitality. The ceremony is replete with symbolic objects and activities. The candles, incense and flowers attract the attention of the unseen powers, the foodstuffs are there to make these powers feel sympathetically inclined. There is little doubt that these prepared dishes take the place of the sacrifices that have been recorded for non-Buddhist Tai-speakers. The tying of a white cotton thread symbolises that after gathering and strengthening the life force of the infant, the increased vitality is firmly bound to the body of the infant.

The simplest medicinal khwan ceremony has been described by Phya Anuman Rajadhon when he recorded how a child may come home distraught after a fall or a scare, and how the mother immediately runs out with a ladle, a bowl and a piece of cloth towards the spot where the incident occurred. Calling the child's khwan, the mother scoops up what she believes to be the khwan, puts it in the bowl and covers the bowl with the cloth. The bowl is passed round and round over the child's head, enabling its khwan to recognise its usual abode. Unspun cotton thread is then tied around each wrist and the child receives a blessing and sometimes a present.[40]

From this description it is clear that the khwan, the element which makes for vitality, is not simply an abstract concept as Wright would have us believe when he states "it is not an entity, but a quality".[41] It should be clear from the ritual that it is both an entity and a quality.

The khwan rituals are not a recent introduction into the culture of the Siamese Tais. Pallegoix describes in quite some detail how these ceremonies are conducted at important stages of life[42] in the famous poem *Khun Chaan*, *Khun Phaan*, written in the first half of the nineteenth century, but depicting rural life during the Ayutthaya period, many references are made to the khwan rituals, both the formal life-cycle events and the purely therapeutic calling of the khwan.[43]

The belief in khwan is widespread in Thailand. In the northeast of the country it has been described by Cripps :

> *riak* khwan (calling the khwan), is a way to make people feel secure and confident, to set the mind at peace. If they are sick they will recover from disease. Were they afraid or depressed, the khwan would be absent; they would waste away.[44]

The most detailed description of the belief in khwan for the northeast is reported by Tambiah. The villagers whom he questioned on khwan explained that when a person is frightened, sick or in trouble, the khwan takes fright and may leave the body. On the other hand, the very act of its fleeing the body expose the khwan's owner to suffering, illness and misfortune.[45] These villagers treat the khwan as one entity when they perform the ritual for its recall. Yet they have heard that there are thirty-two separate khwans but none could enumerate these. As in Central Thailand, the head is considered the pre-eminent residence of the khwan.[46] Unlike the texts used in Central Thailand, the ones of the Northeast mention several separate khwans, namely the khwan of beauty, of the legs, of the shins, of the eyes, of the eyebrows, of other parts of the face and of the upper part of the body.[47] Phya Anuman working through the northeastern texts enumerated khwans of the eyes, ears, mouth, nose, hands, heart, intestines and others, but he also was unable to make up the number of thirty-two.[48]

Some texts for summoning the khwan in the far South of Thailand were checked in the hope of finding an exhaustive list of khwans, but they proved to be similar to the ones used in Central Thailand in that they referred only to the general, single concept and did not mention separate parts of the body.[49]

Central Mekong River Groups

With regard to the Tai Nüa of Southwestern Yunnan, two references were found. Seidenfaden mentions that both the Nüa and the Thai Lü believe that "one or more of their khwans can leave their body and enter other people's making these ill!"[50] Dodd, who was quite familiar with the Nüa reports that "each human soul is divisible by thirty-two khwans. If any of these are absent, disease results".[51] Confirming Seidenfaden's remark, Dodd continues: "If more than thirty-two are present, disease is equally certain."

The summoning ritual is also described by Dodd:

> When it is discovered that any one's khwan, or more of them, have acquired bad habits of wandering and giving the neighbours trouble, the spirit doctor goes through an incantation supposed to bring home the wanderer. Then strings are tied around the wrists, and often the ankles too, to keep the vagrant khwan at home.[52]

The Lü beliefs were mentioned already in Seidenfaden's quotation above. Dodd also has a reference to a relevant belief. He records an anecdote about a set of clothing purchased from a Lü woman. Her husband came to Dodd to ask for the return of the clothing since some of the thirty-two khwans had adhered to it and the woman had fever. Dodd was persuaded to let the man cut off some threads in the hope that the stray khwan would adhere to them.[53] The most detailed statement of this aspect of Lü culture is given by Rispaud. He mentions that the Lü recognise the breath-spirit, or vital spirit (khwan) but as to the number of khwans he reports that the Lü recognise thirty-two khwans on the front part of the body, and thirty on the back.[54]

Rispaud also describes the ritual of calling the stray khwan, or khwans who are seen to have been captured by some invisible power. First the khwan is invited to come back to the body of the patient, food offerings to these invisible powers are believed to help the release. Then the khwan is tied with white cotton thread around the patient's wrists. These threads are not to be broken or cut, but must remain until they drop off by themselves.[55]

The Yuan's beliefs are reported by Chotisukharat. He tells us that the Yuan believe in 32 khwans, and that some of these may be lost through a severe shock or fright. The ceremony of getting the lost khwan back in a sick person is described in some detail. There is a container with gifts for the unseen powers, and the ritual specialist who is called to perform the ritual will take care to chant the traditional text in a pleasing manner, thus enticing the khwan to re-enter the body. Afterwards the specialist binds cotton thread around the wrists, the left side first, symbolic of the return of the khwan, followed by the right side, which symbolises forcing the khwan to remain. Whilst binding, he speaks a good wish. Some people keep the thread around their wrist for three days, but some children carry them there for such a long time that the white cotton may turn quite black with wear.[56]

The people of Bassac in Southern Laos think they have thirty-two khwans, but not even the ritual specialists can give the complete list. In the event of an inauspicious death, some khwans can transform themselves to spirits (phii).[57] There are many descriptions of the Laotian ritual of calling and fastening the khwan.[58] They demonstrate that the Lao people are quite familiar with the elaborations we have thus far encountered. The paraphernalia are identical and the invocations go through similar stages. It is most interesting to note that in some of the prayers a large number of separate khwans are mentioned. On one occasion we encounter khwans for the head, eyelashes, hair, fingernails, feet, eyes, arms, legs, ears, mouth, heart, back, belly, little finger, chin, shoulders, and neck.[59] On another, the separate khwans are those of the hair, head, nose, hands, ears, teeth, spine, belly, little finger, neck, chin and shoulderblades.[60]

Central Upland Groups

The Black Tai also have the idea that a person has a great number of what Lafont calls "khwans". At the end of one of his articles, Lafont gives us an enumeration of all the khwans of a person, for a total of thirty-two, namely the khwans of the skull, forehead, eyes, mouth, nose, ears, neck, heart, lungs and liver, intestines, stomach, shoulders, shoulderblades, belly, armpits, breasts, sides, waist, buttocks, hips, the "swallow-khwan" (which constitutes the capacity to sustain long walks), the "dragon-khwan" (which means one's courage and power), thighs, knees, soles of feet, arms, hands, ankles, wrists, toes, fingers and elbows.[61] Maspero, speaking about the same group of Black Tais, reports that one ritual specialist could enumerate as many as eighty-one khwans, and that even that number may not have been exhaustive. Unfortunately he does not give the whole list, but is satisfied with stating that some khwans are localised and command a part of the body such as the khwans which make sure that the eyes see clearly, and the khwan of the nose located at the nostrils.[62]

It is quite clear that the Black Tai share with many of the other Tai groups the belief that they can lose one or more khwans, that this causes illness and that there is a therapeutic ritual of recalling the khwans. Lafont describes in detail how the ritual specialist who invokes the unseen powers, finds out by divination whether the stray khwan is lost through the influence of a malevolent or a benevolent spirit. An offering is made to the spirit which holds the khwan to persuade it to give this precious substance back. If the specialist finds out that no spirit has the khwan but that it has wandered of its own accord, he coaxes it with inviting sentences and gifts to return to the body. Finally, the khwans are fixed to the body by a long blessing and the tying of a cotton thread, first to the left wrist, then to the right.[63]

The White Tai have beliefs and customs very similar to the Black Tai. Maspero sometimes mentions them in one breath and on one such occasion informed us of the fact that both groups consider a living person to have a great number of khwans.[64] Respaud tells us that they have thirty-two of them.[65] From an entry in a White Tai dictionary which mentions "khhék khhoan = to call one's spirit-souls (whose departure is alleged to cause sickness)[66] we may infer that they possess the therapeutic ritual described in some detail for the Black Tai.

In his monograph on the Red Tai, Robert reports a belief that there are thirty khwans of the body as well as ninety of the head, for a total of 120 khwans. After death, the ninety khwans of the head are destined to go to heaven, whilst those of the body will go to the cemetery. He also reports a short khwan ceremony after the birth of a child, as well as the custom of the Red Tai to murmur "Return home, O khwans" when they are frightened.[67] The extraordinary large number of khwans is confirmed by Boutin, who reports approximately ninety khwans for the Red Tai.[68]

For the Tai Neua Bourlet mentions the fact that they recognise many souls, but he does not provide further details.[69]

Eastern Groups

Abadie gives a summary description of the Tho's conceptions regarding "souls". They are reported to believe in three "subtle souls" called "*hon*" (*hun*) related to the male principle, and seven "vegetative souls" which he calls *via*, which is part of the female principle. Women have nine of these vias. After death, the hun go to the other world, whilst the via remain on earth.[70] Bonifacy, discussing the same topic also mentions that the Tho men have three "souls" and seven "vital spirits" whilst women have nine of the latter. He identifies "soul" with the Sino-Annamite concept hun and states that the Tho use a Tai word *minh*, whilst the vital spirits are Annamite via which correspond with the Tai word *quan* (khwan).[71] It thus appears that the Tho believe in males having three minh and seven khwans and females three minh and nine khwans.

This report is remarkable in several respects. In the first place the concept minh as related to the invisible substances that make up the body is reminiscent of the word min used in central Thailand as a compound with khwan and then it means good luck and prosperity,[72] or it may mean the "tutelary genii of children".[73] According to the Siamese Tai's beliefs, min like the khwan, is an immaterial thing residing in the body.[74]

Moreover, when we note that the Red Tai use the word *mu* or ming as a common prefix before the word khwan,[75] a pattern begins to develop and it becomes likely that the words min, minh and ming are not only related, but that they formed part of the Tai heritage before their dispersion. Naturally, that does not exclude the possibility of it being a loan word from Chinese as Phya Anuman likes to think.

In the second place there is the equation of the Annamite word via, which corresponds with the Chinese p'o, with the Tai concept of khwan. It would have made for a much neater opposition had on the one hand the word p'o been juxtaposed with the Tai phii, or "spirit" and the Chinese hun with the homophonous Tai khwan. The fact that the Tho appear not to do so throws some doubt on the possible relationship between hun and khwan. This will be referred to later in this essay. No further evidence regarding the Tho and their khwans was found.

The last reference with regard to khwans in the ethnographic literature is a mention that the Trung-Cha believe that there are thirty-six vital spirits in each human body, and that these disperse after death, some to the altar of the ancestors, some to the grave.[76]

Summarising the ethnographic survey, it is clear that the concept khwan is universal amongst the Tais, and that everywhere it may be seen related to the concept of "life-force", or "that which makes for vivacity and strength". The idea that various parts of the body may be assigned their own life force, and that consequently the body has a number of khwans is quite widespread. There is no unanimity with regard to the exact number and this is discussed later. The ritual of summoning, feasting and tying the khwans is encountered over the whole area where Tai speakers can be found. We may thus safely surmise that the belief in the existence of khwans, and the therapeutic technique of calling and binding the khwans have been part of the Tai culture since before the Tais spread over the area they occupy today. Outside influences may have been at work in any period, for any individual group. However, the facts that these customs can be found amongst the whole range of Tai speakers, and that they show great similarities in ritual details lead us to the conclusion that they were part of the Tai culture before the spreading of various Tai groups occurred.

The Wider Context

The belief in khwans has many parallels amongst groups surrounding the Tais. Amongst the Karens of Burma, for example, when a prominent man is sick, people may run about with an open cloth in their hands and may suddenly throw the cloth over a bush or a tussock of grass and then close it carefully. The *leip bya,* or "butterfly" of the sick man is supposed to have been captured and the cloth is carefully opened up and shaken over the patient's head.[77] It is clear, however, from Scott's chapter on the "butterfly spirit" that the Burmese do not distinguish between a multitude of leip byas and that there is neither the elaborate summoning-ritual nor the wrist-tying that are so characteristic amongst the Tais.

In Cambodia, people believe in the existence of nineteen "vital spirits" in a human body. If some of these leave the body and lose their way, their owner falls ill. People go out to call and catch the lost spirits, often using a fishing net. The capture and return to the body is a common ritual ending with tying the wrist with cotton threads. Sometimes nineteen threads are used, sometimes nine, seven or three.[78] The ritual has been described clearly by Poree-Maspero and it is striking how during the elaborate ceremonies of *hao pralin* the ritual details are similar to those observed amongst the Tais. They comprise the use of a ritual container, incantations, the use of succulent food and the tying of the wrists with cotton thread. Just like the Tais of central Thailand, amongst the Cambodians the ritual of recalling the souls is used to cure certain types of illness. It is also extended over life-cycle rituals, and it is used, for example, for the goddess of rice during the harvest.[79] The nineteen pralin are made up of ten major vital spirits (corresponding to ten bodily orifices) and nine lesser ones (four representing knowledge and consciousness, four related to the capacity to memorise and the final one standing for the digestion).[80]

Amongst the Vietnamese, the ritual of summoning the "vital spirits" seems to have been reserved for funeral practices and the ritual details are strikingly reminiscent of those of ancient China, where a member of the family, carrying a piece of clothing from the deceased, climbs on the roof of the house, and calls loudly for the souls to return. The custom which comes closest to the one central to this essay occurs when a child has had a bad fall and people believe that part of his spirit has become disengaged. Near the place of the fall seven bowls of rice and seven eggs (or sometimes seven pieces of a single egg) are placed, together with a garment of the child in a winnowing basket. People then call the three subtle spirits (hun) and the seven remaining vital spirits (via) to return. Then the garment is put on the child and he is offered some of the rice and the eggs. When the child is a girl, instead of seven bowls and seven eggs, nine are used, corresponding with the belief that females have nine via.[81] The custom is reminiscent of the Chinese recalling of a child's spirits, discussed below. In other respects too, with regard to the distinction between hun and via as well as the respective amounts of those substances the Vietnamese follow Chinese customs.

For thousands of years recalling the souls has been a custom in China. Ch'un Yuan wrote around the beginning of the third century B.C. a poem called *Chao hun*, the "summons of the soul",[82] and there is evidence that the ritual has been performed until the present day. Chao hun was used in ancient China for both the calling back of a wandering soul of a sick man and to summon the souls of the dead. The latter use has become more known, probably as a result of the fact that it is mentioned in the ancient Books of Rites as a funeral ritual. When a man dies, a near relative holding a garment of the deceased in his hand should climb on the roof and cry out for the dead person to return.[83] The recall of the soul has been also used for the sick. De Groot mentions several instances where this is the case. When a baby is sick, a mother hastens up to the roof of her house and, waving about a bamboo pole to which is affixed a garment belonging to the little one, exclaims several times in succession :

> "My child so-and-so, come back, return home!" In the interim another inmate of the house is loudly beating a gong, to arouse the attention of the soul. After a while the vital spirits are expected to recognise the garment and to slip into it; and so, along with it, they are taken back to the sufferer and placed either upon or at the side of his bed.[84]

It seems that the Chinese custom of calling the soul differs in many ritual details from that of the Tais, there is not the lengthy invocation of various deities, there is no ritual container, no tying of the wrists. On the other hand, the Tais do not generally use an article of clothing, they do not climb the roof of their house or wave bamboo poles. Moreover, the Chinese division of "souls" into three hun, or "superior" spirits and seven p'o or "material" invisible elements (nine for women) which at first sight looks remarkably like the Tai difference between khwan and phii, is quite distinct from that of the Tais. We have noted the interesting case of the sinicised Tho who have adopted the Chinese division, but who have given the p'o the meaning of khwan. Both in China and Vietnam, the p'o are seen as linked with the seven or nine openings of the body, and at least five of these are sensory organs. The p'o, therefore, appear closer to the Tai idea of khwan than the three hun which remain rather vague and abstract concepts and this may explain the case of the Tho.[85]

The Number of Khwans

The survey of customs regarding the summoning of the khwan has revealed an interesting detail regarding the number of khwans the Tais recognise. We found that the Shans believe they have thirty-two khwans and so do the Tais of Northeast Thailand, the Nua, the Yuan and the Lao. In Central Thailand and in South Thailand, people may regard a certain part of the body having a khwan of its own, but no definite number can be assigned. For the Lü, several authors report a number of thirty-two, but another researcher comes up with sixty-two. For the Black Tai there is also disagreement, one author counts thirty-two khwans, another arrived at a total of over eighty. For the White Tai one researcher found the number thirty-two, another found "a great number". The Red Tai have one hundred and twenty. The Neua have "many". The Trung-Cha have thirty-six, and the other eastern groups follow the Chinese system of three plus seven (or nine).

Though the number of thirty-two clearly prevails, it is also clear from the ethnographic literature that it is extremely rare to find a ritual specialist who can actually name the thirty-two khwans. It has been suggested that the thirty-two khwans are none other than the thirty-two parts of the body mentioned in the Buddhist canon.[86] In the *Khuddakapātha*, for example, the *divattiṁsākāram* are enumerated and these have found their way in some of the medical treatises of South-east Asia. A comparison of the divattiṁsākāram with the various lists of the Tais' khwans reveals, however, that they are not related. The Buddhist list of thirty-two parts is much more abstract than any of the Tai listings. In the canon we find parts of the body not specifically localised such as "bodyhair", "nails" "skin", "flesh", "sinews", "bones", "marrow", "membranes", "digestive juice", "pus", "blood", "sweat", "fat", and "lymph". None of these are found in the Tai lists of khwans. The lists contain predominantly specific parts of the body such as hand, elbow, arm etc. Moreover these parts are not themselves khwans. Khwans are the aspect of vitality and health of the particular parts of the body. The Tai belief in khwans thus reveals a quite different perspective of the human body than that which may be derived from the *Khuddakapātha*, and we may safely assume that they are quite unrelated.

Yet it is plausible that many of the Tai groups under the influence of the Buddhist texts[87] have assumed that they possess thirty-two khwans. According to this hypothesis, various Tai ritual specialists, knowing that they had a great number of khwans, and hearing that the Buddhist medical science had divided the body up in thirty-two parts, took it for granted that Buddhist science and Tai medical views were part of one and the same system and that in Buddhist manuals the complete list of khwans was given. The belief in thirty-two bodily signs of a *mahāpurusa* may also have played a role. This hypothesis would account for the fact that there are Tai groups amongst whom it is simply believed that a great number of khwans can be found in the body; these groups have not made the connection with the Buddhist canon. It also accounts for the fact that there is disagreement amongst some Tai ritual specialists, some of them reaching a much greater number of khwans. The latter cases reveal that in actual fact Tai medical principles are at variance with those found in the Buddhist canon.

The ethnographic survey reveals that the Tai way of dividing up the human body differs fundamentally not only from Buddhist ideas, but also from those of the Chinese. The latter distinguish between three "positive" hun and seven (or nine) "negative" p'o. The three hun are "souls", divided up in various manners. One hun may go to heaven to be judged after death, the second could be destined for the ancestor tablet and the third could remain near the corpse in the grave.[88] The p'o seem to be basically linked with the bodily orifices. This Chinese system has been adopted to a certain extent by some eastern Tai groups and many non-Tais in Vietnam. Essentially it is quite at variance with the system of the Tais. The latter in general recognise a much greater number of khwans than the Chinese. The Tais do not regard the bodily orifices as the important seats for khwans, neither do they distinguish between males and females in this respect.

Amongst other populations in South-east Asia, the number of separate "souls" reported is often basically the Chinese system (for example, amongst many of the Man peoples, the Akhas, the Vietnamese and the P'u Noi) or the number of "souls" is simply reported to be seven (on the Malay Peninsula, for people of Melanesia and amongst the Toba-Batak).[89] Even the Cambodians, who at first sight appear to have a promisingly high number of *pralins*, seem to have a system quite different from that of the Tais and essentially a mixture between the Chinese and the Buddhist systems. It will require further comparative studies to establish whether the Tais indeed have an ancient method of perceiving the human body which differs from that of other groups, or whether they represent a view which once was widespread in South-east Asia. At this stage we may conclude that with regard to the number of khwans and their essential character, the Tais appear quite unique in three respects, namely the high number of khwans they may recognise, the system underlying this concept and the positioning on the human body of the khwans.

Tying the Khwans

Though there are rituals to recall "souls" reported for peoples all over Asia, and it could be that such rituals are ubiquitous, the ritual details of the various forms of the ceremony lead us towards hypotheses of links between various cultures in the distant past. The Tai summous of the khwan seems to be very similar in ritual detail to that of the Cambodians, but it is not clear whether this represents a borrowing in the more recent past or whether it indicates a generic link beween the two cultures. In the light of the fact that the ideas behind khwan and pralin are basically dissimilar, I would give more credence to the first possibility.

An interesting ritual detail which may help us place the Tai customs in wider context is the binding of the patient with white cotton thread around the wrists, immediately after the summoning has been completed. Although the Chinese do practise a custom of tying a red thread around people's wrists, this is not intimately linked with a "soul" summons. It is, on the other hand, reported for the P'u Noi of Upper Laos,[90] for the Man of Vietnam, and for the peoples of the Malay peninsula, for the Bagabas of the Philippines, for peoples in Borneo and New Guinea.[91]

Such evidence suggests that, at least for this ritual detail, the Tais conform more to a "Austronesian" pattern than to a "Chinese" sphere of influence. This may be regarded as yet another argument in favour of looking for Austronesian links when we consider the problems of the "origin" of the Tais.

NOTES

1. E.B. Tylor, *Primitive Culture*, Vol. I, (London, John Murray, 5th edition 1929), p. 71.
2. Tai refers to the widespread ethnic group which includes, amongst others, the Ahom, the Shan, Lao, and also the Thais. The latter term refers only to the inhabitants of Thailand.
3. J.M. Brown, *From Ancient Thai to Modern Dialects* (Bangkok: Social Science Association Press of Thailand, 1965) p. 179, looking at sixty dialects of the southwestern branch of Tai languages, considers it possible that these all derived from a parent-language in the 8th century A.D. Recently, Gedney is reported to have estimated the age of Proto-Tai as not older than 2000 years. See J.R. Chamberlain, "A New Look at the History and Classification of the Tai

Languages" in J.G. Harris and J.R. Chamberlain (eds), *Studies in Tai Linguistics in Honor of William J. Gedney*, (Bangkok : Central Institute of English Language, 1975) p. 58. Chamberlain himself tentatively goes back a little further and mentions the third century B.C. as a possible date (Ibid. p. 62).

4. J.F. Embree and W.L. Thomas, *Ethnic Groups of Northern Southeast Asia* (New Haven: Yale University, Southeast Asia Studies, 1950) p. 123; E. Seidenfaden, *The Tai Peoples* (Bangkok: The Siam Society, 1958); F.M. Lebar (et al) *Ethnic Groups of Mainland Southeast Asia* (New Haven, Human Relations Area Files Press, 1964) pp. 187-244; and B.M. Broman, *Early Political Institutions of the Tai: Synthesis and Symbiosis* (University of Washington Master of Arts Thesis, 1968).
5. In this enumeration the groups, such as the Khun, Phuan, Phuthai, Chungchia, Chuang and others for whom no information on the topic of this article was obtained, have been left out.
6. See J. Sarkar "Assam and the Ahoms in 1660 A.D." *Journal of the Bihar and Orissa Research Society*, Vol. 1, 1915, pp. 179-95.
7. G.C. Barua (editor and translator), *Ahom-Buranji : From the Earliest Time to the End of Ahom Rule*, Calcutta: Baptist Mission Press, (1930).
8. No attempt has been made to standardise the transcription of the various Tai languages. For Ahom the transcription of Barua is followed, for Siamese the Haas System has been selected, whilst for all other Tai words the transcription of the relevant sources is repeated. The only exception is made for the word khwan, (in order not to confuse the reader with the many renderings, the word will be spelled in this manner throughout this article, see note 11).
9. P. Gogoi, *The Tai and the Tai Kingdoms: with a Fuller Treatment of the Tai-Ahom Kingdom in the Brahmaputra Valley* (Gauhati: Gauhati University, 1968), p. 122 and p. 290.
10. Fang Kuei Li, *A Handbook of Comparative Tai* (Oceanic Linguistics Special Publication No. 15, 1977) pp. 241 and 271.
11. It would be somewhat confusing to reproduce this word in the various spellings which range from khwān, kwan, k'wan and khuan to q'wan, xwan, khhoan and khoan. Therefore, a fairly neutral rendering of the word has been chosen to represent the concept in all Tai languages and in this essay a uniform khwan is maintained.
12. *Ahom-Buranji*, pp. 16 and 58.
13. Ibid. p. 16.
14. Ibid. pp. 57-8.
15. Ibid. pp. 60, 81 and 100.
16. Ibid. pp. 66 and 251.
17. Ibid. pp. 325-6, 329, 332 and 360.
18. Ibid. p. 73.
19. Ibid. pp. 258-9.
20. Seidenfaden, op. cit., p. 44.

21. Phya Anuman Rajadhon, *Essays on Thai Folklore* (Bangkok: The Social Science Association Press, 1968) p. 202..
22. H.G.Q. Wales, *Siamese State Ceremonies, Their History and Function* (London: Bernard Quaritch, 1931) p. 33.
23. B.J. Terwiel, *Monks and Magic: An Analysis of Religious Ceremonies in Central Thailand*, Scandinavian Institute of Asian Studies Monograph No. 24 (London: Curzon Press, 1975) p. 52.
24. *Phodcanaanukrom chabab raadchabandidsathaan* Bangkok: (The Royal Academy, 1950) p. 185.
25. Anuman Rajadhon, op. cit., p. 202.
26. M.A. Wright, "Some Observations on Thai Animism" *Practical Anthropology* Vol. 15, 1968, p. 5.
27. The fact that the Siamese Tai recognise the concept of a Khwan Myan forms an interesting parallel with the remark in the *Ahom Buranji* on p. 73 where the words which Barua transcribed as *khanmung* are undoubtedly related to respectively khwan and myan.
28. Wright, op. cit., p. 5.
29. Anuman Rajadhon, op. cit., pp. 208-13.
30. ibid., p. 207.
31. R.I. Heinze, "Nature and Function of Some Therapeutic Techniques in Thailand", *Asian Folklore Studies*, Vol. 36, Part 2, 1977, p. 92. (See also her *How to Contain the Essence of Life, A Psycho-Sociological Comparison of a Thai Custom Across Cultures*, forthcoming).
32. Anuman Rajadhon, op. cit., p. 207. See also G.E. Gerini, *Chulakantamangala or the Tonsure Ceremony as Performed in Siam* (Bangkok: The Siam Society, 1976) p. 53.
33. Anuman Rajadhon, op. cit., p. 212; Wales op. cit., p. 33; Heinze, op. cit. p. 94.
34. G.B. McFarland, *Thai-English Dictionary* (Stanford University Press, 1969) p. 706.
35. Heinze, "Nature and Function", p. 94.
36. Anuman Rajadhon, op. cit., Gerini, op. cit.
37. *Plaachon tomjom*, the *chon* fish is sometimes known as serpenthead.
38. Of the 28 varieties of bananas, the tiny *kluaj naam* are often used for ritual purposes. See J.R. Hanks, *Maternity and its Rituals in Bank Chan*, Data Paper No. 51 Southeast Asia Program, Cornell University, 1963, p. 23.
39. Anuman Rajadhon, *Prapheenii kaw khnao Thaj* (Bangkok; Prae Pittaya, 1957), p. 149.
40. Anuman Rajadhon. *Essays on Thai Folklore*, p. 213.
41. Wright, op. cit., p. 5.
42. J.B. Pallegoix, *Description Du Royaume Thai ou Siam*, (Earnborough: Gregg International Publishers, 1969) Vol. II, pp. 54-6.
43. *Seephaa ryan Khun Chaan Khun Phaan*, *chabab haasamudhan chaad* (Bangkok: Department of Fine Arts, 1965), p. 8 et passim.
44. F. Cripps, *The Far Province* (London: Hutchinson & Co., 1965), p. 85.

45. S.J. Tambiah, *Buddhism and the Spirit Cults in North-East Thailand*, Cambridge Studies in Social Anthropology, No. 2, Cambridge: Cambridge University Press, 1970, p. 58.
46. Ibid., p. 223.
47. Ibid., p. 238.
48. Anuman Rajadhon, *Essays on Thai Folklore*, p. 207.
49. *Khati chaawbaan amphoo Sathin phra Amphoo Ranood* (Songkhla: Department of Thai Language, Songkhla College of Education, n.d.) pp. 123-6.
50. Seidenfaden, op. cit., p. 44.
51. W.C. Dodd, *The Tai Race* (Cedar Rapids: Torch Press, 1923) p. 177.
52. Ibid.
53. Ibid., pp. 194-5.
54. J. Rispaud "Sur une tribu des confins sino-laotiens" *France-Asie*, Vol. 10, 1954, p. 750.
55. Ibid., p. 753.
56. Sanguan Chotisukharat, *Prapheenii Thaj Phaagnya* (Bangkok: Odeon Store, 1969) pp. 266-7.
57. C. Archaimbault, *Structures religieuses lao* (*rites et mythes*) (Vientiane: Vithagna, 1973), pp. 183-4. See also Seidenfaden, op. cit., p. 44 and R. Pottier, "Introduction a l'etude des pratiques therapeutiques lao" *Asie du Sud-est et Monde Insulindien*, Vol III, no. 2, 1973, p. 175.
58. Nguyen-van-Lanh, "La metempsycose laotienne et une pratique qui s'y rattache: le sou-khouan", *Bulletin de l'Institut Indochinois pour l'Etude de l'Homme*, Vol. V, pt. 2, 1942, pp. 109-114; Thao Nhouy Abhay, "The Baci" *Kingdom of Laos*, edited by R. de Berval (Saigon: France-Asie, 1959), pp. 128-31; and especially M. Zago, *Rites et ceremonies en milieu bouddhiste lao* (Rome : Gregorian University, 1972), pp. 129-70. The latter provides a short bibliography on the *Khwan* which contains references to Laotian sources which I have not been able to consult.
59. Zago, op. cit., p. 155.
60. Ibid., p. 160.
61. P.B Lafont, "Notes sur les familles patronymiques Thai Noires de So'n-la et de Nghia-lo", *Anthropos*, Vol. 50, 1953, p. 807.
62. H. Maspero, *Le Taoisme et les religions chinoises.* (Paris: Editions Gallimard, 1971) p. 269.
63. P.B. Lafont, "Pratiques medicales des Thai noirs du Laos de l'ouest", *Anthropos*, Vol. 54, 1959, pp. 830-5.
64. H. Maspero, "Moeurs et coutumes des populations sauvages:" *Un-empire colonial francais: l'Indochine*, edited by G. Maspero (Paris: Van Oest, 1929), p. 241.
65. Rispaud, op. cit., p. 750.
66. J. Donaldson and Dieu Chinh Nhim, *Tai-Vietnamese-English Vocabulary* (Saigon: Bo Giao-Duc Xuat Ban, 1970) p. 170. I am grateful to Dr A. Diller for calling my attention to this information.

67. R. Robert, *Notes sur les Tay Deng de Lang Chanh* (*Thanh-hoa-Annam*) Memoire No. 1, Institut Indochinois pour l'Etude de l'Homme, (Hanoi: Imprimerie d'Extreme-Orient, 1941) pp. 38, 42 and 50-2.
68. A. Boutin, "Croyances et superstitions chez les Thay Rouges" *Bulletin des Amis du Laos*, Vol. II, 1938, pp. 65-8, as quoted by Zago, *Rites et ceremonies*, p. 137.
69. A. Bourlet, "Les Thay", *Anthropos*, Vol. 2, 1907, p. 362.
70. M. Abadie, *Les races du Haut-Tonkin de Phong-Tho a Lang-Son* (Paris : Societe d'editions geographiques, maritimes et coloniales. 1924), p. 54.
71. A. Bonifacy, "Les rites de la mort chez les Tho" *Revue Indochinoise*, Vol. I, 1904, pp. 361 and 364.
72. *Phodzanaunukrom chabab raadchabandidsathaan*, p. 717.
73. McFarland, op. cit., p. 650.
74. Anuman Rajadhon, *Essays on Thai Folklore*, p. 208.
75. R. Robert, *Notes sur les Tay Deng.*, p. 38, especially fn. 1.
76. Lebar (et al) op. cit., p. 236.
77. Shway Yoe (J.G. Scott), *The Burman : His Life and Notions* (New York: The Norton Library, 1963) pp. 237-8; see also Ba Han "Spiritism in Burma" Journal of the Burma Research Society, Vol. 47, pt. 1, 1964, p. 7.
78. E. Poree-Maspero (et al), *Ceremonies privees des Cambodgiens* Phnom-Penh: Institut Bouddhique, 1958) pp. 19-22.
79. E. Poree-Maspero, "La ceremonie de l'appel des esprits vitaux chez les Cambodgiens" *Bulletin de l'Ecole Francaise d'Extreme-Orient*. Vol. 45, 1945, p. 145 ff; with regard to the "soul" of the rice, see her *Etude sur les rites agraires des Cambodgiens* (Paris : Mouton, 1962), Vol. 1, pp. 19-21.
80. Poree-Maspero, "La ceremonie de l'appel des esprits vitaux" pp. 146-7.
81. Nguyen-Van-Koan, "Le repechage de l'ame" *Bulletin de l'Ecole Francaise d'Extreme-Orient*, Vol. 33, 1933; pp. 11-34.
82. D. Hawkes, *Ch'u Tz'u, The Songs of the South* (Oxford: Clarendon Press, 1959) pp. 100-9; see in the same work also the poem "Ta Chao" pp. 109-114.
83. Hawkes, op. cit., p. 101. For an overview of the custom in China through the centuries, see J.J.M. de Groot, *The Religious System of China* (Leyden: Brill, 1892) Vol. 1; Book 1, pp. 243-262 and H. Dore, *Recherches sur les superstitions en Chine* (Shanghai: T'ou-se-we, 1912) Part I, Vol. 2, No. 4, pp. 323-331. Textual references can be found in F.D. Lessing, "Calling the Soul: A Lamaist Ritual", in *Semitic and Oriental Studies Presented to William Popper*, edited by W.J. Fischel, (Berkeley and Los Angeles: University of California Press, 1951) p. 280.
84. De Groot, op. cit., p. 243.
85. This aspect has been discussed for Tibet and Vietnam by R.A. Stein, "Le *linga* des danses masquees lamaiques et la theorie des ames"

Sino-Indian Studies. Vol. 5, Pt. 3/4, pp. 208-10.

86. Heinze, op. cit., p. 92.
87. Anuman Rajadhon, *Essays on Thai Folklore*, p. 207.
88. Stein, op cit., p. 208.
89. Poree-Maspero, "La ceremonie de l'appel des esprits vitaux" p. 177.
90. H. Roux, "Deux tribus de la region de Phongsaly" *Bulletin de l'Ecole Francaise d'Extreme-Orient*, Vol. 24; 1924, p. 472.
91. Poree-Maspero, "La ceremonie de l'appel des esprits vitaux", p. 175.

THIRTEEN

J.P. Singh

CHANGING PATTERNS OF TRIBAL GOVERNMENT
A Case Study of the Santal

THE SANTAL are the most numerous of the Scheduled Tribes and comprise nearly 38 per cent of the tribal population of Bihar. Their social and personal life is governed by a well-defined set of political institutions of purely democratic nature which are in striking contrast to modern political institutions. After India's independence marked changes have come about in the Santal village government under the strain and stress of heterogenetic forces. Curiously enough, social scientists have paid little attention to this problem. There is need to study how various agents of change have been operating against the age-old indigenous institutions so as to identify the tendencies for change within the political structures and organisations of a community which has been almost stagnant or immobile for centuries.

It has been my endeavour to make clear the changing patterns of political structure of the Santal and to focus upon factors and forces responsible for bringing about changes in the political structure. The data are based on both synchronic and dychronic facts.

Before the final selection of the villages was made for the present study, over a dozen villages were visited. The purpose was to select two villages as were supposed to have experienced maximum changes in the post-independence era. The changes were presumed to have resulted from the villagers' exposure to the media of mass communication and frequent contacts with non-tribals and local government officials. The two villages selected are not located very far from the metalled road. Most of the changes have come about probably through the non-tribal people who have permanently settled in their villages. Non-tribal villagers appeared to be much more mobile, enterprising and better off than the tribals.

A good deal of difficulty was encountered in establishing rapport with the respondents. *Dikus* (outsiders) are looked upon with great suspicion. I was a Diku. On the second day, I approached two voluntary level workers and one Santal primary school teacher to establish a friendly and closer relationship with my respondents. They accompanied me to the two villages and introduced me to all important persons and village officials. They helped me for three days and then left by mutual agreement. As I stayed in the area for about a year in connection with my teaching work, I got ample opportunity to learn the regional ethos as well as the local dialect. Their awareness considerably helped me in establishing a good communication with the respondents.

When I moved to these villages I had a definite preference for studying a particular aspect of the Santal life and a clear plan of investigation. The non-directed group interview was used to gather data. This method is most appropriate and suitable where the incidence of literacy is low. Administration of any other tool is costly. Besides, the villagers always crowded around me out of curiosity. In the melee, it was difficult to make a personal approach to them as individual respondents.

Only male respondents were interviewed. Dikus are seldom allowed to talk with Santal women, who are of a very shy nature. Besides, they do not play any role in the political activity of the village. Village administration is solely a male affair among the Santal. Women are forbidden from taking part in the meetings of the village council. They are considered chattel, meant for matrimony and progeny, capricious and irresponsible creatures. However, they are allowed to appear as witnesses in the council.

As time is an important factor in the study of the problem of change, studies which were conducted about three decades ago or before independence have been taken as bench-mark data for this study. References to some studies have been made to highlight the changes which have occurred in the "Pax-Britannica" period. Although ethnographic works depend upon several things, like conditions in which field-work is undertaken, the works cited are taken as authentic. Most ethnographic works are generally reliable.

For this study I have concentrated on the village because it is a real social unit, not just an aggregation of individuals. It has an organised system of roles; it draws on the resources of its members and it does things as a unit. Every village has its own history and problems. Sometimes differences between two villages are evident in the cultural ethos also. A feeling of belonging among the villagers for their village not only distinguishes two villages but also implies that a village is a complete whole at social and psychological levels. A villager usually thinks of himself or herself in relation to the village or to other villagers as a group. The village, therefore, has a certain phenomenological reality as a societal thing in itself.

Universe of the Study

The two villages which have been chosen for the present study are Ratansar and Postmara. They are semi-tribal villages in the Baunsi Development Block in Bhagalpur—the chief and the central district of the division of the same name in Bihar. Baunsi is about 50 km south of Bhagalpur on the Bhagalpur-Dumka road. It is also connected by rail—the Bhagalpur-Mandar Hill branch of Eastern Railway. Baunsi is famous for the month-long annual fete at the time of *Makar Sankranti* (January). A *hat* (temporary rural market) is held here every Saturday and Wednesday to which people (including Santals) from neighbouring areas, stretching as far as 16 km, come in sizable numbers for marketing.

I had to get down from the bus at Shyam Bazar situated on the Bhagalpur-Dumka road at a distance of 8 km south of Baunsi to reach Ratnasar and Postmara, which lie south-east of Shyam Bazar at distances of 5 and 3 km respectively. The block development and other officials go to Ratnasar on bicycles, but they have to go to Postmara on foot as the physical topography of that region is quite rugged. Shyam Bazar is a weekly rural market centre. People of both villages come to this *hat* every Saturday for selling and purchasing locally produced consumer goods.

As the villages are nucleated, their population lives in a rather small land area given over to houses. The villages are surrounded by farmlands, agriculture being the main occupation. The villagers speak Santali, a language belonging to the Mundarai group and adherents of Hinduism. Rice and wheat are the important crops grown. Because rainfall is seasonal, only two crops are annually harvested.

The pressure of increasing population on a limited land base has necessitated an ever-increasing temporary migration of villagers for manual work in the off-season. This offers a temporary measure to supplement the family income.

These two villages have developed out of successive migrations of the Santal who originally belonged to the Rajmahal Hills of Santal Parganas (Singh and Singh, 1965). It is, however, difficult to ascertain the exact time of the settlement of these villages because of the lack of any reliable historical evidence. But it is not disputed that the Santal migrated to this region about a century ago for various reasons. The non-tribal people, especially the Hindus, settled in these villages much after the settlement of the Santal in search of cheaper land.

Autonomous Community

The Santal may be considered a politically autonomous community in the sense that they have developed their own administrative and judicial organisations to deal with all kinds of disputes, breaches and social problems. These organisations are governed by the unwritten customary laws, developed, modified and enforced on democratic lines by a panel of village officials under the presidency of a *manjhi*. What is important about the village council is that it has wider jurisdiction than any other civil or criminal court of the modern world. It looks into all kinds of village affairs, whether social, cultural or moral. In other words, it acts as a custodian of the Santal' folkways, mores, morals and all such things which they value.

The Santal, generally speaking, do not like to visit the police station, law court or even the panchayat office, as the government machinery, they say, is not only very costly but also tortuous. They believe more in their own system of justice rather than that of the Diku . People of these villages are reported to have not moved a court even once as yet. They visit the court only when a case involves a Santal on the one hand and a non-Santal on the other; that, too, when the latter takes the initiative to move the court.

Village Council

They have developed a two-tier system of public administration: one at the village level and the other at the pargana level. The village government comprises seven native officials duly elected by the villagers in the month of Magh. They are: *manjhi*[2], *paranik*[3], *jog-manjhi*[4], *jog-paranik*[5], *naek*[6], *kudum naeke*[7] and *gorait*[8], headed by the manjhi. The organisation is known as *more-hore.*[9]

Before the abolition of the zamindari system, the manjhi was appointed as pradhan for the collection of revenue from villagers and for the payment of the rent to the government where rent was payable by the village as a whole. As village chief, all abandoned lands were in his possession. He acted as the custodian of village property, community wells, roads, bandhs, grazing grounds and was endowed with power to requisition village labour to repair these. But all the powers and privileges have got eroded after independence. But the maintenance of the *manjhithan* or *manjhibathan*[10] and the administration of the *jaharthan*[11] are still his important duties, since he continues to be the social and cultural head of the village. Besides the maintenance of the religious estate, he has to see that annual festivals are duly performed and everybody contributes to the ceremonies of birth, matrimony and death. If any serious disease breaks out in the village, he must call a general body meeting and arrange special sacrifices.

As he is the formal head of the village, all important matters, whether social or religious, are brought to his notice, and his opinion and participation are secured. He is the formal spokesman of the village. Any villager can lodge a complaint with him against any fellow-villager. He generally wields much authority and the villagers are expected to obey his commands. Whenever necessary, the headman can summon the village council. While he may significantly influence the opinion of the council by his presentation of a case, the decision is, by and large, of the council and not his. It is his duty to see that the justice is done according to traditional rules. The manjhi may be considered a paternalistic leader. He is in no sense absolute or despotic. The decision-making process is differentiated and dispersed, rather than unitary.

The paranik, next to the manjhi, is another important village official. He may properly be called a deputy manjhi, and is sometimes so closely allied to the manjhi in his general duties that one may confuse him with the manjhi himself. He officiates for the manjhi in the latter's absence if a case is not of a very serious kind.

The jog-manjhi is the third important official of the village council. His duty is to prevent immoral traffic and to see that no scandal arises. He may be called a moral legislator. Dalton observes that "his most important duty is to look after the morals of the boys and girls" (Dalton, 1872 : 213). But compared to the past, his power in the matter of maintenance of the morality of youths in particular, and of villagers in general, has considerably declined. Morality is now more a personal problem than a communal one. Individualisation is gradually on the increase.

The fourth village official is the jog-paranik, who has to officiate for the jog-manjhi when he is absent. Now this official is non-existent. Gorait or godet is another functionary acting as the orderly of the manjhi. His main duty is to inform villagers about the council meeting. Gorait is the only functionary whose functions are still intact. He is appointed by the manjhi for three years, but is liable to be dismissed any time.

The term of all village officials, except of the gorait, is in theory for one year only, but in practice they usually continue for life. However, at the end of every year in the month of Magh[12] all village officials go through the formal process of resigning their office. The manjhi and other officials announce on any evening in the beginning of Magh that they are laying down their offices and those who are interested may come and take them. This is followed by free drinks of *handi* or *pochai*[13], resulting in great merriment. If their services are found satisfactory, their names are again proposed for the same. Persons found inefficient or guilty of any unjust action are always dropped or replaced by new persons who are believed to be honest and efficient. What is important is that they *must* be elected unanimously. In no case can a person be elected if there is a single negative vote against him. Thus, the terms of the manjhi and other village officials are extended every year till their death. The annual renunciation of office and the re-election give the whole business a democratic flavour. It emphasizes village approval and provides an annual occasion for the expression of grievances. Again, when a village official resigns or is dismissed, his successor is appointed by a village meeting.

A manjhi, who was usually appointed a pradhan under the Santal Pargana Tenancy Act, was allotted a sizable area of land which was quite disproportionate to the rent collected by him. For example, if he collected only Rs. 10 or so annually as rent, he got nearly seven *bighas*[14] of land in lieu of this work. If he collected about fifteen hundred rupees, he got around two hundred bighas of land as permanent reward, plus a definite percentage of commission on the collected amount. The land remained in his possession as his personal property during his life-time except in the case of his removal from headmanship, which seldom happened. After his death the son of a pradhan was almost invariably appointed his successor. Thus the *pradhanijot*,[15] passing from one generation to another, contiued to remain the ancestral family property of the pradhan. But all these privileges, functions and powers have come to an end bit by bit with the establishment of the statutory panchayat, civil and criminal courts and the abolition of the zamindari system in Bihar.

Pargana-level Administration

While the first-tier administrative assembly is the village council, the second-tier Santal assembly is the council of neighbourhood which ceased to operate after the introduction of a new form of administration by the central government. This body was known as the council of five manjhis headed by the *parganait*[16] and had jurisdiction over twenty villages. Thus, the Santal villages were federated into a number of large groups. The office of the pargana has a remote history and it is difficult to say how it came into existence.

From all that is known, it may be inferred that the parganait was the social and fiscal head of a tract of country. In the early period, when the country was covered with forests, it was the duty of the parganait to settle new villages and define the boundaries. During British rule, he was made responsible for reporting on criminals. Before the introduction of the regular police, the parganait exercised the power of a sub-inspector of police. As sub-inspector, he could make an arrest. This official status gave him the position of tribal leader.

One of the important functions of the council was to settle inter-village disputes. It adjudicated all matters which the villagers themselves failed to decide. It was the final appellate court of the Santal. As it was a very high tribunal, it sat only occasionally being either convened by the President himself on his own initiative, or on being moved by the aggrieved party.

The introduction of the police, a new form of legal system and the Tribal Block Development Programme affected the police, judicial and revenue powers of the parganait. Though the system of the pargana level administration has been abolished, it still emerges on an *ad hoc* basis when an inter-village dispute arises. It emerges and ends with the emergence and end of the problem.

Hunt Council

Like the pargana-level administration, the hunt council, too, has died. It was so powerful that the final authority of the Santal society was vested in it. It met once a year and was attended by the entire population of the region, covering a number of parganas. The meeting was held in the beginning of the summer season (April-May) because during that period trees of the forest were burnt. The purpose of burning trees was two fold: making place for the council and the symbolic burning of offences. The meeting was presided over by a *dihri*[17] who was at once a priest, a master of the hunt, a provident of the ballot, a leader of the house and chief justice. He was, however, not a permanent official. He was appointed only to conduct the hunt. For two days he used to be the monarch of the meeting and hunting expedition, and there was none to dispute his authority. But after the hunt was over, he resumed his quiet place in the village.

Once the hunt council commenced its business, anyone, aowever low, could speak out fearlessly. Anybody could lodge h complaint against the village council or how the manjhi and the council had imposed a penalty without rhyme or reason, or why the parganas and the five manjhis did not decide properly the disputes about his land and his quarrel with his wife, or where they wrongly or with *mala fide* intention called a person a sorcerer, or why he was excommunicated without sufficient reason, or why the villagers without any cause had blocked his door with thorns (Bodding, 1932-36: 161). People could make any number of such complaints in the hunt council, as it was the highest court of the Santal. There the pargana, the desh-manjhi and the manjhi if complained against, had no power to intimidate anyone. Kolean Harem once observed that at the hunt people judged very righteously, they did not let any injustice to pass at all for the reason that people had great trust in the judgement of the burnt forest (Bodding, 1942: 125).

The introduction of the civil court gave a great jolt to this organisation to the extent of its extinction. Enforcement of new forest laws is also partly responsible for its demise. Nowadays wild game and forests are protected by state laws. The facilities for hunting are almost non-existent. The extirpation of the hunt council is deemed unhealthy in view of the problems confronted by the Santal in a court of law. It was an exemplary institution of direct democracy. It was a poor man's rostrum where delegated power was at discount, and where for one night the final authority was the people themselves. Many respondents advocated revival of this institution. They believe neither in the fairness of the justice meted out to them, nor do they like the legal system of the government, as it is quite clumsy and tortuous. People also detest new laws because they appear to have got a fancy for old things.

Bitlaha,[18] severe punishment, too, has vanished from the scene as a result of the interference of the state government. Bitlaha was meted out to offenders who transgressed the Santal's taboo against sexual relations inside the clan or with an outsider. The first step for holding bitlaha was to secure the people's approval. The manjhi then would inform the pargana. This body acted as a reviewing authority and until it confirmed the decision of the village council, no bitlaha could take place. It was performed by an enormous crowd to the accompaniment and thunder of drums. It had participation by a large number of villagers from neighbouring villages. They came in response to the *dharwak*[19] signal, which was passed from village to village. The exhibition of dharwak had the full force of the command of the Santal. It summoned the people for a definite act. Once issued, it was only with great difficulty that the order could be withdrawn.

No bitlaha is said to have been held in both villages for the last four or five decades. People have heard only such cases of bitlaha which were committed in villages of remote hilly areas a long ago, say, over a couple of decades ago. Though the villagers are quite aware of it, they do not practise it. They consider it as a brute form of punishment. They have largely liberalised their views on such matters. Besides, it has been declared illegal by the government. Once Archer reported that in each year during his time (1942-46) the number of bitlahas in which both the parties were Santal ranged between five and fifteen. During the decade 1953-63, only eight bitlahas were performed and those only in Dumka and Pakur sub-divisions (Raichaudhary, 1965: 881).

Factors of Change

Legislative measures like the Panchayati Raj Act, the Bihar Tenancy Act, the Zamindari Abolition Act and the various laws relating to forests and the introduction of the Tribal Development Block, police stations and civil and criminal courts have put out of gear various political organizations mentioned earlier and undermined the value of their functionaries. It is the Panchyati Raj Act that has affected them much more than any other legislation, as it has provided a substitute for the old village council. As a matter of fact, it has interfered with the Santals' community life to the extent of destroying cultural values on which their political organizations were based. Since their cultural values have not been replaced by new ones or uprooted completely, the village council has not been wholly shattered. It operates side by side with the statutory panchayat. With the Panchayati Raj system spreading and taking roots in tribal society, some sort of adjustment between the traditional and the new set-up of village administration has been going on.

The opening of schools, dispensaries, post and telegraph offices and other government offices engaged in developmental activities, casual visits by the Santal to the weekly market and neighbouring towns, and official visits of the block personnel to villages have greatly increased the opportunity of social contacts, facilitating the process of acculturation. The spread of transportation, communication, media of mass exposure, etc., also have affected the social-cultural life and economic infrastructure of the Santal (Gautam, 1977). The spread of messianic churches has acted as a catalytic agent of change. A similar view has been expressed by Oommen (1977) in one of his studies, *Analysis of Rural Social Change*. All these have consequently affected the political structures and organisations of the Santal because various components of social life in a simple society are interlinked and interdependent in such a manner that change or alteration in one component produces change in the other.

The use of modern utensils, new attire and factory goods, application of fertilizer and new varieties of seeds, interest in vernacular education and white collar jobs, secularisation of belief, knowledge of Hindi, interest in party politics and the shift of village leadership from the old to young educated people[20] are some of the important manifestations of the operation of the process of acculturation and mark the beginning of many more changes in the life of the Santal.

Power is Shared

Oommen's (1970 : 226-39) concepts of "power exerciser" and "power reservoir" seem to be partly useful in understanding the problem of power structure of the Santal society. It is partly because only the former concept appears to be relevant in the sense that the manjhi along with his village officials acts as a powerful authority, especially when the question of execution of the verdict of the council arises, but there is no such group of persons or organisation who can be regarded as the repository of power. The power is, in fact, derived not from any individual but from all the people of the village through democratic election. It is diffused among all villagers, almost equally. Each person is equally powerful in the matter of village affairs. This idea of equality becomes obvious at the time of election of village officials. Even an ordinary individual is capable of interrupting the whole process of election.

Each and every person attending the meeting for the election of the manjhi and other functionaries, except the gorait, is bound to elect them unanimously. Complete unanimity of opinion is always sought. It is really remarkable that every member in the assembly possesses the right to veto the election of the manjhi if he happens to harbour any doubt in the integrity of the candidate. This political system of electing the manjhi and other functionaries is reported to have been working smoothly in the highest democratic tradition among the Santal since time immemorial.

Why the Santal government has been running purely on democratic lines is answered in the following statement of B. Malinowski :

> The primitive State is not tyrannical to its own subject because, first and foremost, we know that a primitive tribe is always a body of people related by bonds of kinship and relationship, by clanship and age-grade, where politically everybody is related, really or fictitiously, to everybody else (Malinowski, 1947 : 253).

The contact of a complex society possessing cultural values and patterns of life of diverse nature with a simpler one is an important factor to cause changes in the simple traditional society. Various contact-situations work as a medium of influence upon the people of a simpler society. Explaining the reason as to why such an interaction takes place, it may be observed that a man enters into a new social association because he knows it to be rewarding, and that he continues his relations with old associations and expands his interaction with them because he actually finds this positively useful.

The tribal institutions have been open for so long to outside influences that they are bound to undergo perceptible changes. Colonialism has acted as a "modernising force" (Apter, 1965). Changes in the political structure of the Santal are coming through the process of syncretisation. The old set of institutions is not being replaced by new ones; rather both are existing together. Neither has the influence of old system yet fully diminished, nor has the new structural frame been wholly internalised. This is because tradition cannot be completely eliminated and certain of its elements survive in one form or the other. Myrdal (1964) has also made a similar observation in the case of a Chinese village. So far as the question of the source of change is concerned, heterogenetic forces are more predominant than orthogenetic ones. In other words, change is more forced from outside than generated inside the system.

NOTES

1. Non-tribals or outsiders are called *dikus*. They are looked upon with suspicion and surprise. This is what the author experienced during the field-work.
2. A duly elected headman is called manjhi. He is also known as pradhan.
3. The paranik is the assistant to the manjhi. In the absence of the manjhi he may be called upon to perform his duty.
4. The jog-manjhi is the moral guardian of the Santal community. He is a deputy to the headman (manjhi). His special function is to preside over the marriage ceremonies. He is incharge of social festivities.
5. The jog-paranik is the assistant to the jog-manjhi. But this functionary is non-existent.
6. The naiek or naeke is the sacral head of the village who is selected by the manjhi alone. He offers sacrifices to the bongas (gods) at jaharthan on behalf of the whole village. He is the spiritual spokesman.
7. The godet, great or gorait is the paid functionary of the village council who acts as an orderly of the manjhi.
8. The kudum-naek is an assistant to the naiek. He performs special sacrifices to the Sima bonga, spirit of the village boundary, with his own blood. He is given a place in the village council by virtue of the office he holds.
9. Village council is called more-hore or moren-hor.
10. It is deemed to be an abode of the spirit of the dead manjhi of the village, and it is the place where the village council usually meets.
11. The sacred grove at the end of the main street of the village. It is usually situated within the boundary of the village. It consists of tall trees which were once a part of the original forest before the site was cleared for the village. Plants or stones of this place are the manifestations of the village deities.
12. The month of Magh (January-February) is the end of the Santal year.
13. Indigenously prepared rice-beer.
14. Bigha is a traditional unit of measurement of land prevalent in the Hindi region of India. This unit is so loose that the land per bigha

varies from region to region. One standard bigha constitutes about 27, 453 sq. ft. of land.

15. The area of land given to a manjhi-cum-pradhan in lieu of rent collected is known as pradhanijot.
16. The head of the inter-village council or pragana who is non-existent now.
17. The dihiri or dehari, the special priest selected for sacrifices to the forest bonga, presides over the "hunt council" or lo-bir sendra attended by the villagers including the parganait, the manjhi, the jog-manjhi, the naeke, etc. He is the highest official selected by the naeks for the annual "hunt council".
18. The bitlaha is the severest kind of punishment typical to the Santal. It is meant for those offenders who transgress the Santal code of conduct with respect to taboos against sexual relations within the clan or outside the tribe. It has, however, died out.
19. Dharwak is a twig or green leaf of sal tree with its leaf stripped to indicate the number of days after which the bitlaha is to be held. The leaf is folded into a cone to symbolise the penis and another is pinned into a groove to symbolise the vagina.
20. In his study of *Leadership in a Tribal Society*, A.C. Sinha reports that the leadership is gradually shifting from old people to young people in Santal villages of even remote areas.

SUGGESTED READINGS

Apter, D., *The Politics of Modernization*. Chicago : University of Chicago Press, 1965.

Bodding, P.O., *A Santal Dictionary*. Vol. 5, Oslo : A.W. Broggers, Boktrykkeri, 1932-36.

———, "Traditions and Institutions of the Santals,". *Ethnographic Museum Bulletin*. Vol. 6, Oslo, 1942.

Dalton, E.T., *The Santals in Descriptive Ethnology of Bengal*, Calcutta, 1872.

Gautam, M.K., *In Search of an Identity : A Case of the Santals of Northern India*. Leiden : The Netherlands (mimeographed), 1977.

Malinowski, B., *Freedom and Civilization*, London : Allen and Unwin, 1947.

Myrdal, J., *Report from a Chinese Village*, Harmondsworth : Penguin Books, 1964.

Oommen, T.K., "Rural Community Power Structure in India," *Social Forces*, 49(2), 1970. pp. 226-39.

———, "Analysis of Rural Social Change", in M.N. Srinivas et al. (eds.), *Dimensions of Social Change in India*, Delhi : Allied Publishers Pvt. Ltd., 1977, pp. 83-100.

Raichowdhury, P.C., *Santal Parganas District Gazetteer*, Patna, 1965.

Sachchidananda, "Bitlaha : Analysis of a Santal Institution", *Man in India*, Ranchi : Vol. 49, No. 3, 1968. p. 281.

Sinha, A.C., "Leadership in a Tribal Society". *Man in India*, Ranchi : 47(2), Sept., 1967. pp. 222-227.

Singh, J.P. and Singh, R.D. 1976, "Santals : A Socio-Economic Study", *Indian Geographical Studies, Research Bulletin*, No. 6. Patna, 1976. p 39.

FOURTEEN

Sarita Bhowmick

THE ANDAMANESE : THEN AND NOW

ANDAMAN Islands are situated along the eastern part of the Bay of Bengal. They comprise 204 tiny islands covering an area of 2,508 sq. miles. The most important islands are the Great and the Little Andaman. The Nicobar Islands lie to the south. The extreme length and width are 219 and 32 miles.

The Great Andaman is about 140 miles long and is divided into four main separate islands by narrow seawater creeks. These separate islands are the North Andaman, Middle Andaman, Baratang and South Andaman, of which the most important are the Interview Island off the west coast, Ritchie's Archipelage on the east, Rutland Island at the extreme south and the outlying North Sentinel Islands.

The climatic condition is tropical, warm and moist with little variation in temperature. April is the warmest month of the year. The highest and lowest temperature in the islands is 97°F and 63°F. The lowest temperature is recorded in January and February. Rainfall is very high—about 140 to 172 inches annually. The greater part of the rain is during the south-west monsoon, which lasts from the middle of May to the middle of November. The north-east monsoon extends over the other six months of the year, which includes the dry and wet seasons.

Owing to heavy rainfall and high humidity, there is a luxuriant growth of forests all over. The average height of the trees is about 100 ft. Various kinds of creepers cover the stems and hang from these trees.

Demographic Aspects

The original inhabitants of these islands are considered to be among the most primitive living tribes of the world. Ethnically some belong to the Great Negrito race, and some others to the Great Mongoloid race. The total population of the Andaman and Nicobar Islands was 30,971 in 1951. The 1971 census put it at 1,15,133. The population can be divided into four main categories. These are:

1. The Negrito and Mongoloid Aboriginals: The penal settlers who, forgetting their traditional cultures, have evolved a new composite culture by mixing with people from different areas of India and neighbouring British settlements.

2. The settlers after Independence: They are a colonised population. They comprise refugees from East Pakistan (now Bangla Desh), Ceylon and Burma and form a distinct community. The Burmese and Bengali styles of life are evident with very little variation in the traditional patterns of these different racial stocks.

3. There are some other groups who have come mostly as labourers. A section of this population is popularly known as Ranchiwalas, consisting of tribal people from different places in Bihar. Besides the Ranchiwalas, groups of labourers have come from Andhra, Tamil Nadu and Kerala. They are engaged in fishing, agriculture, horticulture and in factories.

4. Lastly, the floating population comprising a fairly wide cross-section of Indians who have come here on posting. Among them are some Punjabi families of ex-servicemen who were sent here for permanent settlement in 1971-72.

Aboriginal Population

The aborigines of the Andaman Islands are the Great Andamanese, the Jarwa, the Onge and the Sentinelis. In the Nicobar Island there are two tribes—the Nicobarese inhabiting mainly the Car Nicobar, and the Shopen living in slightly interior areas of the Great Nicobar.

The Greater Andamanese comprise ten tribes, Charian or Chari, Kora, Tabo or Bo, Yere, Kede, Bea, Balawa, Bojigiyab, Juwai and Kol. Each tribe has its distinctive language or dialect. They are scattered from north to south of the Andamans.

The Jarwas live in the western part of the South Andaman Islands and the Sentinelis in the North Sentinel Island. The Onges live in the Little Andaman Island.

The Great Andamanese and the Onges have been in contact with the non-tribals for a long time. The Jarwas and the Sentinelis are still in isolation owing to their hostility to outsiders. According to the 1971 census, the number of Great Andamanese is 24 and that of the Onges 112. The population of the Jarwa tribe is about 250 and that of the Sentinelis about 100. Accurate population figures for Jarwa and Sentinelis are not known, as no census of these tribes could be taken owing to their hostile nature.

TABLE 14.1
Population of the Tribes

Tribes	1901	1911	1921	1931	1951	1961	1971
Greater Andamanese	625	455	209	90	23	19	24
Onge	672	631	346	250	150	129	112
Jarwa	468	114	—	70	56	56	25
Sentinelis	385	117	117	—	—	50	100

The Greater Andamanese, who once constituted 10 tribes, have now only 24 surviving individuals of hybrid groups, racially, linguistically and culturally. They have lost their distinctive dialect and use the Jeru dialect owing to hybridization. Racially they have also changed from the Negrito to a hybrid group.

Reasons for Decline

All small human populations in a primitive stage, particularly at the hunting and collecting stage, tend to have low fertility and high infant mortality. As a result, their number remains more or less stable. They do not show any rapid increase or decrease in numbers unless there is some natural calamity, war or epidemic. The small populations which live in forest, remote islands and other relatively inaccessible places are highly susceptible to certain tropical diseases because they have developed very little resistance to them owing to lack of contact with outsiders and lack of immunity. When a small population is suddenly exposed to extensive contacts with disease and vices of civilization, it is unable to resist the harmful effects. The population dwindles rapidly and soon faces extinction.

This is precisely what is happening to the aboriginal population of the Andamans. The gradual decrease is due to:

1. Occasional confrontation with the British administration.

2. Japanese bombardment of the islands during the Second World War, which killed a large number of the tribals.

3. Low birth rate.

4. Addiction to alcohol and opium as a result of contact with outsiders. This has decreased their fertility and thus reduced the population.

5. Increase in sterility and high infant mortality owing to venereal infection from outsiders.

6. Diseases like measles, smallpox, bronchitis, pulmonary infection, mumps and influenza.

In early times, no welfare measures were taken for the betterment of these aboriginal people or to check their decline. The British wanted to civilise them, but not in a planned way. So we find an alarming decrease in their population. For lack of adequate numbers, they cannot maintain their traditional ways of life, and by contact with outsiders they have gradually moved away from their core culture. This has brought about a transformation in almost all aspects of their lives.

After independence, some welfare work has been done among them by the government. In 1949, the forest department collected the Andamanese people by combing various islands and settled them in a somewhat unplanned manner in the Bluff Island to save them from rapid extinction.

In 1970, a rehabilitation scheme was drawn up and implemented by the Andaman and Nicobar administration for the protection and proper settlement of the Greater Andamanese tribes. They were colonised on the Strait Island.

The Greater Andamanese Tribe

Originally the Greater Andamanese constituted 10 tribes distributed in the North, Middle and South Andaman. They practise a food-gathering economy, i.e., hunting wild pigs and other animals in the jungle, catching dugong, turtle and crustaceans (crabs, crayfish and prawn), collecting molluscs from sea and salt-water creeks, and honey, edible roots, fruit and vegetables. For hunting and fishing, they depend entirely on the bow and arrow, and occasionally on the spear. For capturing turtle, dugong and large fish, they use the harpoon from their canoe and for collection of food products they use a digging stick. The adze is used for scooping out honeycombs and collecting molluscs.

They do not know how to make fire. So they always preserve fire for use. They roast or boil the food collected from the sea or the forest.

The Andamanese are a semi-nomadic people owing to their food-gathering economy. According to Radcliff Brown, the coast-dwellers are more nomadic than forest-dwellers. For their rapid transportation, the coast-dwellers use the dugout canoe. It is of two types: a small one with an outrigger propelled by pedals or by a '*pal*' (sail), and a large one without an outrigger and propelled by oars.

We find three types of camps among them :

1. Communal hut or chief camp or permanent camp consisting of eight huts used for 10 or more years. There is an open place for communal dances.
2. Temporary camp built by them when they are compelled to leave the permanent camp owing to the death of any member. It is used for two to three months.
3. Hunting camp or simple leanto used by them for three to four days.

They use bamboo barrels as water vessels and different types of shells as drinking vessels or dishes.

The Andamanese go about virtually naked. Men wear a rope-girdle of hibiscus fibre. The women wear a sort of small apron made of *Mimusops littoralis* leaves. Every married woman wears a belt of pandanus leaves. It is taken off only when replaced by a new one.

They use ornaments made of shell, bone, and leaves attached to a string. These are worn round the neck, head, knee or wrist. The favourite shell of the Great Andamanese is the *Dentalium octogonum*. Besides, they use clay to paint their bodies. There are three kinds of clay used for decoration: grey—common clay (*odu*); whitefine clay (*tol·odu*)—these two are used by them in everyday life—and red paint *(keyip)* made of burnt iron-oxide and animal fat. It is used on ceremonial occasions, like initiation, mourning, and to decorate the corpse.

Social Life

The Greater Andamanese are divided into tribes on the basis of language. Each tribe is subdivided into a number of local groups, each of which is land-owning. Besides, they recognise division into coast and forest-dwellers on the basis of region. Each local group consists of different individual families having 40 to 50 persons of all ages. The nuclear family consists of the husband, wife and their unmarried children—own or adopted.

According to Radcliff Brown, the average area occupied by each local group is 16 square miles, but some groups have larger or smaller areas than this.

The Andamanese are strictly monogamous. A man may marry in his own local group or tribe or in another group or tribe. Marriage is forbidden between near consanguinal relatives. It is arranged by older men and women. The marriage itself is held always in the evening. On the appointed date, the bride and the bridegroom, with their parents, friends and relatives gather in the dancing ground. The two parties sit separately. The bride and the bridegroom are lectured loudly on their duties in married life. It is followed by instruction by an elderly person. Then the bridegroom goes and sits beside the bride. The relatives and friends weep loudly. The groom attempts to run away. He is restrained by his friends and an elderly man put the bride's and the bridegroom's hands round each others neck. He then makes the bridegroom sit in the bride's lap. This completes the ceremony. It is followed by mass dancing. The next day the bride and the bridegroom are painted with white clay by their friends. They start their life in a new hut especially prepared for them. Marriage by love is not infrequent. Divorce is not popular. A widow may remarry if she wishes. A childless widower may remarry his deceased wife's younger sister.

Birth

At the time of delivery, the husband and the woman's female friends attend on her to the best of their ability. The umbilical cord is severed by a sharp piece of cane or bamboo strip or cyrena shell and buried in the jungle. The newborn is washed with cold water and its skin gently scraped with a shell. After delivery, warm water is given to the mother to drink. She is given different types of food except meat. During its infancy, the child remains in the care of the mother. Children are great favourite among them. They are not only nursed by the own parents, but by every one in the local group. A woman will often suckle the children of other women.

The baby is named before it is born. So the names are common to both sexes.

Death and Burial

The Greater Andamanese believe that disease and death are caused by the spirits of the jungle and the sea.

When a person dies, all the peoples sit around the body and weep loudly. Adult males smear the corpse with mud. Then the women shave its head and decorate it with red paint. The body is then tied with the knees bent and reaching the chin, and the face resting sideways. An acyrena shell is placed in its closed hand. The body is wrapped in a sleeping mat and tied with rope. Then all go to the spot selected for the burial.

There are two ways of disposing of a dead body : (1) burial in a grave dug with the adze and the digging stick. The body is untied and a bow and arrow are left with the corpse; and (2) the body is left on a platform built in a tree. The *Ficus laccifera* tree is mainly used for this. The body is placed facing east. A baby is buried beneath the fireplace with a shell containing its mother's milk. The camp is deserted for three months after the death of a person until the mourning period is over.

At the end of the mourning period, first, the bones are dug up and decorated with red paint. A piece of a bone is worn round the neck by the chief mourner. Secondly, a dance is held in which all mourners join.

Political Organisation

These people have no political organisation. There is a headman or the chief, called *Maia Igla*. He is assisted by the elders or sub-chiefs in organising meetings and the welfare of the local group, and in directing the hunting or fishing party and in choosing land for habitation. After the death of a chief, the deputy chief succeeds him. Social status depends on the skill in hunting and fishing, and on the generosity and hospitality of the individual. The chiefs and the elders and their wives enjoy a superior status in every respect. There is no code of punishment for crime.

The religious beliefs of the Andamanese are animistic. They believe in the spirits of the jungle, sea, storm. Those who possess supernatural power are given a special position in society. They think that earthquakes are caused by the spirits of the ancestors. They worship the ancestors also.

Strait Island

After the monumental work of Man and Radcliff, Brown, attempts have been made by some Indian anthropologists to study the Andamanese tribes. Dr. R.S. Mann of the Anthropological Survey of India has done extensive work among them on which some published material is available. Prof. L.P. Vidyarthi took his students to the island for an exhaustive study. He also has written on some aspects of the island and their people.

The Greater Andamanese colonised the Strait Island in 1970. The island is situated in the Middle Andaman and is about 35 miles from the north-eastern side of Port Blair. It has an area of 1.2 square miles of which 420 acres have been set apart for settlement. One-eighth of this island is hilly and the rest flat land. The land is suitable for gardening and cultivation. It was selected for the resettlement of the Andamanese by the Andaman Nicobar administration and the Anthropological Survey of India. They taught the settlers to grow vegetable and fruit and to domesticate animals. So in the island we now find 750 coconut trees, of which 250 are yielding fruit, and some guava and papaya trees. There is a piggery having 30 animals. There are domestic dogs also. Besides there are deer and luxuriant trees in the jungle, and a variety of fish in the sea.

Inter-island communication is by boat and ship. A ferry service runs twice a week. When the tribals visit Port Blair, they live in the Adibasera, a guest-house constructed for them in 1976.

Population Structure

In 1857 there were 5,000 Andamanese (Radcliff 1920). But in 1906 the population came down to 500; in 1952 to 32, in 1971 to 24; and in 1978 to 23 individuals only. The gradual decimation of these communities has resulted from diseases caused by contact with outsiders and other reasons mentioned earlier.

The population comprises two-thirds males and one-third females. Diseases and disparity in the sex ratio have reduced their vitality and fertility, as also the size of the population. The diseases they generally suffer from are shown in Table 14.2.

TABLE 14.2

Diseases of the Andamanese

Sl. No.	Name	No. affected
1.	Pulmonary tuberculosis	9
2.	Venereal	2
3.	Bronchitis	1
4.	Heart disese	2
5.	Dermatitis	1
6.	Giardia	1
7.	Ascaris	1
8.	Trichuris trichera	2

Almost all males and a few females are opium addicts. Among them 12 are seriously addicted, and 15 are addicted to chewing tobacco.

Demographic details of their marital status, family structure, types of families and literacy are shown in Tables 14.3, 14.4, 14.5 and 14.6.

Among the total number of population of 23, nine are females and 14 males.

The married males belong to the age group 15-20 and married females to the age group 11-15. Among the seven married women, two are childless and one has reached menopause. So we find the shortage of female population in this community.

TABLE 14.3

Analysis of Population on the basis of Age and Sex

Sl. No.	Age-group	Males	Females	Total
1.	0–15	6	3	9
2.	16—30	3	1	4
3.	31—45	—	3	3
4.	46—60	3	2	5
5.	61—above	2	—	2
	Total	14	9	23

TABLE 14.4

Marital Status

Unmarried		Married		Divorced		Widow	Widower
Male	Female	Male	Female	Male	Female		
7	2	4	4	—	1	2	3

TABLE 14.5

Type of Families

Sl. No.	Type of Family	No.
1.	Nuclear family	4
2.	Broken family	4

TABLE 14.6

Literacy

S. No.	Age-group	Literate		Illiterate	
		Male	Female	Male	Female
1.	0—15	3	1	3	2
2.	16—30	—	—	3	1
3.	31—45	—	—	—	3
4.	46—60	—	—	3	2
5.	60–above	—	—	2	—

Widow marriage is popular owing to shortage of females. But, according to Man, "it is by no means unusual for a man, even though he be young at the time of his wife's death, to remain a widower for her sake for many years or even till death, but widows generally marry again when the prescribed term has passed."

There are altogether eight tribal families. The number of their members varies from two to five.

Of the eight families, four are nuclear and the other four broken as one of the married partners is dead or has deserted. Among the four broken families, in two cases the husbands are dead and the widows are living with their children. In one case, a widower is living with an adopted girl and in another one with his son and divorced sister.

Of the 23 individuals in the Strait Island, only four are literate. Among them, three are male and one female in the age-group of 0-15.

Material Culture

After their resettlement, the Greater Andamanese have been provided with new type of huts, free ration, training in cultivation and domestication of animals, clothing and a well-equipped dispensary with a compounder for their medical treatment. For their formal education a social worker and his wife are posted there. They have also been given a sewing machine. All expenses are borne by the administration and the Anthropological Survey. A social worker trained by the Adimjati Sevak Sangha lives there with his wife and four children.

The Adamanese are now provided with corrugated-tin roofed houses, cemented floors and wooden walls. By the side of the houses, a tarmac road has been constructed. At the end of the houses, there is a piggery, three pucca wells for drinking water and one communal hall for meetings. For subsistence they get free ration, i.e., 130 kg of rice, 100 kg of atta, spices and cooking oil per month. Besides, they get tea on special occasions and the women with babies get milk. For fishing they have been given small and large nets and three boats. The social worker, Mr. Bhola Prasad Soni, gives them training in growing fruits and vegetables. They are now producing sweet potato, wild chillie, papaya, pineapple, sugarcane, etc. They sell coconut and papaya to ferry passengers and fish and tortoise to the Bengali families in exchange for rice, wheat and pulses.

In the household they now use utensils made of aluminium, and buckets and mugs made of ploythene. Besides, everyone gets 50 rupees per month except the *Raja Loka* i.e. the king of their group, who gets Rs. 150. The *Biye*, another elderly person, gets Rs. 100 for his other needs, like ornaments, plastic beads, bangles, opium and tobacco.

Every year the government give two shirts, two lungis and two *ghenzi* to males and a lungi and blouse to females. One mosquito net is given to each family. They still wear shell necklaces and decorate their body with 'odu' or common clay.

For transportation, they use the canoes given by the administration. Of the three canoes, one is used by the Raja Loka exclusively and the other two by the rest of the community. Now they are receiving various things like torch, radio etc., as presents from outsiders.

But because of lack of practice and the pressure of the culture of surroundings, they are fast losing their skill in hunting, fishing and making implements for their economy.

Social Life

They have now no local groups or dialects which were once unique features among them. They speak the Jeru language among themselves and Hindi with outsiders.

The Andamanese are monogamous. Marriage is arranged by the elders. After the consent of the elders, the selected male and the female live together in a separate hut.

Most babies are born in hospital or under medical assistance. They have no pollution period taboo on food, but the mother of the baby takes rest until she is completely all right.

The child is named before its delivery or during the pregnancy period. For this reason names are common to males and females as the sex of the child is not known before its birth.

Death and Burial

When a person dies all family members weep loudly. Then they decorate the body and carry it to the place of burial. They have no separate burial ground. They do not leave their huts during the mourning period. After its end, they do not bring the bones of the dead or arrange a communal dance and feast as they used to do before. But they occasionally go to the burial place and leave tobacco leaves and water there for the use of the departed soul.

Political Structure

They have no written social rules and regulations. But for personal and general welfare and trouble-free journey, certain conventions are followed by everyone. Elders are obeyed by all.

In the Strait Island, the Loka has the status of a king. He is respected by all. No crime has been reported among the small population of the Island. When clothes or garments are given by the administration the Loka gets the first preference.

They believe in animism and ancestor worship. They also believe that the two monsoons—north-east and south-west—embody different spirits and when the monsoon blows it is the expression of the anger of its spirit.

The Andamanese of the Strait Island now have no communal hut, communal dances, feasts or festivals. They have forgotten most of their primitive culture and traditions owing to depopulisation and contact with outsiders as also owing to various schemes of rehabilitation being implemented for their welfare and survival. These schemes have changed their habits and ways of life considerably, and are the main causes which have broken their social cohesion and traditions.

We find a three fold transformation among the surviving 23 Greater Andamanese people : first at the physical level; secondly in material culture, and lastly in their social organisation and social environment.

Physical Level

From 1859 to 1862, the British established friendly relations with the Andamanese. Since then the Andamanese have occasionally come into contact with other people. The process is continuing to date. Because of these contacts and interaction, the Andamanese have gradually lost their ethnic identity.

At first they were purely Negritto in origin. But now their physical features show Mongoloid characteristics together with Negritto ones. Of the 23 survivors, four men and five women have typical Negritto features. The physical features of the remaining 14, i.e. four female and 10 male, are of mixed origin. They have contracted various communicable diseases—the main cause of their depopulation.

Material Culture

Regarding material culture and economy, they do not practise any of their traditional economic activity like hunting, fishing and collecting wild products. All their expenses for housing, food, clothing, medical treatment are paid for. So they show less interest in pursuing their traditional economy. They go fishing occasionally for recreation.

The rapid transformation in their economic life has brought a rapid change in their material life also. To sum up :

They use aluminium or enamelled utensils and polythene or plastic ware instead of various types of shells and bamboo pieces, which they used as utensils earlier.

The males wear trousers, shirt and the *ghenzi* instead of the waist-girdle of hibiscus fibre. The women wear lungi and blouse instead of the belt of pandanus leaves. The women have taken to the Burmese dress because of earlier contacts with the Karens. The garments are given to them by the administration. The women wear plastic bangles and necklaces together with shell necklaces and bangles. They still decorate their body ceremonially, but the designs are not as of old. Some men wear a wrist-watch and carry a torch.

They now live in well constructed huts instead of Leanto type communal and temporary huts. Their settlement has metalled roads and a communal hall for dancing and recreation. They have a piggery, dispensary and co-operative stores. They use mosquito-nets instead of repellant juice of leaves.

For transportation from one place to another of the island, ships ply twice a week now. Besides, canoes have also been given to them for short-distance transport and fishing. They traditionally used to make and repair their canoes, but now they have become very lazy and leave the task to the administration.

They previously used to roast or boil their food. Now they prepare it with oil and spices. The food has also more variety.

They take rice, wheat, vegetables, spices, fishes, tea, tobacco, opium etc. instead of only game, honey and tubers and fish.

The social organisation of the Greater Andamanese has completely broken down because of the depletion of population. They are only 23 in number now. As such, they cannot perform their traditional festivals and observe traditional customs. Their social environment has completely changed and so have their social customs, rituals, ceremonies and festivals. But some traditional ceremonies like turtle hunting are still practised. On the debit side we find that :

1. The 10 tribes which constituted the Greater Andamanese population are all extinct now. Only 23 hybrid individuals remain. They have no local groups.

2. They speak only Jeru now instead of different dialects used by different groups earlier.

3. Most marriage rituals are not practised now.

4. They have no birth taboos. They take medical and hospital assistance. Most of the babies are born and taken care of in hospital.

5. They do not leave their huts during the death-pollution period which they did earlier.

6. At the end of the mourning period, they do not collect the bones of the dead. The traditional communal dance and feast are also not observed.

7. For recreation they use radio sets.

On the credit side are only two items :

1. Observance of the name-giving ceremony and paying due respect to the elders as before.

2. Religious beliefs are not affected by various present-day pressures.

Thus it is clear from the above that the Andamanese still live in their traditional ecology with little change to make life easier and comfortable, attempts towards which are being made by the administration. The Adimjati Sevak Sangha is taking keen interest and an ex-military man, Bakhtawar Singh, is looking after the welfare schemes that the administration has introduced. A multi-purpose co-operative society has been organised. The administration gives a monthly allowance, both in cash and kind, to all tribals. There is a dispensary with one compounder. In emergency cases, patients are taken to Port Blair. Every year the tribals are given garments free of cost.

In conclusion it can be said that the Great Andamanese, one of the world's most primitive communities, are on the verge of total extinction. In fact, the people around them are seeing them die stoically despite all facilities given to them. One thing is very clear : that a food-gathering, semi-nomadic hunting tribe, which faced many adverse situations in its long history, has not been able to come to terms with modern progress. Once they enjoyed nature's bounty and were the real pagans. But now, with facilities from all sides, they are the worst victims.

One question arises in this context. Is it their docile nature, coupled with unrestricted external penetration, which has brought about their extinction? There are the hostile Jarawas on the other hand who are trying to resist extinction by isolation and hostility. The administration, social workers and scientists can learn many lessons from the historical transformation of these people, which is still continuing.

SUGGESTED READINGS

Brown, R., *The Andamanese Islanders*, 1943.

Ganguli, Pranab, "The Negritos of Little Andaman Island", *Indian Museum Bulletin* Vol. X, No. 1, 1975.

Man, E.R., *The Aborigines of Andaman Islands.*

Mann, R.S., "Depopulation Among Andaman and Nicobar Aborigines—an Analysis", *Journal of Social Research*, XIV, No. VI, 1978.

Sen, P.K., *Land and People of the Andamans*, 1962.

Vidyarthi, L.P., "Cultural Diversities in the Andaman and Nicobar Islands : A Preliminary Report", "Development Plans of the Tribes of Andaman and Nicobar Islands—An Action Oriented Report", *Journal of Social Research*, Vol. XIX, No. 11, September, 1976.

FIFTEEN

Bhupinder Singh

DYNAMICS OF DEVELOPMENT
The Participative Perspective

THE SAORA, one of the major tribes of Orissa, occupy the remote, hilly and inaccessible areas of Ganjam and Koraput districts. They have had a village council comprising mostly traditional leadership. For about one and a half centuries before Independence, they remained subjects of Oriya Muthaheads *de facto*, though of the British Government *de jure*. They have been exploited in various fields by non-tribals. Since the introduction of the Panchayati Raj system after Independence, the Saora leadership has made attempts from time to time to secure positions of power, but with little success. Their representation has remained poor in the various tiers of the Panchayati Raj system and little influence has been exercised by the tribe on the development programmes. In this paper the findings of a study to ascertain the Saora notion of development, their perception of political processes and framework, the extent of involvement of members of the tribes, and more particularly their leaders, in the development effort are presented. The view is taken, notwithstanding the odds against, that Saora leadership is on the threshold. Suggestions for their active participation and involvement in planning and implementation of development programmes have been made.

The Saora

In the uplands of the two adjoining districts Koraput and Ganjam of the State of Orissa, there live a tribe which may be comparatively unknown outside but which according to historical surmises, occupied a large tract of the country in the hoary past. The Saora is one of the major tribes of Orissa, with a total population of 3,42,757 as per the 1971 Census. However, while all the hill Saora are found only in the aforesaid two districts, the Sabara, Sabar and others not speaking the Saora dialect are found in other districts. The Saora population in the two districts is 1,47,621 or about 43 per cent of the tribe's entire population in the State. The census figures show that it declined from 3.26 lakhs in 1941 to 3.12 lakhs in 1961, whereas in the next decade, 1961-71, it registered increase to 3.43 lakhs or by 9 per cent. Its increase may be compared to the percentage increase in the State of 20.08 for the entire scheduled tribe population and 25.05 for the total population, for the same period.

The hill Saora live in the hill ranges of Eastern Ghats, the highest peaks of which exceed 3,000 feet above sea level, though commonly their height is between 1000 feet and 2,500 feet above sea level. Numerous streams and rivulets flow down from the eastern and western flanks of these hill ranges, the better known being the Mahendra Tanya and the Vamsadhara. Even now these hills are well-forested, though they have been subject to axe-cultivation over a long period of time. Among the forest species, sal (Shorea Robusta) abounds, the other species being Ptercarpus Maraupius (Piasal), Terminalia Tomentosa (Asan), Pongamia Glatera (Karanj), Tamarind, Mohua, etc. Communications are difficult and the preponderant part of both human and goods traffic moves over roads which are sparsely laid out and hardly touch the interior areas. An old railway line passes through the plains area and serves chiefly the purpose of export of local goods outside and import of outside goods.

From the historical stand-point, the heart of the Saora country remained untouched; around, in the plains on both the sides, small zamindaris grew and spent themselves in feuds with each other. In the early decades of the 19th century, the British power exerted itself to bring about amity among the warring principalities and in the process pressed their troops right up to the hills to ensure that the Saora tribe was not used by the numerous factions or that the tribe itself did not make periodic incursions into the plains in search of plunder or to seek reprisals. By the middle of the 19th century, peace had descended on the area. The agents in the hills of the erstwhile zamindars became intermediaries between the Saora and the British Government not only for collection of land revenue, but for many other matters. They were called "Mutha-heads" after *Mutha*, indicating a territory, or *Bissoyia*. The Mutha-heads acted for over a century not only as intermediaries but as members of a ruling class *vis-a-vis* the Saora, as their socio-political leaders. With the advent of Independence came the abolition of the intermediary system and gradually the Mutha-heads began to lose their power and prestige. The establishment and growth of the statutory Gram Panchayat system dealt a severe blow to their authority and influence.

Up in the hills, a Saora village is made up of linear streets, often irregular, more or less conforming to the existing slopes. The houses in the streets are built cheek by jowl and touch each other. Many of the villages are homogeneous in the sense that the inhabitants may, predominantly, be Saora. Another community living in these hills is the scheduled caste community called the "Pano" in the Ganjam district and the "Dom" in the Koraput district. The members of this community often live in separate villages, as Puttasingi village, or where there is a mixture the two communities live in separate quarters in a village. Thirdly, there is the Oriya community of comparatively recent settlement. The example of Gumma village may be cited where the Pano live in one quarters and the Oriyas live in a different quarters. It is remarkable that despite their co-existence for a long time, the identity of separate villages or separate quarters in the same village has been retained.

Basically, the Saora are agriculturists. They practise both settled agriculture and shifting cultivation. In the hills and valleys, settled agriculture is characterised by an outstanding feature i.e. terrace cultivation. The terraces have been built on the slopes,throughgenerations ofhard labour and skill. The chief advantage is that while making full use of the available hill slopes they enable the waters of perennial hill streams to be tapped for cultivation throughout the yearas they descend from one terrace to another. The terrace walls have been rivetted and packed with stones and boulders which have stood the test of time. Old records suggest that independent observers have marvelled at the skill and ingenuity which have carved out the terraces. Besides terrace cultivation, the valleys have been utilised for plain cultivation. The chief crop grown is paddy, followed by millets. Shifting cultivation has been practised by the Saora since olden times. The foresters and administrators have often lamented that the Saora have been responsible for the denudation of the mountain and hill slopes. Nevertheless, even that Saora family which has adequate terrace and plain land does not consider its agriculture complete unless it is able to undertake shifting cultivation on a strip of land. Settled and shifting cultivation appear to be complementary to each other. The crops of shifting cultivation, namely small millets, pulses and oil-seeds are not only food crops, but some part is utilised also as cash or barter crops. In fact, shifting cultivation has made deep inroads into the economic, social and religious life of the Saora. Apart from agriculture, collection of minor forest produce like tamarind, Mohua, Karanj seed, etc., is another important avocation, but this activity falls more to the lot of women and children. Animal husbandry is not important; in fact, milk is taboo in certain parts of the Saora country. It deserves mention, however, that some Saora tracts have specialised for many decades in horticulture, particularly cultivation of citrus fruit.

Socially, the Saora have no exogamous totemic clans. The main exogamous unit is the extended family descended from a common male ancestor called "Birinda", based on patrilineage. Birinda is equivalent to lineage. It comprises a few families related to each other by blood. Usually, more male ancestors among the Birinda members are traced back to not more than two or three generations. An interesting fact about Birinda is that when a woman marries, she retains her affiliation to the Birinda of her origin. Another, that the Saora are polygamous; when a man dies, a step-son may marry his step-mother, provided there is no serious incompatibility.

Earlier, the Saora villages were unilineal in composition. Each village reclaimed some land in the near-by hill slope and the members of the lineage parcelled out among themselves plots of land which they could cultivate and manage. With the increase of population and inter-village migration, the villages have become large and multi-lineal in composition.

Saora aristocracy consists of the families of the secular

chief and, where they exist, of the "Buyya" priests. Secular chiefs are known by various names, the most common being "Gomango". "Mondal" may be the head on the Ganjam side, but may also be the Gomango's assistant. The Gomangoand the Buyya are not only the most wealthy but in the past they were recognised by the government and used to receive an official turban which was greatly prized. The Gomango was the most important as the secular head of the village and an intermediary between the government and the people; it was by his orders that the villagers went to work for officials or Bissoyis. In Koraput district, he was the arbiter in matrimonial disputes and had the final say in the allocation of rent.

In the distant past, when the Saora society was of the unilineal-bands multi-family aggregates, it might have had the characteristics of an egalitarian society. When the population increased and when the Saora changed their migratory to sedentary habits, villages grew and they settled down therein on permanent basis.

The Saora had and still have in their society a well-organised political system. For each Saora village there was a village head-man, the Gomango, a religious head-man, the Buyya, and few assistants such as Dissari (astrologer), Gunia (Shaman or doctor diviner), Barik (messenger). By virtue of their knowledge in their respective fields, they wielded authority in the society. The head-man had considerable power of maintenance of law and order, peace and good government in a village. The other secular and religious officials at the village level were guardians of the socio-cultural, economic and religious norms of the Saora society. These influential persons were revered, respected and their offices were by and large, hereditary.

With elaboration of political organisation in course of time, the egalitarian character of the society was modified. The present Saora society conforms to the characteristics of rank society (Fried, 1967, p. 100). The Gomango is a position which is not occupied by a person other than an elder male member of the Gomango family in order of seniority. The position of the Buyya is similar in respect of succession. Although the Gomango and the Buyya are men of influence and wield authority and power, they are not authoritarian in their decisions on problems concerning village affairs. The decisions taken at the village meeting are arrived at in consultation with village elders.

Religion plays an important part in the life of the Saora. There is hardly any activity in the village which is beyond the purview of the spirits keeping a watch over them. Transactions of landed property, construction of new houses, agricultural operations, marriage ceremony, detection of crime must have appropriate religious rites performed. Super-natural sanctions operate. The machinery of social control plays a significant part in promoting conformity with accepted moral standards of the contemporary society. Failure to comply with the ethos and value-system arouses the wrath of the super-human beings and creates conditions for divine punishment during the life-time of the culprits. The Saora religion is both a drain and an incentive on his economy. The sacrifice of animals, e.g. buffalo, pig, fowl designed to appease the deities on the occasion of disease or death etc. followed by feasting of food and drink, cost a lot and the Saora is not usually in a position to defray the expenses in cash. He has to go to the local Dom to buy the animal on the promise to pay in kind at the time of the next harvest. Usually, the tribal is unable to extricate himself out of indebtedness. The ceremonies also make serious inroads into the time of the family or families. On the credit side, religion is an incentive to produce more in agriculture so that its demands can be met.

In the recent Saora history of which we have some records "Fituris" or minor rebellions have occurred chiefly against the Dom or Pano community whenever exploitation reached an intolerable limit. The Dom, the cleverer of the two, being in contact with the outside world and having a higher literacy percentage, have also been acting as intermediaries between the Saora and external agencies like the government, the traders, the contractors, etc. As middle-men, it has been their tendency to exploit the Saora. When the exploitation became unbearable, the Saora retaliated spontaneously by organising raids of mobs on Dom village or quarters. The "Fituris", therefore, have been spontaneous violent outbursts of protest against socio-economic oppression.

National Policy and Tribal Development

Before Independence, the State functioned more or less as an agency for collection of revenue and maintenance of law and order. The concepts of public good and advancement were scarcely relevant. After attainment of Independence in 1947, the national government has been turning more and more towards development and welfare of the people. Rational economy is being geared towards increasing production, higher gross national product and higher per capita income. Experience in the first four five-year plans indicated that effort for a general rise in standards did not concomitantly ensue in equitous distribution of the national income among the various sections. Hence, as a matter of deliberate policy, greater effort has been directed towards advancement of the weaker and poorer sections of the society. In this context, during the fifth Five Year Plan period, a new strategy has been launched for tribal development. Areas of tribal concentration in the country i.e., with more than 50 per cent of tribal population have been located and with the help of larger investments and physical effort, the aim has been to bridge the gap of tribal and non-tribal economic disparities. Quite often, the ultimate objective has been spelt out as bringing the tribals to the national main-stream. The concept of tribal sub-Plan within the Fifth Five Year Plan envisages pooling of all available fiscal and personnel resources and making use of them for a total integrated effort. In States having substantial areas of tribal concentration, units have been identified for such effort each comprised of a few Community Development Blocks. These have been called Integrated Tribal Development Projects (ITDPs). An ITDP has become a focal point in the planning and implementation process. The lowest administrative unit of execution is the Community Development (or Tribal Development) Block, in existence in the country for the past two decades and more. In the organisational structure of the CD (or TD) Block, the team leader called the Block Development Officer (BDO) is assisted by a number of extension officers in each of the fields like agriculture, animal husbandry, cooperation, industries, education, engineering, etc. The grass-root workers have been the village level workers, so far multipurpose but now being split up into two groups, namely multipurpose and agriculture-specialist, under the recent Benor plan. Needless to say, the most vital link in the entire chain is the basal, namely that of VLW.

Tribal Mosaic

The mental and psychological make-up of a people is composed, *inter alia*, of their historical experiences and this is an aspect which, notwithstanding requisite empathy, few outsiders can sense and share. The ethos of the tribal world sets it off against the stereo-typed modernity of the non-tribal world; within it, there is a rich mosaic of cultural and socio-economic diversity among the different tribal communities. The individuality of one tribal makes it conspicuously different from another, being heightened by isolation and other environmental factors, leading to development of distinctive lines of evolution. Cognisance has to be taken, therefore, of the personality of each tribe for determining the course of its growth and development. It is expressed in one way through participation of the prominent members of the tribal community in the forums charged with programme formulation and watching implementation.

Participation in Development

In fact, peoples' participation has been an indivisible element of the original community development concept. Statutory Gram Panchayats were introduced and a Sarpanch became the leader of elected representatives, for a group of villages. The Sarpanches became members of the Block-level Committee and one of them was chosen as the Chairman of the Committee known as Panchayat Samiti. Thus, the Panchayati Raj system was built into the community development movement.

Mention has been made earlier of the traditional political organisation in the Saora country. The Gomango, the Buyya, the Dissari and other hereditary functionaries along with some village elders formed the village council which took decisions in politico-socio-economo-religious spheres. Outside this indigenous matrix, came in the Oriya Bissoyis or Mutha-heads, the overlords of the earlier part of nineteenth century who became intermediaries in the later part. The elite of the area, "the political class" of Mosca (Parry, 1969, p. 30), comprised of the traditional Saora village leader as well as the Bissoyis operating in the background of an almost egalitarian society, have been turning their attention to the new institutions which have opened up new political and economic vistas. But, often, the Bissoyis, the Pano and other non-tribals have captured posts or positions at the Panchayat, Panchayat Samiti and Zilla Parishad levels, since reservation of seats does not obtain for those bodies.

The Saora Perception of Development and Political Culture

At this stage, it is worthwhile taking stock of the concept of development as envisaged by the members of the Saora tribe and comparing it with the notions of development entertained by the State. In an investigation conducted in the area, it appeared that in the view of both the Saora and the non-Saora, the components of development in order of decreasing importance were irrigation, education, roads, agriculture, drinking water and electricity. They thought that for an ideal village land, irrigation and agriculture were the basic essentials, followed by schools, health institutions and drinking water facilities. In an area which comprises of uplands and plains, terrace, shifting and plains cultivation, the value of irrigation seems to have acutely realised. The level of literacy is very low being 10.19 per cent as per the 1971 Census; it is for this reason, perhaps, that education is prized highly.

Investigation conducted revealed disconcertingly that about one-third of the respondents had not heard of the Panchayati Raj institutions and that only 8 per cent among them had heard of five year plans. But a redeeming feature was that a high percentage among them could tell the names of the Sarpanch and the local MLA and were familiar with national leaders like Gandhiji and Jawaharlal Nehru. Further, the interesting fact emerged that about two-thirds of the respondents had voted in the Panchayat, State and national elections, indicating substantial evidence of political interest. But only a handful among them stood for election. Nine out of 172 Saora respondents contested forward membership, Sarpanchship and Chairmanship of Panchayat Samiti, out of whom seven lost and two won. A majority of the respondents were not clear in their thinking about the purpose and functions of Panchayati Raj institutions; quite a number thought that they were meant for distribution of Taccavi (agriculture) loans and financial assistance. That the links between the Saora mass and the Panchayati Raj bodies are tenuous is also borne out from the fact that persons who were elected as peoples' representatives to the Panchayati Raj bodies were mostly the politically-oriented non-Saora. Not one out of eleven Chairmen of the Panchayat Samities in the Saora country was a Saora and out of the 159 Sarpanches in these Blocks only 40 were Saora. This points to the necessity for extending reservation (already available in respect of seats of the Legislative Assembly) to the district, Block and Panchayat tiers.

In the sub-Plan areas, during the Fifth Five Year Plan period ITDPs have been set up and committees at ITDP level comprised of officials and non-officials to advise on planning, supervise implementation and effect coordination have been constituted. At the State level, in some States a sub-committee of the Cabinet has been set up to guide and direct tribal development. The detailed pattern varies from State to State. But the fact remains that non-official participation, particularly of the Saora, has been below par. The objective ultimately is that the plans should grow from the village level and spiral up towards Block, ITDP, district and state levels. The plans must be a reflection of people's needs and aspirations and progressive movement towards that ought to be made. The views and findings of the Asoka Mehta Committee on Panchayati Raj Institutions are relevant in this regard.

The conditions in the Saora country call for attention. In the historical past, through its leadership, the Saora tribe gave expression to its thought-trends, *inter alia*, in the form of "fituris" or minor rebellions, at a point in time and geography the tribe could not contain the severity of oppression and exploitation by other communities. These have continued, in one form or another, during the post-Independence era also, (Das, N. 1967-68, pp. 45-52). At the same time, inevitably, the members of the tribe got involved in the community development and Panchayati Raj movements. But, as we have seen, after more than two decades, their representation in the different hierarchical tiers has been rather feeble. Nevertheless, it will not do to minimise the impact of these movements as well as that of the continuous, ostensibly imperceptible, interaction which has gone on these decades between the tribe and external agencies.

In the early seventies, a violent Marxist-Leftist movement called the Naxalite movement swept through parts of the country. It was a traumatic experience. The larger part of the Saora country was engulfed in it. Apparently, it has not left any traces behind and it seems that it failed to strike roots. But this may be deceptive and it is possible that the impress it left behind in the minds particularly of the leading members of the community may not be easily erased.

The Government of Orissa launched a scheme called purchase-sale-fair-price shops (PSFS) scheme in the mid-sixties. The purpose was to purchase from the tribals their surplus commodities and sell to them their consumer necessities at fair prices. Encouraged by its result, a co-operative society called the Tribal Development Co-operative Society (TDCS) was formed in 1972 which took over the shops under the aforesaid scheme. Subsequently, the Society has been converted into a Corporation and has been designated as Tribal Development Co-operative Corporation (TDCC). The impact of the scheme has been highly beneficial in parts of the Saora country. There are some shops functioning under the Corporation which have become a veritable bee hive of activity, particularly those which have on their staff Saora employees. The example of the branch at Badakalakote near Gumma stands out in this connection (Singh, 1977, pp. 229-243). There is a Saora youth employed as salesman in this shop and he has infused tremendous amount of life and energy into it. The shop attracts crowds of Saora men and women carrying basket-loads of tamarind and Mohua on their heads filing through woods and dales. It is a refreshing experience to witness the scene. In stark contrast, the shop at Jaltar, hardly 10 miles away across the country, presents a dismal and disheartening picture, chiefly on account of the apathy of the employees there who are all non-Saora. But one may hasten to add that the popularity of the Badakalakote shop is not only due to Saora elements in employment there. It is also due to the fact that the philosophy of the TDCC is supported and backed by some elements of Saora leadership.

The Leadership

It may bear emphasis that resentment against exploitation has run through the Saora society as historical undercurrent and "Fituris" have been spontaneous release of protests against exploitation. It would appear that, in the past, after the upsurge of each such protest, things settled back with perhaps little difference to the socio-economic order. In other words, no action programme followed on the heels of the open revolt. But this does not mean that the leadership of the Saora society has not concerned itself with long-term measures. The simple and direct philosophy behind the TDCC has inspired a band of Saora leaders and workers to advocate amongst the Saora mass dealings exclusively with the TDCC and virtual boycott of their economic exploiters, particularly the Pano or the Dom. In course of time, this thought-trend promises to snowball into a movement. The traditional leadership comprised of the Gomango and the Buyya are in sympathy with it; actually, it is spearheaded by one Sarpanch named Kirtan Sabara and his associates (including ex-MLAs and present MLA) mostly semi-literate, but actively conscious of the exploitation and the need for pulling the tribe out of it. Kirtan Sabara may be likened to a "natural leader" of the concept of Spear (1977). His is a crusade against economic oppression and in favour of participation in the development process set in motion by the government. One difficulty which the band faces is that the level of literacy is so low, being 10.1 per cent as per the 1971 Census, that the mass-media have little relevance. Hence, for a long time to come they will remain unutilisable and opinion leadership will have to play a predominant role in the area. In the investigations which were conducted, the respondents felt that "Hats" or market centres are nodal points for dissemination of information. It is, therefore, not difficult to see that the most important means of diffusion of the message of the State will be through word of mouth. It is necessary, therefore, to identify opinion leaders, "gate-keepers" of Levin (1958), to study their strategy and to devise effective modes of communication.

There are a few signs that Saora leadership is on the threshold. It was found during the investigation that the highest number of leaders was associated with villages which had an intermediate score of village development in terms of irrigation facilities, agricultural development, educational and health institutions, market centres, etc; villages with lower and higher scores had fewer number of leaders. This led to the interpretation that there is a stagnation level which has to be crossed before the take-off stage of development is reached. There is also evidence to show that when the village size grew, say upward of 900, monomorphism (or leadership with singular function) made a marked appearance, but polymorphism (leadership with multifunctional character) was the rule in smaller villages (Merton, 1957). Further, in villages with Saora and non-Saora population, polymorphism increased with increasing Saora concentration. These are pointers of tendency to modernisation and support the threshold idea.

On the whole, it would appear that some traditional leaders like the elders of the village council, unable to reorient themselves and confined to village councils, are fading out. Some others, particularly the younger, not set in the old mould, exhibit adaptability and have been taking to the new institutions. In fact, as indicated hereinbefore, there are signs of emergence of Saora leadership at the Panchayat and Panchayat Samiti levels. But, there is little impact of it at the State level. There is a lone Saora member in the Legislative Assembly. Presently, the tribe has no representation in the Orissa Council of Ministers. Links with other tribal groups, as a result of this, are not strong and there is little thought of pan-tribal identity.

A Frame and Perspective

The present writer has stressed elsewhere that both in the planning and implementation processes, tribal leadership should assume a direct role or, at least, should be associated (Singh, 1977). Development of each tribal family being the ultimate aim, we have to start from grass-roots. It has, hence, been suggested that at the Panchayat-level a committee should be formed comprising of the Sarpanch, a ward member and a Panchayat Development Officer (a Government employee) to deal with all manner of issues relating to planning and implementation. It is assumed that in the predominantly tribal areas both the Sarpanch and the ward member would be tribals; if not, regulatory measures need be adopted to ensure it. This

Committee should have nexus with the Panchayat Samiti (at the Block level) and the ITDP-level Committee which has on it M.Ps., M.L.As., Chairman Panchayat Samitis etc. This scheme could give (a) practical shape to the concept of planning from below and (b) effective expression to the needs and aspirations of the people.

The suggestions made in the preceding paragraph rest on the existing framework of Panchayati Raj structure which does not take adequate care of the crucial operative level, viz., the village. In the scheme of statutory Gram Panchayats, the village is represented by one or more ward members in the Panchayat, a body constituted for a group of villages. In order to make the village a focal point of development, a body needs to be established for it. In some of the tribal areas, as for example, the Saora country, traditional village councils have been functioning. Reference to this has been made earlier. These village councils as such or a set of new bodies composed of the traditional village leaders and the elected ward members could be entrusted with development works whose execution will be greatly facilitated thereby. These village-level bodies could also be relied upon to make appropriate suggestions to the Panchayat-level committee for programme formulation. Their constitution would fit in with the concept of Jaya Prakash Narayan who would like to avoid "elections to executive officers on the present majority-minority pattern which is divisive and disruptive process" and could be made to conform to "selection by general consensus of opinion, or sometimes by drawing lots" (1960, p. 51).

In the present state of the Saora society, when its leadership is on the threshold of a new phase of its life, it will be ideal to start the experiment, coinciding with the commencement of the Sixth Five Year Plan. This should yield rich dividends.

SUGGESTED READINGS

Das, N., "Saoras and Panos of Ganjam Agency : A Study into Social Interrelationship"; *Adibasi*; Bhubaneshwar, 1967-68, Number Three, 45-52.

Fried, M.H., *The Evolution of Political Anthropology*. New York : Random House, 1967.

Levin, K., "Group Decisions and Social Change" *Reading in Social Pcychology*, Mascoby, Newcomb and Hartley. New York : Holt Rinehart and Wingstom, Inc, 1958.

Merton, R.K., *Social Theory and Social Structure* : Amerind Publishing Co., 1957.

Narayan, Jayaprakash, *A Plea for Reconstruction of Indian Policy* : Wardha, 1960.

Parry, G., *Political Elites*; New York : Praeger Publishers, 1969.

Singh, Bhupinder, "Tribal Development at Cross-Roads : A Critique and a Plea", *Man in India*, Volume 57, Number Three, July-September 1977.

SIXTEEN

Stephen Inglis

CHALLENGES OF CULTURAL READJUSTMENT
A Canadian Effort

CULTURAL readjustment is involved in such movements as the gradual return of the control of countries to their inhabitants (or to sections of them), return of confiscated portions of countries to their original owners, and the still intermittent recognition of aboriginal rights, the rights of minorities etc. Cultural readjustment is also involved in the movement toward increasing access of important cultural materials to countries and the people (or their descendants) who originally made them. These movements are in large part a reaction to and readjustment of treaties made, borders drawn, and ideas formulated during the colonial era. The impetus for change has been increasing communication, politicization, and refusal by dominated countries or peoples (often by force) to submit to continued oppression or deprivation.

The impetus for change has also been the increasing recognition of the importance of cultural diversity and cultural heritage in a world speeding toward a rather frightening homogeneity. In the increase in this concern, anthropology has played some part.

It is generally recognised that many peoples, especially those of countries (Third World) which experienced colonial domination and those of "primitive" tribal societies (Fourth World)—(Greyburn, 1976 : 1) have had the majority of their arts, from great historical monuments to handicrafts, taken away. Much was purchased "legally", but much was also acquired as war booty, through grave robbery or outright theft. These objects are now for the most part housed in great museums, the majority in Europe and North America, and in the private collections of the wealthy. Despite the laws designed to stop the flow of cultural arts, especially from the poor countries to the rich, the flow continues. The days when "the archaeologist or art dealer captured the popular fantasy as a romantic bucaneer engages in a kind of scientific treasure hunt" are now fading. However today in Africa, Latin America, Asia, Oceania and even Europe, "modern pirates with substantial resources, using modern techniques. . ." (M'Bow, 1978 : 4) systematically spoil and rob archaeological sites and plunder entire material cultural heritages.

UNESCO Chief's Appeal

Amadou Mahtar M'Bow, Director-General of UNESCO, appealed on 7 June 1978, for the "return of an irreplaceable cultural heritage to those who created it." Citing the "vicissitudes of history"—which have seen the drain of cultural material from some parts of the world for hundreds of years and "unbridled speculation" fanned byprices currentlyprevailing in the art market—he has called on governments, and museums, as also librarians, art gallery owners, journalists, historians, critics and writers to create a climate whereby peoples who have been deprived of their cultural heritage might "ask for the return of at least the art which best represents their culture, which they feel are most vital and whose absence causes them the greatest anguish." It is pointed out that the peoples whose material cultural heritage has been largely removed have suffered not only material loss, but also loss of "a memory which would doubtless have helped them to greater self-knowledge and would certainly have enabled others to understand them better."

The logic seems hard to argue with. However delegations requesting token returns or even loans, temporary exihibits or information still regularly return home empty-handed. What are some of the arguments used against this type of co-operation ?

Perhaps the most pervasive sentiment behind the refusal to consider international repatriation claims is that "great art is universal" and not the property of any single culture. This idea crystallized during the enlightenment when bringing the art of other cultures to Europe was thought to be a reflection of reason and scientific progress. More scientifically advanced people were seen to have "better use" for anything that could be considered a reflection of man's genius. The "universal laws of property" continue to be invoked by countries which have amassed large quantities of precious material which once belonged to others. By returning material to the confiner of its original national boundaries (most often to developing or "Third World" countries), it is argued that the universal value of cultural material to art and science is diminished. Those who would ask for the return of cultural material are admonished for selfishness, as it is argued rather patronisingly that it is because the material can be seen in the great museums of the world that it has been acknowledged as "great art"—i.e., the original owners are graced by the presentation of their art in major galleries in more developed countries! There they are more accessible to more people, regardless of their accessibility (or lack of it) to those in the culture in which they were made.

Another historical basis and continuing justification for great international collections (and argument against return) is that great art must be "saved". During the age of exploration and colonialism in Africa, Asia and South America, this involved saving or preserving works of art or cultural properties threatened by wars, natural disasters or "unstable" governments, usually by shipping them to Europe. These were "rescued" at a time when they would otherwise have "perished". This attitude has persisted and is prevalent among museum collectors today.

Debates on specific historical incidents continue, for example the famous "rescue" of the Parthenon sculptures by Lord Elgin (Ward 1977, Forgey 1970). Whether one supports or condemns these rescues much of the burden upon great western museums of saving world art has now shifted to preserving it. Very few of the great museums are willing to return or even loan material to developing countries because they fear that these will not be cared for in a way which ensures preservation. The object has become the primary concern and its preservation a major responsibility of the technologically sophisticated museum.

Most museums can document the "legal" nature of the transactions leading to the acquisition of much of the material in their collections, and this has often been used as a basis for the refusal to consider repatriation claims. Despite the previously mentioned sentiment that great art is universal, ownership is now often legally attributed to the people of the country in which the museum is located or to that state itself. That the legal basis of acquisition during periods of recognised oppression and coercion is still supported is a curious paradox and one which places the entire issue of historical legality in question. In any case, claims are most often being made on the basis of known cases of thefts, seizures, or war booty, and there seem to be ample recorded cases of these types of acquisitions (and many still being researched) to keep the issues open for some time to come.

By participating in any sort of repatriation of material, museums implicitly acknowledge that the material was in some way improperly in their possession. Thus, any transfer is embarrassing if not incriminating. Worse still, any transfer establishes a precedent whereby every other museum sees its foundation eroded, if ever so slightly. The spectre of a reverse flow of cultural material to countries of origin looms with every act of repatriation, however small.

Despite these general and widespread constraints many museums have begun the process of co-operation with museums and governments of developing countries. Incidents of the return of museum objects have taken place recently between Belgium and Zaire, New Zealand and Papua New Guinea, Sweden and Kenya, the U.S.A. and Panama and Guatemala to name a few (Fradier, 1978). Many more requests are under consideration.

Organisations such as the International Council of Museums (ICOM) are deeply involved in establishing guidelines and standards for the future. It seems inevitable that international museum repatriation will become more closely linked with political readjustments and alliances, and will grow in importance. But it remains to be seen whether real cultural co-operation, such as the exchange of museum training and technical skill as well as material, will foreshadow and help to guide new trends in more general cultural policy or will follow begrudgingly in their wake.

Readjustment in National Context

Many of the considerations and constraints prominent in the negotiations for return of cultural material to the countries of origin are also relevant to another phase of readjustment. Increasing access to material of cultural significance is an issue not only between countries but also between cultures or peoples within specific countries. Aboriginal peoples or minority groups within many countries have been victims of the loss of materials of significance to their cultural heritage, often to a national government controlled by a dominant or more sophisticated sector of the population of their country. Often this loss has been co-incident with a programme of the national government toward assimilation of minority groups, their alienation from original territory, and encouragement to adopt national norms of religious, economic and social life.

One area where native groups lost or gave up vast quantities of material of cultural importance during a relatively short period of time was on the North-west Coast of North America, much of which is now part of Canada. This occurred during the 19th century. The volume of collecting North-west Coast material and the intensity with which it was sought is only now being seriously estimated (i.e. one North-west Coast collector, G.T. Emmons, gathered and shipped away over 15,000 specimens during his career) (Cole, 1978 : p. 6). Most material went immediately or has subsequently gone to private collections or museums, including the National Museum of Canada. Museums commissioned collectors and competed briskly for native artifacts which became available. Although much of the type of material collected was, from early contact with outsiders made to be sold on the market, much became available as a result of the decline in the traditional way of life, especially ritual and ceremonial life, in the face of modernisation and the pressure from missionaries and the government to give up the "old ways". Much was also available due to the drastic decline in population of native people through epidemic diseases and the general trauma of the changes introduced and often enforced by Europeans. The ironic possibility exists that museums, while attempting to record the material culture of a "vanishing people", actually hastened the cultural decline. Many groups of native people in Canada are now in the process of negotiating readjustments over aboriginal rights to resources, legal rights and ownership of land.

One particularly well-documented incident of the loss of cultural material by North-west Coast native people is the confiscation, by agents of the Canadian government, of ritual masks, clothing and other instruments from some Kwagiutl tribes in 1922. Since that time a portion of this material has been stored in the National Museum in Ottawa. As some of the confiscated material is being returned to the Kwagiutl, a brief survey of the history of this case and its implications will be a useful framework for considering the issues of readjustment in the national context.

The Kwagiutl are one of the large ethnic or language groups of North-west Coast people. Their villages are located on the northern part of the inside of Vancouver Island. They have become well-known among anthropologists for their vigorous art style and for their particularly elaborate version of a social event—the potlatch—common to groups throughout the North-west Coast area. The potlatch is "a gathering of important guests invited in order to witness some important event, such as the assuming of a new name, the completion of a house or the erection of a totem pole . . ." (Duff, 1958 : 58). It is characterised by a display of wealth by the host and a distribution of gifts to guests in order of rank.

Various descriptions of the potlatch have emphasized different functions. Among these are the social function by which the status and rank of a great number of related and neighbouring people are periodically reiterated and legitimised; the economic function, by which wealthy men redistribute their surplus throughout their communities and established debt-credit obligations; the religious or spiritual function by which the ritual cycle of secret societies and the arts flourish and are elaborated. All these aspects and many others as well are part of the potlatch and there seems to be general agreement that it was a central feature of Kwagiutl culture before outsiders arrived on the North-west Coast, although after the time of contact potlatches probably became "more numerous and larger . . ." (Duff, 1958 : 59).

Many of the missionaries and Indian agents of the government in the late 19th and early 20th centuries viewed the potlatch as barbarous perpetuation of backward customs and an orgy of waste and laziness. They had great difficulty in keeping track of native people for whom they were responsible, because those people might be absent from their village for weeks or even months, potlatching. There was a feeling among administrators that the potlatch retarded their avowed mission of teaching thrift, temperance, and "civilized ways" to the Indians. They assumed, quite correctly, that the suppression of the potlatch would be an important step toward eliminating the traditional way of life of the Kwagiutl people.

Section 149 banning the potlatch was inserted in the Indian Act in 1884. The first charges were laid under the section in 1889, and charges continued to be brought through the turn of the century. There were prosecutions every year from 1913 to 1922. Most were dismissed for lack of evidence and convictions were usually suspended. Despite the prohibition, potlatching among the Kwagiutl continued (often covertly) throughout this period and right up to the present, although it very nearly died out during the 1930s and has experienced a limited revival recently.

During the winter of 1922, Dan Cranmer of the Nimpkish Band at Alert Bay, hosted a potlatched at Village Island, his wife's ancestral home, and a quiet place removed from the government authorities at Alert Bay. Preparations were made secretly. Most of the 300 guests came from Village Island, Alert Bay or the southern most Kwagiutl village of Cape Mudge. The police and Indian agent nonetheless learned of the potlatch and arrested many of the participants. Frustrated up to this point, the authorities were determined to make this a test case and to secure convictions. Thirty-four people were eventually charged under the act, with such crimes as distributing gifts, dancing, or giving a speech. Sentences of two to six months were handed down. In addition to jail sentences the government authorities compelled people of the three major groups present to surrender many of their masks, ritual costumes, and other paraphernalia, whether it had been used at the potlatch or not, in an attempt to stop the continued use of this material in traditional performances. Threats of further prosecutions and jail sentences were used to ensure co-operation.

A nominal sum was paid for each item to make the transaction a "sale". The material was gathered at Alert Bay and in 1923 shipped in seventeen crates to the National Museum of Canada in Ottawa. Lists were made at the time by the Indian agent in Alert Bay and by the Director of the National Museum. Other counts of the material seized survive in the memories of old people who were involved or whose families were. The problem in dealing with these lists is that descriptive terms were not standard and it is not clear if some items with multiple parts were listed as a unit or separately.

In any case, the National Museum is in the process of returning to the Kwagiutl the material in their possession which was taken in the aftermath of the 1922 potlatch. This unfortunately accounts for only about half (and possibly less) of what was originally seized. Some of the balance was sold without authorisation by the Indian agent to an American museum collector. Some other material is in the possession of another Canadian museum, which has so far been reluctant to co-operate.

After years of negotiations, grant applications, and struggle, the material is back on the North-west Coast, awaiting transfer to museums now under construction in both Alert Bay and Cape Mudge. The material is being divided according to which village the descendants of people who lost a particular piece now belong. Descendants of people from Village Island (now abandoned) who gave up material have been asked to choose in which museum they wish their pieces to be displayed. By taking a broad look at some issues raised by this case we may begin to seek some guidelines for considering national readjustment.

Legality and Ownership

It seems that in terms of the law as constituted in the 1920s, the seizure of the potlatch goods was an illegal action, contrary to the spirit if not the letter of the law. Money was paid to the owners but the transaction was initiated under duress, i.e., the threat of more trouble and imprisonment. Kwagiutl families in effect ransomed their chiefs and important persons with their ritual goods.

Many other materials were obtained from native people during periods of time when laws were, according to today's standards, unfavourably biased against them. Often they had for practical purposes, no legal rights. Nonetheless, under the situation prevailing at the time, most material collected from them was obtained "legally". Much of the traditional wealth of the North-west Coast peoples became part of museum collections during a period when native cultures appeared to be dissolving completely; the word often used at the time was "vanishing". Disease, displacement, and pressure by government and religious officials was taking a heavy toll. It is apparent from the tone of official correspondence of the time that many non-Indians, and Indians too, felt that traditional native culture of any kind would soon be a thing of the past. These were the general conditions under which the massive transfer of material took place.

The section of the act banning the potlatch was quietly dropped in 1950s. Would it be just to cite this archaic law now as a justification for the refusal to consider a repatriation claim from people who, as a result of the law, lost material important to their cultural heritage? If a museum is to seriously assess the conditions under which its material was acquired (both the legal situation and its cultural context), it must also be prepared to consider grievances and new proposals and to participate in readjustments with respect to those conditions in light of today's beliefs and standards.

Regardless of the legal conditions of acquisition, museums tend to assume ownership of material they saved "when no one else cared". Museum collections are, in addition to many other things, conspicuous symbols of superior technology and foresight. The audacity of a cultural group who, having once neglected materials of cultural importance, (now "priceless relics") would now ask for their return, shocks the museum purist. Furthermore, the problem of who, among the descendants of the original owners or makers, should get the ownership is a very real issue, and one which makes any repatriation an extremely sensitive transaction.

In the Kwagiutl case, it could be argued that the National Museum, because of the nature of the confiscation, never established full ownership, from the Kwagiutl side there has been a "continuity of claim" in the sense that they never relinquished their ownership completely and continued intermittently to press for return. The record of what was taken and from whom has survived to the present. As Duff and others have pointed out, the cultural complex in which these materials were used never died out completely among the Kwagiutl, and is still evolving (Duff 1970). It is in part the long-standing rivalry, especially among the two major groups receiving material back from the National Museum, which has created the dynamics and the determination by which the whole process of return has been carried this far.

Accessibility of Material

One of the standard arguments for the refusal to consider repatriation claims involves concern for the accessibility of the material. Museum people have pointed out that in national museums, material is available to *all* the country's people, all Indians, to scholars and to all future generations. In the case of the potlatch collection, the particular geographical circumstances resulted in the material being moved and stored (in Ottawa) over 4,000 miles away from where the Kwagiutl live. This material has thus been virtually inaccessible to the Kwagiutl since its confiscation. One wonders if a museum visitor survey would not reveal that accessibility to national museum holdings in Ottawa does not mainly benefit a very small and select class of non-Indian Canadians in any case. Perhaps large national museum institutions will have to relinquish some of the hypothetically exercised responsibility to "all citizens" to serve special interest groups more directly (including people of cultures from which much of their material originated). When accessibility involves a 4,000 mile journey, it should logically be the elite and mobile class of museum visitor and the grant-funded scholar who makes the trip rather than people from small and localised communities.

The question could be asked : "How accessible are museum objects in most large institutions anyway?" The fact is that in most major museums, including the National Museum of

Canada, much of the collection is in storage and is rarely if ever accessible to the public. It is difficult to believe that the potlatch collection, photographed, published, and highlighted in museums built especially to house it will be less accessible to the Canadian public than it was in the storage vaults of the National Museum.

One argument used against considering repatriation is that the claimants will not use the material in the "traditional way" (Museums Committee, 1970). In such cases, the museum anthropologist, presumably knowledgeable of the traditional context, judges that the object maintains its integrity to a greater extent in the museum collection than in the hands of the acculturated descendants of the original owner. Such judgments may be based on sentiments expressed in statements like "we in museums now know more about native art than the natives and can appreciate it more fully". It has been difficult to convince claimants of this point of view in some cases. That many Indians realise that there is "no escape from the mass culture in which we all participate" and that it is "a source of pride that their cultures are so prominently displayed in ethnographic museums" (Museums Committee, 1970) does little to offset or negate the wishes of many others that this "source of pride" be brought closer to home, and into their control, for whatever use they see fit.

On the other hand, few museums would ever consider the return or recirculating of parts of their collections without assurances that they *wouldn't* be used in traditional ways, i.e., without assurances about the physical use, care, storage and display of the objects. In the case of the potlatch collection, the National Museum set certain conditions for return of the material, involving sums of money to be raised, building standards for the museums to be built, trained personnel for their operation and so forth. In these ways the use of these materials i.e. to be housed in museums meeting at least certain national standards, has been dictated to conform to mass culture approval rather than their traditional use (which in certain cases involved destroying ritual goods before large audiences). There has been general co-operation from native recipients in attempting to meet the National Museum guidelines. As modern Canadian communities, both native villages in which the new museums will be located look upon the institution as well as the material in it as a source of pride.

This is not to suggest that the transfer of material from Ottawa back to the North-west Coast is simply a geographical one. Most of the potlatch collection consists of ritual materials; masks, costumes, and noisemakers, some of which will be reintegrated to some extent into present-day Kwagiutl ritual life. Kwagiutl potlatching has been revived to some extent as has the production in traditional arts and interest in traditional knowledge generally. These important possessions of previous generations are the type of wealth which was the source of strength in a former time, and remains so today.

The experience of negotiating for the return of this collection has had other important consequences. Some native people have received training in connection with museum work and have created what may prove to the useful liaisons with other museums. Further experience in dealing with government agencies (although most native people are already expert) can only aid further negotiations.

The implications of the successful repatriation of the potlatch collection to the Kwagiutl may well extend to future native claims, not only for museum material, but also in outstanding issues of aboriginal resource rights and land claims.

Fears of Museum People

Perhaps the most central factor in the consideration of "cultural readjustment" in the museum context is the self-interest of museums and museum people themselves. Every act of repatriation, in the opinion of some, "poses a threat to the integrity of museum collections everywhere" (Fenton, 1960). Naturally, museums cannot operate without material and some sense of security. There is fear of a landslide. "Some museum anthropologists have predicted that the day will come when museums are forced to return everything of native origin in their collections" (Ward, 1977). In 1970, the Museum Committee of the A.A.A. (comprising a powerful group of well-known museum anthropologists) issued a concise statement which neatly summarises their self-interest. This was in response to the attempt (subsequently successful) by a group of native people in the United States to reclaim some important cultural materials from a state museum. The anthropologists wrote : "As scholars whose researches depend on great ethnographic collections of now largely vanished primitive peoples of the world, we urge the preservation of such mementos of culture in museums. We deplore the principle of returning such treasures. . . etc."

These views appear somewhat archaic when framed against the realities of contemporary culturallife. Most museums in fact hold much more material than they can ever show, look after, or use in any way, no matter how esoterically. Most will never be "requested back" by anyone. The world has changed. Many cultural groups have disappeared or have been completely absorbed by others and those claims which can be firmly established with some documented basis (as many as there may be) will probably never seriously threaten the "material base" of great museum collections. On the other hand, museum anthropologists must be ready to acknowledge that certain sections of their collections are not simply the residue of "largely vanished" peoples, no matter how much more convenient it would be if they were. Museums may in these cases have to consider the possibility that, rather than owning these materials for all time, they have been "holding" them during a time when they might otherwise have been unwanted, lost or destroyed, or during a period when the museum felt it had rights, which in fact don't exist for all time.

Museums must be ready not only to observe and interpret cultural process, but to take a more active part in it, in some cases by returning, recirculating or making available museum objects and information. Collection policy oriented toward this aspiration may become less treasure-oriented and laden with "ownership" concerns. The museum endeavour may in this way eventually become a dynamic process with a two-way flow of meaning and material.

Two thousand years ago, the Greek chronicler, Polybius, hoped that ". . . the conquerors of the future will learn not to despoil the towns they take, and will refrain from turning other nation's misfortunes into embellishments for their own country." It may be added that it should as well be hoped that dominant populations within particular countries will also refrain from turning their minority countrymen's misfortunes into embellishments for their ways of life, and where this has happened a reassessment and readjustment will soon begin.

SUGGESTED READINGS

Cole, D., "The Bowls are no Longer There" : *Ethnological Collecting on the North-west Coast*, Unpublished paper, 1978.

Duff, W., *The Indian History of British Columbia, Volume I, The Impact of the White Man.* Anthropology in British Columbia Memoir, No. 5, B.C P.M.. 1965, Unpublished letter, 1970.

Fenton, W., "The Museum and Anthropological Research". *American Anthropologist*, Volume III, No. 4, 1960.

Forgey, B., "Lord Byron Cried 'Rape'. . ." *Museum News*, Volume 48, No. 10, June, 1970.

Fradier, G., "Return to Homeland". *UNESCO Courier*, July, 1978, (31st Year)

Graburn, N.H.H., *Ethnic and Tourist Arts*, Berkeley : University of California Press, 1976.

M'Bow, Amadou-Mahtar, "An Appeal by Mr. Amadou-Mahtar M'Bow, Director-General of UNESCO", *UNESCO Courier*, July, 1978, (31st Year).

Museums Committee : American Anthropological Association, "An Illusion of Religiosity ? *The Indian Historian*, Volume 3, No. 2. Spring, 1970.

Ward, P., "Ownership of Collections", *Museum Round Up*, No. 67, Summer, 1977.

SEVENTEEN

Bhabesh Chakraborty and
Sumita Kundu

THE VANISHING CRAFTS OF CHOTANAGPUR

UNLIKE the Northern Gangetic alluvial plains with its caste-based agricultural population, South Bihar, rather the Chotanagpur plateau, has been aptly called by Col. E.T. Dalton, as the great living anthropological museum in India'' with a predominantly tribal population pursuing, among others, varied agricultural and industrial occupations. It is a land of ever-rising wooded hills interspersed with picturesque green valleys and sandy ravines. It is characterised by varieties of ecological, ethnological, linguistic and cultural situations. The tribal culture-linguistic zone as classified by Vidyarthi (1977)[1] has 94.30 per cent rural tribal population (3,355,608) as per 1971 Census although Chotanagpur villages are essentially multi-caste and multi-tribe in character. The centrally located district of Ranchi (18,214.91 sq. km) as a constituent district of Chotanagpur administrative division serves not only as the administrative pivot but ethnically represents Chotanagpur in miniature as all the thirty Scheduled Tribes (ignoring the unclassified ones) of Chotanagpur are found here in varied numbers. Chotanagpur alone represents 64.24 per cent of the total tribal population of Bihar (4,932,767) and the district of Ranchi in its turn is the home of 44.40 per cent of tribal strength of Chotanagpur (3,415,608). As per 1961 Census enumeration, Chotanagpur has 95.22 per cent of the total strength (1,669,811) of eight tribal communities (namely, the Asur, Birhor, Baraik/Chick Baraik, Kharia, Lohra/Lohara, Mahli, Munda and Oraon) representing different stages (i.e., hill cultivation type, forest hunting type, plains agricultural type and simple-artisan type), of culture the district of Ranchi in its turn represents 78.79 per cent of those tribal communities residing in Chotanagpur. Table 17.1 shows the concentration of the aforesaid tribals in Chotanagpur and Ranchi.

TABLE 17.1

Concentration of Tribals (Concerned) in Chotanagpur/Ranchi

Sl. No.	Community	Population (1961 Census) Bihar State	Chotanagpur Division	% of col. 4 to col.3	Ranchi District	% of col. 6 to col.4
1	2	3	4	5	6	7
1.	Asur	5,819 (7,026)	5,803	99.72	4,999	86.14
2.	Birhor	2,438 (3,464)	2,438	100.00	947*	38.84
3.	Chick Baraik	30,770 (33,476)	30,766	99.99	29,311	95.27
4.	Kharia (including Hill Kharia)	106,240 (127,002)	102,801	96.80	93,426	90.88
5.	Lohara/ Lohra	92,609 (116,828)	87,100	94.05	69,928	80.28
6.	Mahli	67,979 (74,452)	47,075	69.25	24,359	51.74
7.	Munda	628,931 (723,116)	624,277	99.26	465,093	47.54
8.	Oraon	735,025 (876,218)	689,768	93.84	564,774	81.88
		1,669,811 (1,961,582)	1,590,028	95.22	12,52,837	78.79

Note: *Birhor at Hazaribagh District—1,233 (43.44%).
Figures in parenthesis—1971 Census, data for other spells, not available.

Source: Census of India 1961, Vol. IV (Bihar), Part V-A, Special Tables for Scheduled Castes and Scheduled Tribes.

As classified on the basis of culture types and economic specialisation (Vidyarthi 1964)[2], normal groups like the Oraon, Munda and Kharia (except the Hill Kharia) of the plains-agricultural type are essentially settled agriculturists. The small groups like the Asur and Hill Kharia (10,241 as per 1971 Census) of the hill-cultivation type are traditionally iron-smelters and shifting cultivators. The Birhor of the forest-hunting type are bark rope-makers, though linguistically, historically and racially they are related to the Munda. Among others, the Mahli comb-maker (an offshoot of the Santal), the Baraik/Chick Baraik cotton weaver, Lohra/Lohara blacksmith of the simple artisan type reside with their specialised services in farm villages ordinarily among their clients.

Prior to Independence some sporadic individual research contribution continued to come mainly from missionaries, travellers' account, administrators, census superintendents and non-professionals. These, of course, provided the base data for studies to be undertaken scientifically by researchers in future. Some valuable contributions to the knowledge of artisans came among others, from Beverly (1872)[3], Dalton (1872)[4], Risley (1891)[5], Roy (1925)[6], Laccy (1932)[7], Archer (1942)[8], and Elwin (1942).[9] These are only illustrative and not an exhaustive list of significant works. The novelty of the post-Independent era is represented by theoretical study followed by field and action-oriented research. To quote a few significant examples out of many references may be made to the works of Sinha (1961)[10], Saraswati and Behura (1966)[11], Vidyarthi (1968)[12], Sinha (1968)[13], and Williams (1968)[14]. In short, these carry promising indication of vitality and hope for qualitative as well as quantitative development in various fields of cultural anthropology and ethnological study.

It is universally acknowledged that in the tradition-bound peasant society of rural Chotanagpur, craftsmen (both tribal and non-tribal), though numerically not so significant, play a very vital role in socio-economic and ritual life. As a minor social group they extended specialised services and finished goods, ordinarily on reciprocal basis, to their patrons. In exchange they receive traditionally fixed amount of paddy and/or money. Both the major and minor social groups, particularly in the relatively unopened region, remain functionally integrated in the local framework of an agro-based economy. These days, of course, *jajman-parjan* (client-clientee) relationship in the socio-economic sphere varies from region to region and craft to craft.

With the gradual decay of some crafts this socio-economic and ritual interdependence gets naturally disturbed and thus not only cultural distinctiveness is lost but also group solidarity and functional integration at the regional society get weakened. Therefore, there is an urgent need for identification of native skill, mainly with reference to various economic activities, innovative adaptation, rejection after adaptation. Anthropologists, rather cultural anthropologists, have a pivotal role to play in the revival of native craft and skill.

Objectives of Study

With the objectives of ascertaining the existence of artisans (both tribal and non-tribal), particularly the Asur-ironsmelter and the Baraik/Chick Baraik cotton weaver as craftsmen and the role of anthropolcgists in the changing situation, a survey was undertaken during 1966-68 in three purposively selected regions (the south-east region with Marungtoli, Bamhani, Katatoli of Goratoli and Etrey under the territorial jurisdiction of the newly created Murhu police station forming a part of the Ranchi plateau; the north-west region with Banari, Jahup-Kokortoli, Barki Samdari, Hearag, Chingri, Beti and Norma of the Bishunpur police station comprising a part of the Bishunpur ecological valley and margin and lastly the south region with Vikratoli of Lachragarh in the Kolebira police station and Gerakel and Samdega in the Bano police station forming a part of the greater Chotanagpur Plateau) in three different directions of the periphery of a district (Ranchi). Each region in its turn was composed of three to seven semi-contiguous villages located ordinarily under the territorial jurisdiction of a police station (very often coterminus with a Tribal Development Block). The south-east region is situated at a distance of 42 km to the south of the district and divisional headquarters (Ranchi) and 10 km away from the sub-divisional headquarters (Khunti) on the busy Ranchi-Jamshedpur (via Chaibasa) all-weather metalled road. Similarly, the north-west region is served by the 154-km Ranchi-Netarhat (via Ghagra) metalled road and thereby enjoys contact of intermediate nature as traffic to Netarhat, a summer resort, is seasonal. Banari, hub of commercial activity of the region, is on the Ranchi-Netarhat road at a distance of 130 km away from Ranchi Town and stands only 6 km away from the block headquarters (Bishunpur), 25 km from the sub-divisional town (Gumla) and 130 km from the district and divisional headquarters (Ranchi). The south region, which is remotely connected with the sub-divisional headquarters (Simdega) and the district and divisional headquarters (Ranchi) by road, stands midway between the Kolebira and Bano blocks on the 16 km long Kolebira-Bano (via Lachragarh) partially metalled road. The state bus plies twice a day in dry weather. Happily enough, the recently constructed Ranchi-Hatia-Rourkela broad gauge section of South-Eastern Railways passes through the region.

Methodology

Information regarding age, sex tribe/caste/community, occupation, marital status, etc. was recorded on schedules. Through genealogy, the structure of the family (with composition) was ascertained. Heads (irrespective of sex) of the families were interviewed personally through a pretested structured interview schedule. In case of broken families (that is where husband or wife was dead) relevant information was collected in respect of both the partners from the surviving member. Data thus collected were processed. There was also a provision for checking, and discrepancy, if any, was removed. The unit of the study was the family which "is a social group characterised by common residence, economic cooperation and reproduction. It includes adults of both the sexes, at least two of whom maintain a socially approved sexual relationship and one or more children own or adopted of the sexually cohabiting adults" (Murdock 1958 : 1)[15]. Therefore, friends and others who may normally take food from a common kitchen but are not related (either through consanguineal or affinal ties) do not come under the purview of a family. Such persons were excluded from the scope of the study. Under the present survey 891 families (of which 492 belong to one or other artisan community) with a population of 6,536 have been covered.

Universe of Study

The relatively opened Munda dominated south-east region is inhabited, among others, by the Baraik/Chick Baraik Swansi/Panr—cotton weaver, Ghasi (Majhi)—fisherman (now bamboo worker), kumhar—potter, Turi—Basket (Big) maker and Lohar/Lohra—blacksmith. The comparatively unopened Oraon dominated north-west region is typically characterised by the presence of the Asur—ironsmelter and shifting cultivator, Birhor—ropemaker and Mahli—comb maker and basket (small) maker. Here the Ghasi, Lohar and Swansi/Panr are absent. Loss of specialised services of these craftsmen is made good by other artisan communities of the regional society. Lastly, the least opened south region is peopled with the Baraik/Chick Baraik, Ghasi (Majhi), Kumhar and Lohar/Lohra. These are the communities—tribal and non-tribal—which are of primary concern to this study. In addition to all these, there are others which include both the numerically strong major and culturally distinct minor communities. The Munda—settled agriculturist alone claim 38.50 per cent of 1816 and 40.18 per cent of 1558 respectively in the south-east and south region while the Oraon—settled agriculturist too are with 62.79 per cent of the total population (5,673) of the north-west region. Amongst minor communities references may be made to the Ahir—cowherd, Bania—trader, Chamar—tanner, regular Napit (Nai)—barber and Muslim—settled agriculturist (having faith in Islam) irrespective of regions they are found. In two out of the three regions reside the Bhogta/Gorait—coir rope maker, Kherwar—settled agriculturist Rajput (Thakur/Rautia) landlord and warrior and Teli—oil presser reside. The Bhuiya-Kharia (both being plains cultivator), Brahmin—priest, Birjia—iron worker (now bamboo worker), Dhobi—washerman and Majhi—headman are found in one out of three regions. Tribals among craftsmen (mainly, the Baraik/Chick Baraik, Lohra, Asur, Birhor and Mahli) practise tribal animism, while other social groups—Scheduled or non-Scheduled (the Ghasi, Swansi/Panr, Turi, Kumhar and Lohar) have faith in Hinduism. But, in practice, religion of artisan can be said to be a mixture of both animism and Hinduism. Some of these communities (namely, the basket-maker, potter, weaver and blacksmith) may be categorised, as per Nesfield's occupational ranking scheme, under artisan castes. Their social status, too, varies. Risley, however, put the artisan castes (co-eval with metallurgy) like the Lohar under the 'clean Sudras' and the Ghasi under the unclean 'feeders'.

Population Details and Workers

Table 17.2 shows distribution of population in all the three regions and proportion of artisans to total population in each region. Though the strength of artisans varies from one region to another, but nowhere they form less than 25 per cent of the regional population. Again, the proportion of individual artisan communities varies from one region to another, and even within a region one differs significantly in strength from another. For the agro-based economy, the presence of the Lohar/Lohra is a must mainly because of the *jajman-parjan* relationship but they nowhere represent a great number of families. The proportion of the Lohar/Lohra to total artisans is almost insignificant, what to speak of total population of the region. Among artisans the Turi together with the Ghasi claim 41.61 per cent in the south-east region and the Baraik/Chick Baraik alone account for 32.41 per cent in the south region. Similarly, the Asur represent 71.52 per cent of artisans in the north-west region. Further, both sexes amongst artisans are almost of an equal strength when all the three regions are taken into account. Except in the north-east region, females out-numbers their male counterparts, though not by a very considerable margin. Besides minor variations, this trend holds good in the case of other communities.

It is worthwhile to mention that the labour force includes all employable persons (irrespective of sexes) aged between 16 and 64. Workers include those who (irrespective of sexes) are aged between 16 and 64 and are actually engaged in one occupation or other. But among artisans there are persons aged below or above that range who are workers but not full-fledged. They are the earning dependents. For convenience such workers have been treated as non-workers. In other words a majority of dependents are such persons who are required to be fed either partially or wholly by earning members.

TABLE

Distribution of artisan population

Sl. No.	Community	South-East Region				North-West Region			
		No. of family	Population			No. of family	Population		
			Male	Female	Total		Male	Female	Total
1	2	3	4	5	6	7	8	9	10
1.	Asur (S.T.)	—	—	—	—	210	596	534	1130 (71.52)
2.	Birhor (S.T.)	—	—	—	—	8	14	17	31 (1 96)
3.	Chick Baraik (S.T.)	3	5	8	13 (2.42)	19	56	61	117 (7.40)
4.	Ghasi (Majhi) (S C.)	20	42	41	83 (15.49)	—	—	—	—
5.	Kumhar	31	86	96	182 (33.96)	11	32	40	72 (4.56)
6.	Lohar	3	7	7	14 (2.61)	14	32	32	64 (4.05)
7.	Lohra (S.T.)	2	5	4	9 (1.68)	—	—	—	—
8.	Mahli (S.T.)	—	—	—	—	19	48	43	91 (5.76)
9.	Swansi (S.C.)	21	49	46	95	— (17.72)	—	—	—
10.	Turi (S.C.)	26	72	68	140 (26.12)	18	38	37	75 (4.72)
	Total	106	266 (49.63)	270 (50.37)	536 (100.00)	299	816 (51.64)	764 (48.36)	1580 (100.00)
	B. Others	131	688 (54.75)	592 (45.25)	1280 (100.00)	499	2122 (51.84)	1971 (48.16)	4093 (100.00)
	Proportion of craftsmen to "others"	44.73	27.88	31.32	29.28	37.47	28.11	27.93	27.85

Note : S.T. stands for Scheduled Tribe.
S.C. stands for Scheduled Caste.

17.2

in different regions

South Region				All Regions			
No. of family	Population: Male	Population: Female	Population: Total	No. of family	Population: Male	Population: Female	Population: Total
11	12	13	14	15	16	17	18
—	—	—	—	210	596	534	1130 (45.00)
—	—	—	—	8	14	17	31 (1.23)
34	59	69	128 (32.41)	56	120	138	258 (10.27)
26	61	55	116 (29.37)	46	103	96	199 (7.93)
15	44	48	92 (23.29)	57	162	184	346 (13.78)
2	3	4	7 (1.77)	19	42	43	85 (3.39)
10	30	22	52 (13.16)	12	35	26	61 (2.43)
—	—	—	—	19	48	43	91 (3.62)
—	—	—	—	21	49	46	95 (3.79)
—	—	—	—	44	110	105	215 (8.56)
87	197 (49.87)	198 (50.13)	395 (100.00)	492	1279 (150.94)	1232 (149.06)	2511 (100.00)
261	579 (49.78)	584 (50.22)	1163 (100.00)	891	3389 (51.85)	3147 (48.15)	6536 (100.00)
25.00	27.77	25.33	25.35	35.57	27.40	28.13	27.76

Family Size

Table 17.3 shows variations in the average size of the family of the artisan and others. In general, the average size of the artisan's family (5.10) is smaller than that (7.34) of "other communities," when regional differences are ignored. But both

TABLE 17.3

Variation in average family sizes

Sl. No.	Community	Regions			
		South-East	North-West	South	All
1	2	3	4	5	6
A.	*Artisans*				
1.	Asur	—	5.38	—	5.38
2.	Birhor	—	3.87	—	3.87
3.	Chick Baraik	4.33	6.15	3.76	4.61
4.	Ghasi	4.15	—	4.46	4.33
5.	Kumhar	5.87	6.54	6.13	6.07
6.	Lohar	4.67	4.56	3.50	4.47
7.	Lohra	4.50	—	5.20	5.08
8.	Mahli	—	4.78	—	4.79
9.	Swansi	4.52	—	—	4.52
10.	Turi	5.38	4.17	—	4.89
	Total	5.06	5.28	4.54	5.10
	Others	9.77	3.94	4.45	7.34

in the north-west and south region the average size of the artisan's family is bigger than that of "other communities", although by a shallow margin. Among artisans the family size of the Kumhar and the Turi in the south-east region and of the Asur, Baraik/Chick Baraik and the Kumhar and Lohra in the south regions exceed the regional averages and the small family norm as envisaged under the National Family Planning Programme. In fact the Kumhar's family everywhere is the largest in size. Among others, a number of helping hands (of both the sexes) of the family is required in course of manufacturing varied types of wheel-made pottery. Crude as well as elaborate technology of pot-making till date requires many hands. Moreover, sex division of labour is in operation in different stages of its manufacture. In pot-making too, trade secrecy cannot be disclosed to all, particularly unmarried female members of the family. Besides there are cultivating Kumhars who need labour of members of family in cultivation of paddy and other cereals.

The average size of an artisan's family is 5.1 of which 3.35 are actually workers against 3.74 employable persons. Therefore, for a family of 5.1 members 0.39 and 1.36 remain unemployed and dependent respectively. In short, as many as 1.75 members are to depend on 3.35 working members for their livelihood. The dependency rate thus stands at 52.24 per cent when all the regions are taken into account. On region-wise analysis it is seen that dependency rate is maximum (53.48 per cent) in the north-west region while it is minimum (31.33 per cent) in the south region. The south-east region (with 47.95 per cent in the sphere under reference) stands in the middle. Thus it is seen that there exists a big gap between employable persons and persons actually engaged in one occupation or other. In the north-west region out of 5.28 members in a family 3.44 are workers and another 0.49 could have been engaged in some occupations. Corresponding figures of employable persons in the south-east and south region stand at 0.17 (out of 3.42) and 0.21 (out of 3.00).

The sex-wise analysis shows that the size of dependents among females is everywhere smaller than that of males, although by small margin. It varies from 48.35 (in the case of the north-west region) to 49.37 per cent (in the case of the south region). What is most striking is that excepting the north-west region, the proportion of female workers elsewhere is more than that of their male counterparts. It varies between 50.67 per cent (in the south region) and 50.88 per cent (in the south-east region). In the south-east region proportion (50.88 per cent) of female workers is more than that (49.12 per cent) of their male counterparts. When individual artisan communities are brought into picture, it is seen that the Baraik/Chick Baraik with 71.67 per cent female workers stand at the top while the Turi with 36.98 per cent in the sphere under reference are at the bottom. The north-west region presents a slightly different picture. Here the proportion (48.55 per cent) of female workers is less in comparison with male workers. As many as 59.03 per cent of the Birhor workers are female while the corresponding figure for the Lohar is 42.66 per cent. The

TABLE 17.4

Average size of labour force, workers and non-workers amongst artisans

Region	Community	No. of family	Labour force			Workers			Non-workers		
			M	F	T	M	F	T	M	F	T
1	2	3	4	5	6	7	8	9	10	11	12
South-East	Chick Baraik	3	0.67	1.67	2.33	1.66	1.67	2.33	1.00	1.00	2.00
	Ghasi	20	1.70	1.35	3.05	1.55	1.20	2.75	0.55	0.85	1.40
	Kumhar	31	2.10	2.26	4.36	1.97	2.13	4.10	0.81	0.96	1.77
	Lohar	3	1.33	1.33	2.66	1.33	1.33	2.66	1.00	1.00	2.00
	Lohra	2	1.50	1.00	2.50	1.50	1.00	2.50	1.00	1.00	2.00
	Swansi	21	1.52	1.71	3.23	1.42	1.67	3.09	0.91	0.52	1.43
	Turi	26	1.84	1.88	3.72	1.80	1.85	3.65	0.96	0.77	1.73
Total		106	1.77	1.82	3.59	1.68	1.74	3.42	0.83	0.81	1.64
North-West	Asur	210	2.17	1.92	4.09	1.78	1.65	3.43	1.06	0.89	1.95
	Birhor	8	1.13	1.50	2.63	1.13	1.50	2.63	0.62	0.62	1.24
	Chick Baraik	19	2.32	2.37	4.69	2.26	2.21	4.47	0 68	1.00	1.68
	Kumhar	11	1.91	2.36	4.27	1.73	2.27	4.00	1.18	1.36	2.54
	Lohar	14	1.64	1.21	2.85	1.57	1.14	2.71	0.71	1.14	1.85
	Mahli	19	1.89	1.63	3.52	1.84	1.63	3.47	0.68	0.63	1.31
	Turi	18	1.61	1.50	3.11	1.56	1.44	3.00	0.56	0.61	1.17
Total		299	2.06	1.87	3.93	1.77	1.67	3.44	0.96	0.88	1.84

South	Chick										
	Baraik	34	1.26	1.44	2.70	1.20	1.44	2.64	0.53	0.59	1.12
	Ghasi	26	1.61	1.50	3.11	1.50	1.42	2.92	0.85	0.69	1.54
	Kumhar	15	2.00	2.13	4.13	1.73	1.80	3.53	1.20	1.40	2.60
	Lohar	2	1.00	1.50	2.50	1.00	1.50	2.50	0.50	0.50	1.00
	Lohra	10	2.30	1.60	3.90	2.10	1.60	3.70	0.90	0.60	1.50
Total		87	1.61	1.60	3.21	1.48	1.52	3.00	0.78	0.76	1.54
All Regions		492	1.92	1.81	3.73	1.70	1.65	3.35	0.89	0 85	1.74

Note : M—stands for Male.
F—stands for Female.
T—stands for Total.

Asur with 48.1 per cent in this sphere exist in the middle. The south region strikes a balance and here the proportion of workers is almost equal (50.88 per cent) in both the sexes. The Lohar with 60 per cent female workers stand at the top while the Kumhar with 36.83 per cent in the sphere exist at the bottom. The Baraik/Chick Baraik claims 54.55 per cent as female workers.

The proportion of non-workers amongst females varies from 48.35 per cent (in case of the north-west region) to 49.37 per cent (in case of the south region). Again, in the north-east region it is maximum (61.62 per cent) with the Lohar and minimum (45.64 per cent) with the Asur. The Chick Baraik with 59.62 per cent non-workers among females stand only next to the Lohar. In the south region, the Kumhar with 53.85 per cent female non-workers stand at the top. The corresponding figure for the Ghasi is 44.80 per cent (which is minimum). The Baraik/Chick Baraik with 52.68 per cent in the sphere stand next to the Kumhar. In the south-east region the proportion of female dependents is minimum (36.26 per cent) for the Swansi and maximum (60.91 per cent) for the Ghasi.

Here half of the dependents amongst the Baraik/Chick Baraik, Lohar and Lohra are female. All these become evident from Table 17.4.

Table 17.5 presents a consolidated picture showing distribution of workers in traditional and contemporary occupations. Traditional occupation today, in general, claims 44.34 per cent and remaining workers (53.66 per cent) are attached with one or other contemporary occupation. So far as individual artisan community is concerned, the Asur of the Bishnupur ecological margin have workers to the extent of 25.97 per cent who are associated with ancestral callings (skill for which is acquired by the "see and learn" method). Ironsmelting as an ancestrol occupation has become a matter of the past as there are only two Asur ironsmelters who even hesitate to disclose their professional identity to outsiders. With the gradual extension of forest codes to the locality of the Asur, they have had to abandon their age-old *purkhetipesha* (ancestral calling) of ironsmelting with native technology and slowly take to settled cultivation unlike *daha/kurao* shifting type (Leuva 1963).[16] Now 56.39 per cent of the Asur workers practise

TABLE 17.5

Distribution of Workers in different occupations (Primary)

Sl. No.	Community	No. of Workers	Traditional									
			Iron-smelting	Rope-making	Weaving	Wood-crafts	Pot-making	Black-smithy	Comb-making	Basket-making	Mid-wifery	Total (Col. 4 to Col 12)
1	2	3	4	5	6	7	8	9	10	11	12	13
1.	Asur	720	2 (0.28)	—	—	112 (15.55)	—	45 (6.25)	—	—	28 (3.89)	187 (25.97)
2.	Birhor	21	—	16 (76.19)	—	3 (14.29)	—	—	—	—	—	19 (90.48)
3.	Chick Baraik	182	—	—	60 (32.97)	—	—	—	—	1 (0.55)	—	61 (33.52)
4.	Ghasi	131	—	—	—	—	—	—	—	70 (53.44)	16 (12.21)	86 (65.65)
5.	Kumhar	224	—	—	—	—	146 (65.18)	—	—	—	—	146 (65.18)
6.	Lohar	51	—	—	—	2 (3.92)	—	14 (27.45)	—	—	8 (15.69)	24 (47.06)
7.	Lohra	42	—	—	—	1 (2.38)	—	22 (52.38)	—	—	3 (7.14)	26 (61.90)
8.	Mahli	66	—	—	—	—	—	—	40 (60.61)	—	4 (6.06)	44 (66.67)
9.	Swansi	65	—	—	37 (56.92)	—	—	—	—	—	—	37 (56.92)
10.	Turi	149	—	—	—	—	—	—	—	88 (59.06)	14 (9.40)	102 (68.46)
	Total	1651	2 (0.12)	16 (0.97)	97 (5.88)	118 (7.15)	146 (8.84)	81 (4.91)	40 (2.42)	159 (9.63)	73 (4.42)	732 (44.34)

TABLE 17.5 (*Contd.*)

Sl. No.	Contemporary										
	Own cultivation	Share-Cropping	Labour agri. & day	Mat making/Leaf cup making	Fuel collection	Cattle tending	Musical instrument making	Fishing	Business	Service	Total (Col. 14 to Col. 24)
	14	15	16	17	18	19	20	21	22	23	24
1.	406 (56.39)	—	114 (15.83)	—	—	—	—	13 (1.81)	—	—	533 (74.03)
2.	1 (4.76)	—	1 (4.76)	—	—	—	—	—	—	—	2 (4.52)
3.	19 (10.44)	16 (8.79)	72 (39.56)	1 (0.55)	—	—	—	—	7 (3.85)	6 (3.29)	121 (66.48)
4.	2 (1.53)	—	3 (2.29)	5 (3.82)	—	—	13 (9.92)	22 (16.79)	—	—	45 (34.35)
5.	45 (20.09)	8 (3.57)	14 (6.25)	2 (0.89)	—	—	—	—	4 (1.79)	5 (2.23)	78 (34.82)
6.	2 (3.92)	—	9 (17.65)	2 (3.92)	2 (3.92)	—	—	—	6 (11.76)	6 (11.76)	27 (52.94)
7.	8 (19.05)	—	3 (7.14)	—	5 (11.90)	—	—	—	—	—	16 (38.10)
8.	4 (6.06)	—	8 (12.12)	6 (9.09)	—	—	4 (6.06)	—	—	—	22 (33.33)
9.	—	4 (6.15)	5 (7.69)	—	—	12 (18.46)	—	—	5 (7.69)	2 (3.08)	28 (43.08)
10.	19 (12.75)	—	11 (7.38)	5 (3.36)	—	4 (2.48)	—	—	8 (5.37)	—	47 (31.54)
Total	506 (30 65)	28 (1.69)	240 (14.54)	21 (1.27)	7 (0.42)	16 (0.97)	17 (1.03)	35 (2.12)	30 (1.82)	19 (1.15)	919 (55.66)

plough and/or spade cultivation for growing maize, millets and potato with inputs like fertiliser—organic and inorganic. Ironsmelting and woodcraft as a cottage industry collapsed due to close contact with the industrial world yet at one time it brought wealth and happiness to thousands (Elwin 1942).[17] Indigenous iron known as *bom loha* produced from the crude *bhatti* (furnace) has been increasingly replaced with 'English' or factory iron. Elwin holds that when fuel (i.e., logs of raw sal wood) was plentiful, much iron was smelt but now the roar of the *chapua* (foot bellow) is silent. Previously finished iron products used to move from the *pat* (level hilltop) to the plains, but now the movement has totally changed its direction. Among others, cheap spade and ploughshare made of factory iron today climb up the *pat* from plains. Ironsmelting in a crude way still survives beyond the knowledge of forest rangers and guards in a limited sense and on subsidiary level at Kujam and Ranjharia on the *pat*. In olden days ironsmithy and ironsmelting amongst the Asur went side by side. The former attracts only 6.25 per cent of the Asur workers. Woodcraft (with 15.55 per cent of workers) too loses its ground. The Birhor because of their sentimental attachment with ancestral callings like rope-making, continue to be the rope-workers, although rope and rope articles when sold from the settled site in the local inter-tribal market amongst limited buyers do not bring them any fair return particularly in slack season. Among others, lack of bargaining power compels them to sell goods even below the cost of production. Coir rope and synthetic rope, as brought by *pharias* (intermediaries) in the village market, are the cheap substitutes of bark rope. Cotton weaving with the traditional loom by the Baraik/Chick Baraik has already become unpopular among its patrons. As a result less than one-third of the Baraik/Chick Baraik workers are actually weavers. Unskilled labour (with nearly 40 per cent workers) is the common occupation by which the Baraik/Chick Baraik in the south-east and north-west region earn their bread, of course, thereby they on an average get lesser remuneration than that of a day labourer. "Because of development of a communication network at both the south-east and north-west regions cheap and attractive mill-cloth has flooded the village market and is found to suit the taste of people of all ages. The old and the young, who ordinarily have no choice for the selection of fabrics use the Baraik/Chick Baraik woven cloth. Too much dependence on imported yarn (coloured or simple) has considerably crippled the art of weaving. Abstinence of the technique of manufacturing yarn from cotton has resulted in the loss of creative work" (Chakraborty 1972: 46).[18] The Swansi, with their relatively superior technology in cotton weaving, survive with 56.92 per cent weavers. Fabrics woven by them are relatively fine but a bit costly, multicoloured and with designs to suit the need of all ages. On the contrary, the Baraik/ Chick Baraik woven cloth is coarse and relatively unattractive, but it enjoys seasonal demand for its ceremonial and ritual value. Cultivation of own land and share-cropping are their second line of earning. Business in cotton cloth and service, though with fewer number of working units, are coming into the picture. Water pools and collections are few and far between in the south-east region. The Ghasi hardly find here opportunities to eke out their livelihood as fishermen. In practice, few of them (16.79 per cent) today are fishermen. Most of them (53.44 per cent) have taken up basketry (small sized) as a primary occupation. The Turi, whenever found, are essentially basket-makers (large-sized) and the females amongst them in particular are adept in midwifery. Some amongst the landed Turi (12.75 per cent) practise cultivation while others amongst the landless Turi (7.38 per cent) are purely labourers. Many of the Mahli (60.61 per cent) are comb-makers and not basket-makers as in West Bengal. As a matter of fact, basketry (large-sized or small-sized) faces minimum competition from synthetic products particularly in the south region but this is not exactly so with the comb-making Mahli of the north-west region, where the plastic comb poses a cut-throat competition with the reed comb of the Mahli. Happily enough, the utility of the reed comb still remains. The Lohar and Lohra everywhere flourish as blacksmith but the proportion of blacksmiths in relation to their agriculturist patrons is more than what is needed. So some of them under compulsion have taken to cultivation of the tiny plots they own while others among the landless have taken to road-building and stone-breaking work. However, business in hardware and service attract some of the Lohar workers.

TABLE 17.6

Generation-wise distribution of primary occupations amongst the Asur of the North-West Region

Sl. No.	Occupation	Generation										Grand total
		Ascending more than one		Ascending one		Ego		Descending		Total		
		D	Al	D	Al	D	Al	D	Al	D	Al	
1	2	3	4	5	6	7	8	9	10	11	12	13
1.	Iron-smelting	6	—	4	—	1	1	—	1	11	2	13
2.	Blacksmithy	1	—	—	3	—	16	—	26	1	45	46
3.	Own cultivation	—	—	9	5	—	93	—	308	9	406	415
4.	Wood craft	—	—	2	2	2	67	—	43	4	112	116
5.	Midwifery	5	—	2	5	—	15	—	8	7	28	35
6.	Labour	—	—	2	—	—	28	—	86	2	114	116
7.	Fishing	—	—	—	—	—	—	—	13	—	13	13
	Total	12	—	19	15	3	220	—	485	34	720	754

Note : D—denotes dead.
Al—denotes alive.

TABLE 17.7

Generation-wise distribution of primary occupation amongst the Baraik/Chick Baraik of different regions

Sl. No.	Occupation	Region	Generation: Ascending more than one		Ascending one		Ego		Descending		Total		Grand total
			D	Al	D	Al	D	Al	D	Al	D	Al	
1	2	3	4	5	6	7	8	9	10	11	12	13	14
1.	Weaving	S-E	1	—	1	—	1	3	—	2	3	5	8(3.80)
		N-W	1	--	1	1	4	12	—	7	6	20	26(12.32)
		S	2	—	3	2	7	22	—	11	12	35	47(22.27)
		T	4	—	5	3	12	37	—	20	21	60	81(38.39)
2.	Basketry	S-E	—	—	—	—	—	—	—	—	—	—	—
		N-W	—	—	—	—	—	—	—	1	—	1	1(0.47)
		S	—	—	—	—	—	—	—	—	—	—	—
		T	—	—	—	—	—	—	—	1	—	1	1(0.47)
3.	Midwifery	S-E	—	—	—	—	—	—	—	—	—	—	—
		N-W	—	—	1	—	2	—	—	—	3	—	3(1.42)
		S	—	—	—	—	—	—	—	—	—	—	—
		T	—	—	1	—	2	—	—	—	3	—	3(1.42)

1	2	3	4	5	6	7	8	9	10	11	12	13	14
4.	Own Cultivation	S-E	—	—	—	—	—	—	—	—	—	—	—
		N-W	1	—	1	—	—	5	—	4	2	9	11(5.21)
		S	—	—	—	—	—	6	—	4	—	10	10(4.74)
		T	1	—	1	—	—	11	—	8	2	19	21(9.95)
5.	Share cropping	S-E	—	—	—	—	—	—	—	—	—	—	—
		N-W	—	—	—	—	—	2	—	4	—	6	6(2.84)
		S	—	—	—	—	—	1	—	9	—	10	10(4.74)
		T	—	—	—	—	—	3	—	13	—	16	16(7.58)
6.	Labour	S-E	—	—	—	—	—	—	—	2	—	2	2(0.95)
		N-W	—	—	—	—	1	4	—	34	1	38	39(18.48)
		S	—	—	—	—	—	1	—	31	—	32	32(15.17)
		T	—	—	—	—	1	5	—	67	1	72	73(34.60)
7.	Mat/leaf cup making	S-E	—	—	—	—	—	—	—	—	—	—	—
		N-W	—	—	—	—	1	1	—	—	1	1	2(0.95)
		S	—	—	—	—	—	—	—	—	—	—	—
		T	—	—	—	—	1	1	—	—	1	1	2(0.95)
8.	Business	S-E	—	—	—	—	—	—	—	—	—	—	—
		N-W	—	—	—	—	—	2	—	2	—	4	4(1.90)
		S	—	—	—	—	—	—	—	3	—	3	3(1.42)
		T	—	—	—	—	—	2	—	5	—	7	7(3.32)

TABLE 17.7 (*contd.*)

1	2	3	4	5	6	7	8	9	10	11	12	13	14
9.	Service	S-E	—	—	—	—	—	—	—	—	—	—	—
		N-W	—	—	—	—	1	—	—	6	1	6	7(3.32)
		S	—	—	—	—	—	—	—	—	—	—	—
		T	—	—	—	—	1	—	—	6	1	6	7(3.32)
	Total	S-E	1	—	1	—	1	3	—	4	3	7	10(4.74)
		N-W	2	—	3	1	9	26	—	58	14	85	99(46.92)
		S	2	—	3	2	7	30	—	58	12	98	102(48.34)
		T	5	—	7	3	17	59	—	120	29	182	211(100.00)

Note : D—denotes dead.
Al—denotes alive.

Occupation Mobility

We have examined the distribution of existing workers among artisans in different primary occupations. We are now mainly concerned with the distributions of Asur workers (both dead or alive) in different generations. Before late, it is perhaps worthwhile to state that persons in the age-group of 16—35 have been placed under the descending generation. Persons in the age-group of 36—40 have been put under the ego's generation and those beyond 64 years and their age-mates who at the time of survey were dead but whose families were represented either in the ego's generation or below that have been placed under generation one and ascending generation more than one.

With the appearance of occupations like own cultivation of settled type among the Asur, an ever-increasing number of workers (6.1 per cent of 754) in different generations are found to be attached to smithy (rather blacksmithy). Of course, in olden days ironsmithy and ironsmelting went side by side, but these days ironsmelting is progressively disappearing. Own cultivation alone claims more than half (55.04 per cent) of workers and is the principal means of subsistence for the ego's generation and below that. By that it does not necessarily indicate a very happy trend as the cultivated land on the *pat* is mainly unterraced and such land in course of time becomes temporarily unfit for plough cultivation and/or spade cultivation due to heavy soil erosion by the rains. Labour (essentially unskilled) as an occupation is fast gaining ground. On the contrary, woodcraft has already started showing a decline.

The Baraik/Chick Baraik and traditional weavers irrespective of regions claim only 38.39 per cent of 211 workers (dead or alive) when all the generation levels are considered. The Baraik/Chick Baraik weavers are relatively more in proportion in the south region than elsewhere. Conversely, labour (mainly unskilled) with 34.6 per cent of workers emerges as an occupation of ever-increasing strength in the descending generation, in general, and in the north-west region in particular. Own cultivation on tiny plots of partially terraced land attracts only 9.85 per cent of workers mainly belonging to the ego's generation and below that as the Baraik/Chick Baraik are essentially landless in both the north-west and south regions where some (7.5 per cent) among them at the same generation level survive with land let out on *sajha* (share-cropping) basis. Slogans like 'he who owns plough owns land' have further curbed the opportunities for getting cultivable land within easy reach on sajha basis. Occupations like business and service (each with 3.32 per cent of workers) are additions in the ego's generation and below that in both the regions (north-west and south).

Rank Order of Occupations

Table 17.8 and 17.9 present an idea of the rank order of occupations pursued by the Asur and Baraik/Chick Baraik respectively in different generations.

TABLE 17.8

Rank order of occupations in different generations amongst the Asur

Sl. No.	Occupation	Generation			
		Ascending more than one	Ascending one	Ego	Descending
1	2	3	4	5	6
1.	Iron-smelting	I	III	VI	VII
2.	Black-smithy	III	IV	IV	IV
3.	Own-cultivation	—	I	I	I
4.	Woodcraft	—	III	II	III
5.	Midwifery	II	II	V	VI
6.	Labour	—	V	III	II
7.	Fishing	—	—	—	V

Among the Asur, cultivation of settled type as a contemporary occupation enjoys an unparallel position and holds the first rank order right from its appearance in one generation above the ego. On the contrary, ironsmelting as a traditional occupation holds the first position in ascending generation more than one, but progressively loses its rank order through different generations till it occupies the base position in the descending generation. Thus a downward trend of occupations like ironsmelting is visible irrespective of generation levels. Midwifery and blacksmithy are two other ancestral

TABLE 17.9

Rank order of occupations in different generations amongst the Baraik/Chick Baraik

Sl. No.	Occupation	Ascending more than one	Ascending one	Ego	Descending
1	2	3	4	5	6
1.	Weaving	I	I	I	II
2.	Basketry	—	—	—	VII
3.	Midwifery	—	II	V	—
4.	Own cultivation	II	II	II	IV
5.	Share-cropping	—	—	IV	III
6.	Labour	—	—	III	I
7.	Mat/leaf cup	—	—	V	—
8.	Business	—	—	V	VI
9.	Service	—	—	VI	V

callings of the Asur. The former with the second rank order and the latter with the third rank order in the generation ascending more than one have failed to retain their respective positions in generations to follow. At length in the descending generation blacksmithy occupies the fourth place while midwifery has been placed at a still lower level. Amongst contemporary occupations labour (mainly unskilled) with its emergence in the generation immediately above the ego occupies the lowest position but in the generations to follow, it improves its position to a great extent occupying at length the second highest position in the descending generation. Thus an upward trend of occupations like labour in relation to rank order is visible in all generation levels. Position of woodcraft is better in the ego's generation when it occupies the second highest position but in generations immediately above and below the ego it finds its place at the third rank order. Lastly, fishing with the fifth rank order is a solitary addition in the descending generation.

Similarly, among the Baraik/Chick Baraik weaving as a traditional occupation holds the first position up to ego, but in the generation below ego it loses its own position to labour. Cultivation continues to enjoy the second highest position up to ego but loses its position in the descending generation when it occupies the fourth position. Besides these two, there exists no other type of occupation either in the ascending generation more than one or in the generation immediately above the ego. Five other types of occupations are additions to ego. Of these, labour (mainly unskilled) with third rank order in ego occupies abruptly the first position in the generation immediately below ego but other lose their respective positions step by step in successive generations.

Role of Anthropologists for Revival of Native Crafts

Anthropologists, more precisely cultural anthropologists, are social doctors who are professionally equipped with adequate knowledge. Without any break they are to take care of both preventive and curative aspects of social weaknesses. For maintaining socio-economic and ritual interdependence between artisans and "other communities" of the regional society identification of native skill in craftsmanship and use of the same for overall socio-economic betterment and promotion of integrity of the people are a must for social scientists. On empirical findings they are to diagnose, among others, bottleneck in technology and see the scope of exploitation of raw material, marketing and development of finished goods and prescribe remedial measures—both short-term and long-term—for continued prosperity of artisans so that native skill acquired by the 'see and learn method may' not be lost. On the contrary, experiments are to be launched for gradual improvement in skill and technology after keeping an open eye on the changing situation.

Among others, enhancement in literacy rates is the passport to prosperity. By that they can themselves better understand the whole situation both in theory and practice. Literacy (both with and without educational standard) varies from one region to another. It is maximum (15.04 per cent) in the north-west region and the minimum (5.35 per cent) in the south region. Female literacy is proverbially poor everywhere. It is 5.1 per cent in the north-west region and 0.87% in the south-east region. There is, however, no female literate in the south region.

Attainment in literacy is poor, indeed, with all individual artisan communities. It is more so with the cotton weaving

Baraik/Chick Baraik. The literacy rate among them in the south and north-west regions stands at 10.28 per cent and 11.85 per cent respectively. The less we speak of female education among them, the better. It varies between 1.67 and 3.71 per cent. At the district (Ranchi) level, only 20.22 per cent of the Baraik/Chick Baraik are literate, as per 1961 Census. Further, only 20 per cent of school-age students (6-11 years) attend primary education from within and outside the scheduled age-group.

The ironsmelting Asur in their turn stands with 16.96 per cent literacy, of which 5.46 per cent go to the credit of female literacy. The 1961 Census, however, recorded literacy to the extent of 4.57 per cent among the Asur of Ranchi district. Only 5 4 per cent of the expected school-age students attend primary education. The problem which the Asur face is of multi-dimensional nature and cannot be solved simply with the establishment of one or two residential schools imparting general education in *pat*. Craft-based and employment-oriented education is the need of the hour (Bose 1970).[19] Inclusion of certain amount of skill of head and hand in school curriculum, at least on an experimental basis, particularly for the literate Asur and Baraik/Chick Baraik, is a must. For the illiterate, of course, primary education should be made free and compulsory so that parents and guardians do not treat school-age boys and girls as economic units. Textbooks for the primary stage should have references to their own environment (forest, hills, rivers etc.) and in the script they prefer. Medium of instruction, particularly at the early stages of education, should be the mother tongue to make it understandable and attractive to the young mind.

Age-old simple but useful crafts like ironsmelting and cotton-weaving can be revived at least as secondary means of livelihood although in his *The Asur*, Leuva says, "their (Asur's) traditional occupation has not much scope for revival" (1963)[20]. In contrast, Elwin's blessing is for its revival. In his *The Agaria*, Elwin remarks, "No Mahatma has arisen to revive it. The interests of big business on the other have combined to suppress it" (1942)[21]. For a one square meal a day, if not two, artisans in general, the Asur and Baraik/Chick Baraik in particular require very badly a second source of income to fall back upon.

Now inherited skill of artisans, if not utilised, may vanish altogether from society when our move is to make unskilled labour into skilled and/or semi-skilled. Further, at the existing situation artisans as a weaker section of regional society should have in the occupational field (particularly in craft) all possible types of government protection, some of which are listed below :

For Ironsmelting

It is paradoxical that we take care of the forest but not of men who are directly dependent on it. For ironsmelting with crude tools, implements and technology charcoal fuel is required. This should be made available to registered Asur ironsmelters. Forest coupes, from where fuel for smelting iron can be supplied should be opened nearest to the Asur plant. These may be leased out to labour cooperatives. Here Leuva states, "when the government are wedded to the policy of doing welfare work for the Scheduled Tribes, they should not grudge to forego a little income of forest resources" (1963)[22]. Registered Asur ironsmelters should be permitted to exploit, with little or no royalty, locally available raw materials like *gitti* (ironore), sand and limestone. The revenue lost on this account can be commensurable to welfare. Then with charcoal iron from the Asur bhatti, a training-cum-production centre (for blacksmithy) be established on the *pat* as the Asur are also adept at smithy. The success of such a scheme depends, on types of help (including upgradation and innovative adaptation) to be extended to the Asur for revival of their ancient craft. Communication facilities to and from the Asur plant may be taken as one of the prerequisites for the development of this simple but very useful village industry. At present unmetalled but jeepable roads are there for picturesque waterfalls and dak bungalows but not for sites where Asur plants (i.e. at Kujam and Ramjharia on the *pat*) exist today.

For Cotton Weaving

Some of the suggestions for revival of cotton weaving namely, bringing out technological improvement in the hand-operated *hata* (wooden loom), assured supply of standard yarn at fixed rate, sale of multidesigned and partially subsidised finished goods through weavers' cooperatives (with limited government control and revolving capital), establishment of fresh training-cum-production centres and revitalisation of existing one at Dudri (Murhu) in the south-east region are applicable to the Baraik/Chick Baraik. For master craftsmen among them, some payment against orders, if required, may be made in advance which may be recovered at final payment on delivery of finished goods to cooperatives. The objective behind the establishment of a few training-cum-production centre in areas with concentration of the Baraik/Chick Baraik is to promote the cause of weaving and thereby acquaint trainees with latest technique and design. The art of making textile fabrics attractive and less costly by manipulation of partly sophisticated tools and use of multicoloured design and embroidery should be included in training. A follow-up programme on successful completion of training is a must so that trainees may have scope for proper socio-economic rehabilitation, a spirit of self-reliance and revival of respect for ancestral calling; otherwise schemes, however good and need-based, may meet an unwanted fate.

With the revival of native skill and craft, the will to live among artisans by creative work will be strengthened. Consequently, idleness, dullness and unwillingness to shoulder the burden of life will be gradually removed. Indeed for revival of indigenous craft there lies ample scope for further research. Any effort in this direction, we are sure, will help in revitalising the native skill and craft. This can fruitfully be done by undertaking research-cum-action programme (with social scientists in general and anthropologists in particular) in each region for uniterrupted walfare of artisan communities. In short, artisan communities will remain under constant studies and on empirical findings schemes for their socio-economic betterment may be executed as and when required. The programme should have provisions of flexibility for facilitating readjustment as per local situation. Besides process can maintain an effective communication link between artisan communities and administration at different levels.

NOTES

1. Vidyarthi, L.P., *The Peasant Organisation in India*, Ranchi : Council of Social and Cultural Research, 1977.
2. Vidyarthi, L.P., *Culture Contours of Tribal Bihar*, Calcutta : Punthi Pustak, 1964.

3. Beverly, H., *Report on the Census of Bengal, 1872*, Calcutta, 1872.
4. Dalton, K.T., *Descriptive Ethnology of Bengal*, Calcutta, 1872.
5. Risley, H.H., "Tribes and Castes of Bengal," *Ethnographic Glossary* Vols. I & II, Calcutta, 1891.
6. Roy, S.C., *The Birhors : A Little Known Jungle Tribe of Chotanagpur*, Ranchi, 'Man in India' Office, 1925.
7. Lacey, W.G., *Census of India, 1931 Vol. VII Bihar and Orissa Part-I, Report*. Patna : Superintendent Govt. Printing, 1932.
8. Archer, W.G., *Census of India, 1941, Vol. VII, Bihar*. Simla, 1942.
9. Elwin, V., *The Agaria*, London : Oxford University Press, 1942.
10. Sinha, S., B.K. Dasgupta & H.N. Banerjee, "Agriculture, Crafts and Weekly Markets of South Manbhum". *Bulletin of the Anthropological Survey of India* (Calcutta) 10, 1, 1961.
11. Saraswati, B.N., and Behura, N.K., *Pottery Technic in Peasant India*, No. 13, Calcutta : Anthropological Survey of India, 1966.
12. Vidyarthi, L.P. (ed.), *Applied Anthropology in India*, Allahabad, Kitab Mahal, 1968.
13. Sinha, D.P., Culture Change in an Intertribal Market, Bombay: Asia Publishing House, 1968.
14. Williams, B.J., A Model of Band Society in American Antiquity (Washington) 29: 4:2, 1974.
15. Murdock, O.P., *Social Structure*, New York: Macmillan Company (fourth printing), 1958.
16. Leuva, K.K., *The Asur*, New Delhi, Bharatiya Adimjati Sevak Sangh, 1963.
17. Elwin, V., *Ibid*
18. Chakraborty, B., "Vanishing Crafts of Artisans of Chotanagpur", *Bulletin of the Cultural Research Institute*. (Calcutta), 1972.
19. Bose, N.K., *Report of the Commissioner for Scheduled Castes and Scheduled Tribes* (1969-70), Nineteenth Report, Delhi, 1970.
20. Leuva, K.K., *Ibid.*
21. Elwin, V., *Ibid.*
22. Elwin, V., *Ibid.*

EIGHTEEN

Pavla Strukelj

ADAPTABILITY TO CIVILIZATION
Gypsies in Slovenia

THE GYPSIES in Slovenia originated from the three main gypsy tribes which had dispersed all over Europe many centuries ago.

In Slovenia there are the Sinti group of gypsies who emigrated from Germany and Austria, the Hungarian group from Hungary and the ones who wandered across from the south-eastern part of our republics.

The ethnological field-work which has been done so far among these colourful tribes considers firstly, the question of the adaptability to the modern way of life.

The gypsy groups in Slovenia were nomads in the distant past like similar other groups all over the world. These nomadic habits still persist among a few groups. The majority of our gypsy groups, however, have settled down in large and small villages. In these smaller communities we can observe that gypsy families keep together mainly in the interests of economy. Urbanization is also one major factor that we must take into consideration while studying the changing social system and life-style of the gypsies in Slovenia. Many of the changes in the common life of all gypsies in Europe began after the Second World War. Hence research in the cultural changes is very important.

As I said I am going to speak about the adaptability to the modern life of our gypsy groups. These new forms refer to the economic and cultural goods. This problem will be dealt with in some aspects.

The socialist system of our society which has thoroughly changed the life of all our people after the Second World War has had a great influence on the transformation of the gipsies in Slovenia.

The gypsy village communities spring up everywhere but we must say that they are still dependent on the parish authority and the social workers to a high degree. To this extent they are a part of the mainstream of national life.

The different sources of livelihood of the gypsy settlers form the new social structure of their communities. To earn their own living some of the families nowadays practise the old crafts or other activities as they had done in the past. A step towards change among some families shows itself in the cultivation of fields. These people grow some vegetables and other agricultural produce necessary for their consumption. But for their cultural development and for the improvement of their financial condition there is need for gainful employment of our gypsy people. So we can say that some of our gypsy families work for their living to a large extent as obtained from the data at the field-work. They can be employed permanently. The number of professional qualified gypsies grows larger and larger, too.

The study of the cultural connections of our gypsies as compared to the other people in Slovenia yielded a good deal of data. It is known that these mutual connections are relatively modest in some aspects but, we must, however consider them.

During our field-work we observed that on the one hand our gypsies kept their original cultural characteristics; for instance some manners and customs, believing in the supernatural beings and some ethnical traditions; and on the other hand we note how the gypsy adapts himself to modern culture and modern ways of life.

The village gypsy settlers that built their homes near the farmers adopted some of their customs (for instance in the celebration of a child's birth and in weddings, and funeral rites). The situation of the employed gypsies with regard to their traditional customs gave us some different data. These families abandon the old customs or they simplify them. In the case of child birth for instance, it is important only that the child gets a name.

The marriage ceremonies by our gypsies are preserved in part, but to some extent they have adapted themselves to the nuptial rites of the Slovene people. But nearby all are simplified now. Some of the gypsy people don't get married at a registrar's office because they feel, namely, that it will do if they are married by their own traditional custom. The registrar's office treats such marriages as a concubinage, indeed. And so in the registrar's offices and in other card-indexes such married couples are registered as single.

For the most part, lhe original gypsy customs in Slovenia were kept at the death of a member of the family. They believed in the transformation of the dead into vampires. The rites of burial are like that by the Slovene people.

The cultural development of our gypsies becomes more and more important in some respects. First of all we must mention their interest of modern dance and music. The members of gypsy orchestras usually play both the traditional melodies and the modern songs. There are some professional gypsy musicians too in Slovenia; they play in orchestras. One of them is a very famous and popular singer and composer of modern songs. We should also mention the occasional gypsy musicians who play at the popular festivals.

A word about gypsy women here will not be out of place; they are very skilled in making small trinkets and souvenirs. The interest in such work is quite new among them but the latter data should be taken into account, too. Most of the objects made in this manner are very attractive. We notice that the woman is precise, the colour on the object go well together and the use of the material shows how inventive these women are. Actually such ornamental products are made by the unemployed gypsy women. Let me cite some of these examples : a bunch of artificial flowers, a typical star made from cardboard covered with printed and many coloured fabrics, further the modelling of the designs in straw on wooden plates. The gypsy women sell these products in the vicinity of fairs or other places of amusement.

Gypsy homes are often decorated with religious pictures and statuettes. Gypsies in Slovenia follow the Christian faith; hence it isn't unusual to find such pictures and statuettes in their homes placed on chests or set on little altars. Many such figures figurines were probably gifted to them by fellow gypsies who were perhaps the artists or artisans who carved them. In addition to these, family photographs also adorn the walls particularly in the living room. Occasionally it is not unusual to find film posters or pictures of pop singers. Striking examples of modernization and urbanization !

I have also come across homes of these colourful people which have life-size dolls dressed up in long flowing dresses placed among decorative, embroidered antimacassars and cushions on sofas in the living rooms or on beds. Window-boxes with potted flowering plants and walls decorated with needlework and game trophies complete the picture. The gypsy is simple in his tastes and is often pleased with pretty, inexpensive objects with which he beautifies his home.

Leisure as we understand is perhaps doesn't apply very strictly to the gypsies as a whole. Not many of them have steady jobs which they do within regular hours each day. But some generalizations can be made in this context based on the kinds of recreation that the gypsy both old and young indulge in when not at work. The gypsies are by nature a gay fun-loving people with an inborn feeling for music and the rhythm of dance. Music and dance are an essential part of their lives and are fully brought into play at festival time, both religious and public not to talk of marriages and other joyous family events. Here too, however, urbanization and modernization have wrought changes in their lives.

Young gypsies like to watch various sports. Further they celebrate holidays as the religious and public festivals. They spend their annual holidays celebrating some important family events, for instance baptism, engagements and weddings. The gypsies visit their relatives and friends or go to the village fair where they do business, hawk their wares, act as horse brokers and amuse themselves in many different ways. The gypsies also come to the rural annual festival because there they can find many entertainments.

The play and recreation of gypsy children has undergone changes today. The children go to school where they get new friends, learn new games and other amusements in the new circumstances. In the past, for instance, these children usually played with discarded bicycles, old baby-carriages often found in dumps or with old pots and pans and so on. Nowadays the young parents buy toys for their children from shops, for instance a baby car, a baby-carriage, or a doll.

We should mention that the urbanisation extended into the country and systematic employment are the causes of the changes in the gypsies' everyday life in Slovenia. The workday of the employed gypsies is divided into work and rest just like with other Slovene working people. The collected data during the fieldwork reveals that the employed gypsies usually spend their annual holidays at home. The gypsies employed abroad return home for holidays and most of them build new houses or renew the old ones during that time.

The young gypsy people have recreations similar to the other Slovene youth. They like to play football (in one of their villages there is a football team which competes with other local teams). All gypsies like to go to the movies; the girls are interested in love stories but the boys prefer adventure.

The radio and television are significant mass media which have captured the fancy of one and all today. We noticed a lot of these sets among the gypsies.

These excellent public means of communication are suitable for illiterate gypsies, too. Some families whose members are employed compete in buying TV sets. Poorer families make efforts to buy radio-sets operated on battery cells at least if not on mains. We noticed radios in almost all gypsy homes even those in tents.

As we said, the radio and television impart a lot of information about events both at home and abroad more clearly than the newspaper. Gypsies enjoy television because they get both picture and sound. But it is necessary to add that TV sets are not always within the reach of these families. These are therefore greatly valued as status symbols.

We should also mention some bigger industrial products which can be seen in the gypsy villages latterly. The most usual are the motor cars and washing machines. Motor cars are used at work as well as in their free time. But bicycles are the chief means of transport of the average gypsy men and children. The gypsy musicians were the first to buy motor cars because they earned a lot of money by playing in orchestras and bands. Then the gypsies employed abroad began to buy them too because they could afford to. In their villages we can see cars of different types and sizes. It is necessary to point out again that the above mentioned industrial products have brought about big changes in the life of our gypsies.

Concluding our discussion on the cultural changes in the life of Slovene gypsies we can say that in the present study we have attempted to explain the general cultural influences which are the main reasons for the changes in the gypsy way of life in Slovenia.

We especially wanted to call attention to the fact that urbanisation and the use of all sorts of industrial products of modern society have changed the identity of the gypsy today. Modernity has spread among them through the mass media of radio and television. This has brought changes in their indigenous culture and way of life. It is obvious that there are social differences among the gypsy families which arose from various reasons e.g. the ability of the individual gypsy, unsuitable location of their settlements, the language, the illiteracy—especially of the women and finally the employment problems of these people. I should like to point out that these problems apply in general to all gypsy people. These changes must be considered from the point of view of their attempts to adapt themselves to changing conditions of life today.

INDEX